ADVANCED LEGAL ANALYSIS AND STRATEGIES FOR BAR PREPARATION

ASPEN COURSEBOOK SERIES

ADVANCED LEGAL ANALYSIS AND STRATEGIES FOR BAR PREPARATION

TWINETTE L. JOHNSON

Professor of Law
Director of Academic Success
University of the District of Columbia
David A. Clarke School of Law

MARCIA GOLDSMITH

Professor of Legal Writing
Saint Louis University School of Law

 Wolters Kluwer

About Wolters Kluwer Legal & Regulatory U.S.

Wolters Kluwer Legal & Regulatory U.S. delivers expert content and solutions in the areas of law, corporate compliance, health compliance, reimbursement, and legal education. Its practical solutions help customers successfully navigate the demands of a changing environment to drive their daily activities, enhance decision quality and inspire confident outcomes.

Serving customers worldwide, its legal and regulatory portfolio includes products under the Aspen Publishers, CCH Incorporated, Kluwer Law International, ftwilliam.com and MediRegs names. They are regarded as exceptional and trusted resources for general legal and practice-specific knowledge, compliance and risk management, dynamic workflow solutions, and expert commentary.

I dedicate this book to my students. Just by virtue of your desire for assistance in conquering the bar exam and your belief that I could help, you have given me so much. You are the spark that started this effort and the energy that keeps me dedicated to it.

— Twinette Johnson

To the students who frequented my office and whose questions and concerns prodded my interest in writing this book. Also, to my wonderful family, my husband Hal and my boys Jacob and Benjamin, thank you so much for your support and your pride in the finished product.

— Marcia Goldsmith

Summary of Contents

Contents   *xi*

Acknowledgments   *xv*

PART I   CRITICAL PREVIEW

CHAPTER 1: The Time Is Now! Welcome to Bar Study!   3

CHAPTER 2: Before You Start: Preparing to Study   9

CHAPTER 3: Engaging from the Start: What to Do about
            Those Lectures, Commercial Subject Outlines,
            and Other Bar Materials   23

PART II   ORGANIZING ACTIVITIES

CHAPTER 4: Creating a Bar Exam Study Schedule: Bar
            Study Is Not "Gone with The Wind" and
            YOU Are Not Scarlett O'Hara!   41

CHAPTER 5: The MPT: A Winner of a Test   49

CHAPTER 6: The MEE: You Write! Therefore You Are . . .   151

CHAPTER 7: The MBE: The Multiple Choice
            Portion of the Bar Exam   181

CHAPTER 8: Final Study Days: A Macro Organizing Exercise   203

PART III REACHING YOUR GOAL

EPILOGUE   Believe You Will Pass the Bar Exam   217

APPENDIX A: MPT Answers   221

APPENDIX B: MEE Answers   269

APPENDIX C: MBE Answers   303

Contents

Acknowledgments   *xv*

PART I   **CRITICAL PREVIEW**   1

CHAPTER 1   **The Time Is Now! Welcome to Bar Study!**   3

Introduction   3
A. What Is the Bar Exam?   4
B. The Three Step Engagement Process   4
    1. Critically Previewing Material   4
    2. Completing an Organizing Activity   5
    3. Reaching a Goal or Producing a Product   6
C. Conclusion   7

CHAPTER 2   **Before You Start: Preparing to Study**   9

Introduction   9
A. Creating the Right Study Atmosphere   10
    1. Money Matters   10
        a. Paying for Your Commercial Bar Prep Course   11
        b. Bill Paying   12
        c. Maintaining Health Insurance/Accessing
           Medical Care   12
        d. Child Care/Loved Ones   13
    2. Working While You Study for the Bar Exam   13
        a. Take a Leave of Absence   14
        b. Shift from Full-Time Work to Part-Time Work   14
        c. Consider Leaving Your Current Job Situation   14
    3. Family Members and Loved Ones   15
    4. Study Space   15
B. Determining (or Re-Determining) How You Learn   16
C. Assessing Your Skills   17

  D. Evaluating Your Substantive Knowledge of Bar
     Tested Subjects   20
  E. Choosing the Commercial Bar Exam Study Course That's
     Right for You   21
  F. Conclusion   22

CHAPTER 3 **Engaging from the Start: What to Do About Those
           Lectures, Commercial Subject Outlines, and
           Other Bar Materials?**   **23**
  Introduction   23
  A. Step 1: Critically Preview by Reviewing the
     Topic and Watching the Lecture   24
  B. Step 2: Organize the Lecture Notes by Producing
     a Processing Product   26
     1. Choosing a Processing Product   27
        a. How Does My Learning Style Influence
           What Processing Product I Choose?   27
        b. Does the Lecturer's Presentation Align with
           How I Learn?   28
        c. What Else Besides the Law Should
           My Product Include?   29
     2. The Different Types of Processing Products   29
        a. Outlines   29
        b. Flashcards   31
        c. Flowcharts and Tables   31
        d. Sticking with the Lecture Notes   31
     3. Active Memorization   32
  C. Step 3: Reach Your Goal by Putting the
     Processing Product to Work   36
  D. Conclusion   37

PART II   **ORGANIZING ACTIVITIES**   **39**

CHAPTER 4 **Creating a Bar Exam Study Schedule: Bar Study
           Is Not "Gone with the Wind" and YOU Are
           Not Scarlett O'Hara!**   **41**
  Introduction   41
  A. Critical Preview – Building Your Knowledge Base   43
  B. Organizing Activity – Expanding Your Knowledge Base   43
  C. Reaching the Goal – Producing a Realistic and
     Workable Bar Study Schedule   47
  D. Conclusion   48

CHAPTER 5 **The MPT: A Winner of a Test**   **49**
  Introduction   49
  A. Critically Previewing   51

	B.	Organizing Activity	53
		1. What Is an Outline?	53
		2. Don't Skip This Step!	53
		3. Start with the Task Memo	54
		a. Tone	54
		b. Fact Statements	55
		c. Legal Analysis	55
		d. What Not to Discuss	55
		e. Special Instructions Beyond the Task Memo	56
		4. Use the Task Memo to Create Headings for Your Outline	56
		5. Turn to the Other Parts of the Packet	57
		6. Where to Write Your Outline	58
	C.	Producing the MPT Product	58
	D.	Conclusion	60

CHAPTER 6 The MEE: You Write! Therefore You Are . . . — 151

Introduction		151
A.	Critically Previewing	153
B.	Organizing Activity – Reading the Facts and Creating an Answer Outline	154
	1. Visual Organization	155
	2. Substantive Organization	156
	3. Sketching in the Law and Facts and Reaching a Conclusion	157
C.	Reaching Your Goal—Producing a Clear, Concise, and Correct Essay Answer	158
	1. Using CRAC, CIRAC, or IRAC to Produce Your Final Essay Answer	158
	a. Issue or Beginning Conclusion	158
	b. Rule	159
	c. Application	160
	d. Conclusion	161
	2. When You Can't Remember or Just Don't Know the Law	161
	3. When You Know the Law, But Aren't Sure of the Outcome	162
	4. Practice, Practice, Practice	163
	Alternative Ways to "Work" Essays	163
	5. Using the Allotted Time to Finish Every Essay	163
D.	Conclusion	164

CHAPTER 7 The MBE: The Multiple Choice Portion of the Bar Exam — 181

Introduction		181
A.	Critical Previewing	182

	B. Organizing Activity	182
	1. IRAC Processing	183
	2. Do You See Your Answer in the Answer Choices?	184
	C. Reaching Your Goal —Choosing the Correct Answer	185
	D. Timing	185
	E. Conclusion	186
CHAPTER 8	**Final Study Days: A Macro Organizing Exercise**	**203**
	Introduction	203
	A. What Should I Do During My Final Days of Bar Study?	204
	1. Assessment Categories – There, Almost There, Nowhere	205
	a. Assess Your Strengths Regarding Each Bar Study Topic	205
	b. Be True in Your Assessment – Honesty Really Is the Best Policy	207
	B. Now That I Know Where I Stand on Each Topic, How Should I Build My Final Days' Schedule?	208
	1. Scheduling Your Subjects According to Assessment Category	209
	2. When Can I Stop Studying for the Bar Exam?	212
	C. Conclusion	212
PART III	**REACHING YOUR GOAL**	**215**
EPILOGUE	**Believe You Will Pass the Bar**	**217**
	You Can Do This (Pep-Talk and Loud Cheer)	217
	You Have to Believe Too (Embrace Self-Efficacy)	218
	Be Resilient (Handling Tough Times)	218
	Take Care of Yourself (You Are the Whole Package)	219
	Conclusion	220
APPENDIX A:	**MPT Answers**	221
APPENDIX B:	**MEE Answers**	269
APPENDIX C:	**MBE Answers**	303

Acknowledgments

Twinette Johnson
Heartfelt thanks go to my research assistants Rahnesha Williams and Roxy Araghi for their unwavering belief in this project, student centered feedback, and consistent willingness to help in bringing this book to life.

Marcia Goldsmith
Thank you to my diligent and extremely helpful faculty fellows, Chris Miller, Jackie Coffman and Adrian Mehdirad. They worked very hard to insure we had a quality product. The time and effort that they expended in helping us research and edit this textbook was very much appreciated.

National Conference of Bar Examiners, Multistate Bar Examination (MBE), Torts (MBE-OPE 4), Contracts (MBE-OPE 4); Multistate Essay Examination (MEE), Torts (February 2008, February 2009, February 2010), Contracts (July 2007, July 2009), Agency (July 2001, July 2002, February 2003, July 2004, February 2005); Multistate Performance Test (MPT), *Whitford v. Newberry* (February 2002), *In re Madert* (February 2002), *In re Al Merton* (July 2002), *Acme Resources, Inc. v. Black Hawk et al.* (July 2007), *Logan v. Rios* (February 2010). Copyright © 2001–2013 by the National Conference of Bar Examiners. All rights reserved. Reprinted by permission.

ADVANCED LEGAL ANALYSIS AND STRATEGIES FOR BAR PREPARATION

PART I

CRITICAL PREVIEW

CHAPTER 1   Welcome to Bar Study
CHAPTER 2   Preparing for Bar Study
CHAPTER 3   Engaging from the Beginning

The Time is Now! Welcome to Bar Study!

INTRODUCTION

You knew this time was coming. Even if you were not sure what it was or what it would take to be prepared for it when you started law school, you knew it was coming. You may not have even been sure of what state you would work in, but you knew it was still coming. You've planned your graduation celebration and envisioned roused and proud loved ones and the toasts they'll make extolling you, and you will still know what is coming—what was always coming. You've always known you would have to prepare for and take a state bar examination. Well, the time is now.

Like it or not, your future, as a practicing attorney, involves taking a bar exam. But, this does not have to be scary or ominous. In fact, you've already taken an important step in this process by enrolling in a class that focuses on bar study and/or taking the time to read this book. You are already engaging in the bar study process. Now, you simply need to understand the nuts and bolts associated with studying for and passing the bar. And, with the right guidance and attitude toward the process, you can pass your state bar like thousands of other applicants each year.

There is a process to preparing for and taking a bar exam. In the following chapters, we will lay out the process for you in great detail. We will use a step-by-step engagement process to demonstrate how much of the strategies and techniques used in your law school study can be transferred to bar study. We will use this engagement process to help you understand and manage the work that goes into preparing for a bar examination. You will see how the engagement steps can assist you with preparation (from making a schedule to working practice problems) for success on the bar exam. This is our ultimate objective.

A. WHAT IS THE BAR EXAM?

Before we delve into the three-step engagement process, some of you may actually be wondering what exactly a bar exam is. You probably already know that you need to take a state bar exam to practice law. But, do you know what that entails? Do you know the components and test forms associated with a bar exam? Do you know how long you will have to study to take the exam? The best answer to all of those questions is, "It depends." Below is a description of bar exams generally.

> **BOX NOTE 1-1**
>
> ***Typical Bar Exam Structure***
> - DAY ONE   Essay Practice Test(s)
> - DAY TWO   Multiple-choice Test

Bar exams typically last for two to three days depending on your jurisdiction. The test forms used typically are essay, multiple-choice, and practice or performance test. In most jurisdictions, there is a day of essay testing and a day of multiple-choice testing. If your jurisdiction uses the practice/performance test, it is usually administered during the essay day.

Most students begin studying, in earnest, for the bar exam soon after graduating from law school. That means in most cases you have between eight to ten weeks to assimilate the bar study material and practice questions in the hopes of being ready for what may be the biggest closed book exam of your life. That's what this entire book is about—getting you ready for that experience and facing your bar exam future with confidence. As you read each chapter, you will learn more about the bar exam and its potential testing forms. You may be wondering at this point how you can possibly be ready for your exam in only eight to ten weeks. Rest assured, law graduates like you pass their bar exams every year. The process described below will get you started on that path.

B. THE THREE STEP ENGAGEMENT PROCESS

The three-step engagement process includes (1) critically previewing material, (2) completing an organizing activity, and (3) reaching the goal or producing the product. While we have developed this three-step process, what the process asks you to do is not too different from what you have already done over the course of your years in law school.

> **BOX NOTE 1-2**
>
> ***Engagement Steps***
> 1. Critically Previewing
> 2. Organizing Activity
> 3. Reaching the Goal or Producing the Product

1. Critically Previewing Material

The critical preview is critical. It is what you do to begin to prime your brain to receive additional and more detailed information. Have you ever attended class without completing the reading or assigned exercises? Were you able to follow along with the professor's lecture or the class discussion? Did the answers to the exercises make sense to you? Were you able to discern any deeper meaning from the discussion of cases or hypotheticals? Was it difficult to be confident about your notes and outline on whatever was covered that day?

For most of us, not preparing for class made it extremely difficult to fully participate in the class discussion. In many instances, a lack of preparation for class could have the cumulative effect of making us not ready for the final exam. The same is true when it comes to preparing for the bar exam. During bar study, you will attend or watch a new lecture almost every day. That means you will learn a new or part of a new topic every day. What that also means is that you will encounter vast amounts of information at a rapid pace and thus must have a system in place for assimilating it. The critical preview is an important part of this system. It is in essence your class preparation—your attempt to prime your brain to receive the information provided in those lectures.

So what does critically previewing involve? Depending on the particular task at hand, it could involve reading a table of contents or outline, listening to a lecture on the topic, reading the call of a question, skimming fact patterns, working questions, or many other activities. We'll discuss this more in the context of each bar study task in the following chapters.

2. Completing an Organizing Activity

This requires organizing the material you just took in (after your critical preview) so that you can memorize it and use it to answer questions appropriately. This should be very similar to what you did in law school. After each class, you attempted to read over that day's notes and "make some sense" out of them. After you finished a topic, you outlined it. You gathered your course book, your notes, and necessary supplements and attempted to pull together something that would be a handy tool for memorizing the principals of law and practicing issue spotting and analysis. You may have also outlined answers to questions as you worked problems. For instance, as you worked exam essays in preparation for your law school final exams, you may have devoted a portion of the allotted time for writing that essay to outlining your answer. You may have, in your outline, identified the applicable issues, jotted down a few words that would help you remember the rule, and noted the facts relevant to the particular issue. You may have completed this outline on scratch paper, in the margins of the exam document itself, or in the text of your exam answer.

You will complete similar tasks as you prepare for your bar exam. After attending or watching each bar lecture, you will have generated a set of notes. Those notes will be the primary tool you use to assimilate and memorize information. Chapter 3 will discuss in greater detail your options for organizing those notes.

As you study for the bar, you will also be tasked with working many practice problems. Certainly, your ultimate goal is to get these questions correct but to do that you must also have a system in place. Part of that system is organizing your thoughts and thus your answer prior to writing your actual answer. As you read this text, you will explore the many ways in which you can engage in the organizing activity while working practice questions.

3. Reaching a Goal or Producing the Product

You engage in each of the preceding steps so you can reach your ultimate goal and/or produce the required product. This will change depending on what task you are faced with. For instance, if you are pulling together your notes, your goal is to produce a product that will allow you to memorize the law and answer questions appropriately. If you are working an essay or multiple-choice question, your ultimate goal is to be able to spot issues, recall the appropriate law, and write a concise well-reasoned answer under time constraints. If you are practicing your test strategy, your goal is to be able to marshal the information so that you can produce whatever product has been assigned.

Chapters 4-7 will discuss each of these engagement steps in the context of the particular bar exam task. Each chapter will thus provide you with an opportunity to learn and understand the steps. But more importantly, the work you do in reading the chapters and working through the exercises will put you well on your way to establishing a method for bar exam preparation and ultimately for bar exam success.

BOX NOTE 1-3

The Overall Bar Exam Study Process in Three Engagement Steps

Critically Preview Through Context Building/ Critical Reading
- Reading commercial bar prep outline prior to attending/watching lecture
- Working questions
- Listening to an audio summary of the lecture topic
- Attending commercial bar prep lecture/taking notes

Organizing Actvity/Building a Knowledge Base
- Processing (outlining, flashcarding, flowcharting, other processing activities, or any combination) lecture notes from bar class
- Working Essay questions—every day
- Reading and/or outlining answers to Essay questions
- Working MC questions—every day
- Reading answers to all MC questions
- Reviewing/changing outline, flashcards, flowcharts, etc., by incorporating any useful

information (rule statements, examples, organization principals) into your processing product if working questions reveals a lack of understanding of a subject area or topic
- Memorizing material
- Working MPTs—frequently and consistently
- Reading answers to MPTs and assessing whether your chosen strategy for completing the MPT is effective

Reaching a Goal/Producing a Product
- Able to memorize material
- Able to demonstrate knowledge of material and understanding of substantive organization principals and analysis patterns in essay writing and multiple-choice question answering
- Able to execute techniques that allow you to answer essays, multiple choice questions, and MPTs adequately and in the allotted time

---

C. CONCLUSION

This book, which sets out a guided method of studying, facilitated by the three-step engagement process, will assist you as you work through all the tasks necessary for adequate bar exam preparation. Each necessary step, whether it is preparing your life for study, processing and memorizing information, or testing yourself on that information, is meticulously spelled out in the subsequent chapters. Each chapter will act as a guide to help you put your best foot forward on the road to bar exam success.

CHAPTER 1 RECAP

▶ *THE BAR EXAM*
- DAY ONE Essay Practice Test(s)
- DAY TWO Multiple-choice Test

▶ *THREE ENGAGEMENT STEPS*
- Critical Preview
- Organizing Activity
- Reaching the Goal/Producing the Product

Before You Start: Preparing to Study

INTRODUCTION

Have you ever planned an extended vacation? What did you do to prepare? Did you have to secure a passport? Did you have to buy plane tickets and arrange lodging? Did you have a travel companion you needed to coordinate with? Did you have to make arrangements for your children? Did you have to arrange for bills to be paid? Did you need someone to watch your house and pet or gather your mail during your absence? If you've ever had to make these arrangements before a trip, you know that taking care of these matters before you leave allows you to focus fully on enjoying your trip and all associated with it.

While bar study is certainly no vacation, some of the same preparation principles apply. This chapter will review preliminary measures you should take before beginning your bar exam studies. The main objective here is to guide you through establishing a healthy study environment and performing a critical assessment of your study skills and substantive depth of knowledge *before* your bar study period begins. To do this, you will need to think about your personal and financial obligations. You will also need to think about the courses you have and have not taken during law school. Your ultimate goal in assessing these things is to determine how each of them could potentially impact your bar study. Doing so will ensure that nothing negatively impacts your bar exam preparation. Take this pre-preparation seriously and you will be well on your way to having a productive and fruitful bar exam study experience.

BOX NOTE 2-1

You Can't Have Too Many Minds When Preparing for the Bar Exam

In the movie, *The Last Samurai*, an alcoholic United States Army Captain traveled to Japan as part of a paid military contingent charged with training Japanese soldiers to resist Samurai warriors. During an early skirmish, the Captain was captured by the Samurai. The Samurai leader ordered his fighters not to kill the Captain, but instead to bring him to their home base. As the Captain toured the Samurai grounds, he saw several Samurai warriors practicing their fighting craft. He also saw young boys emulating the practicing warriors. The Captain looked on with curiosity and joined the boys' play fighting. A Samurai spotted the Captain and challenged him to fight him instead of the boys. The Samurai bested the Captain, landing his wooden sword harshly on the Captain during each round. A younger Samurai gave the Captain some much needed advice. He told him he had too many minds. When the Captain seemed confused by this, the young Samurai showed him how he was minding everything except the fighter in front of him. He was minding the passersby, those looking on, and even the surrounding animals. After realizing he was not focused enough on the task at hand, the Captain blocked out all surrounding distractions. When he fought the Samurai again, the Captain countered the Samurai's every move.

The Last Samurai. Dir. Edward Zwick. Per. Tom Cruise. Warner Brothers Studio, 2003.

And so it goes with bar study. Use the tips in this chapter to help clear or manage anything that might significantly distract you from bar exam preparation.

A. CREATING THE RIGHT STUDY ATMOSPHERE

It is critical that before you start preparing for the bar exam, you *prepare* your life so you can have an optimal learning environment. Studying for the bar exam is usually done over an eight to ten week period. You can expect that you will spend six to seven days a week studying for the bar and that you will spend at least eight to ten hours (or more) per day in that endeavor (in subsequent chapters we will explore what we mean by the word *studying*). It is important that you come into this "marathon" in the best shape of your life. That means you need to get your mental, personal, and financial state in shape.

1. Money Matters

Do you currently have a plan for financing your bar study? How will you pay for your commercial bar course? How will you pay your living expenses (rent, mortgage, utilities, food, health insurance, child care, etc.)? In short, how are you going to finance your study time? Use the information below to guide you in writing a detailed budget that sets out your financial obligations and accessible money during the bar study period.

a. Paying for Your Commercial Bar Preparation Course

Bar study is an expensive enterprise. You must consider how you will pay for your bar exam course. But we may be putting the cart before the horse here. So, let's take a step back. First, should you take a bar exam course at all? In most cases, the answer to that question is a resounding yes. Let's do a quick unscientific, but hopefully insightful, assessment using Exercise 2-1.

EXERCISE 2-1

Think about courses you took in your first and second year of law school. under the Third Year column, put a check next to the courses you think you could take a timed closed book quiz on today and score a grade of B or above on.

FIRST/SECOND YEAR	THIRD YEAR
Torts	_____
Contracts	_____
Property	_____
Criminal Law /Pro	_____
Civil Procedure	_____
Constitutional Law	_____
Evidence	_____

At this stage, most of us would not be able to place many checks in the Third Year column. This is the main purpose of the commercial bar preparation course. It helps you to review the information you learned during those courses. It does most of the work in categorizing and chunking the information so that you can practically hit the ground running in terms of assimilating and memorizing the information. And because the commercial course is squarely focused on preparing you for the bar exam, it will provide you with a suggested study schedule, thousands of bar exam or bar exam type questions and sample answers, and strategies and tips for success on the bar exam.

In short, even if you took every bar class in law school and even if you scored well in those classes, you still need the bar course to help you review, organize, and study the information in a way that will help you maximize your short bar study period and be successful on a bar exam.

Now, back to our regularly scheduled program on paying for your commercial bar preparation course. Some students save for this over the course of their time in law school. If you have not done so, consider contacting commercial bar course providers to determine their fee schedules. You may be able to secure a commercial loan to cover the cost of bar study. If you cannot secure a commercial loan, perhaps you can secure a loan from family members.

In any event, when you contact the commercial bar course providers, ask about any available discounts or scholarship programs. Determine if there is any job you might do for the commercial bar prep company to offset the costs. If you truly cannot afford a course and may end up without one because of costs, talk to the administrators or faculty at your law school. They may be able to assist you in finding an affordable course that fits your needs.

b. Bill Paying

Paying bills is a fact of life for most of us and that fact does not cease to exist just because you are studying for the bar exam. Now is a good time to think of all your financial obligations and to calculate how much they will cost over the course of the bar study period. Think also of what resources you have or will have that will allow you to meet those obligations.

If you can, consider delegating bill paying to a spouse, significant other, or trusted family member. If you prefer to retain responsibility for paying your bills, consider paying your bills in advance (for at least the eight to ten which comprise your study period). If you choose this method, make sure your service provider or creditor will treat your payments like advance payments and count them toward each individual month. If paying up front is not possible or if it makes you uncomfortable, consider automating your bill payments (through your bank or creditor) during your bar study period. In this way, you retain responsibility but don't have to be too closely involved on a monthly basis. Each option has its pros and cons. You may feel uncomfortable relinquishing responsibility, or you may find relief in doing so. Weigh the pros and cons of each option and decide *now* which you will use for paying your bills during bar study.

> **BOX NOTE 2-2**
>
> ***This is not your grandparents' bar exam. It may not even be your parents' bar exam.***
>
> While they may mean well, be wary of employers who attempt to convince you that you can work during bar study simply because they worked during bar study and passed the bar exam. The bar exam has expanded its coverage of topics and skill sets over the years. In addition, jurisdictions are increasing pass cut scores and continually looking for other ways to add rigor to the bar exam. In short, you could be sitting for a very different and more difficult exam than lawyers who took the exam a few generations or even one generation ago.

c. Maintaining Health Insurance/Accessing Medical Care

Assess your health coverage and determine whether and how that coverage will extend during your bar study period. Determine whether your law school or the university your law school is attached to provides health care services you can access as an alumni studying for a bar exam. Have a plan in place before you start bar preparation. Many universities offer gap health care insurance, and many will allow you to continue to use student health services (typically for a fee) during your bar study period. Be aware of your options and make a plan for paying for medical care should you become ill during bar study. If you become ill or sustain an injury during your bar preparation time, you don't want to compound the situation by not having a clear plan for how to access medical services and pay for them.

d. Child Care/Loved Ones

If you have children, consider how you will spend time with them and also ensure that their needs are met during your bar study period. Bar study requires a significant amount of time. If you have young children, think about how you will provide childcare. Perhaps, you plan to adjust childcare responsibilities with your parenting partner such that you shift most of the responsibilities in that area. Perhaps there is a trusted family member who can assist you during your bar study period. For instance, if you are currently responsible for coaching your child's sport's team or driving your child to piano lessons, you might consider assigning these duties to someone if you feel continuing them would detract from your bar study. These same principles apply if you have adults whose care you are responsible for. If you do not have "free" help you can rely on, make sure you consider other alternatives and any potential costs associated with them. As with all things in this category, you want to consider and plan now so that you can fully focus on your bar study with the knowledge that your little ones and/or loved ones are well cared for.

2. Working While You Study for the Bar Exam

The best-case scenario for effective bar study is that you do not work. Period. The demands of bar study leave little time for many things including dealing with the responsibilities that come with employment. This is because, in many instances, work duties can be unpredictable. Tasks may take longer than expected. Your very presence in the office may lead to more projects or assignments than anticipated.

But, for some, due to financial reasons or for reasons related to job security, not working during bar study may not be a realistic option. Before you decide whether you fit into this category, consider carefully the risk you will take by working during bar study. Compare the costs of failing the bar with not working during bar study. The costs of failing the bar exam include not being able to secure a legal job requiring a law license, potentially losing the job you already have, and the cost of retaking the exam (including applying to take the bar exam again and any costs associated with preparation and living expenses while studying again). The added expense and worry associated with failing a bar exam may not be worth the short-term goal of making money while getting ready for the bar exam

If you have a job already that you must maintain, consider the following options.

a. Take a Leave of Absence

Try negotiating an eight to ten week leave of absence with your employer. If you cannot take that much time off, consider another arrangement that allows you to take less time off but still gives you time during crucial study periods. For instance, students often report that bar study intensifies in July. This is mainly due to an increase in the number of subjects covered at that point and undoubtedly because of the added stress of the bar exam drawing nearer. Perhaps you can negotiate a one-month absence use it to take July off from work. Any time off from full-time work can be extremely helpful to your bar exam preparation. Make sure you approach your employer with your request well in advance of the bar study period or as soon as possible. This will help your employer plan for your absence and thus increase the chance that your employer will allow it.

b. Shift from Full-Time Work to Part-Time Work

If a leave of absence is not possible, consider shifting from full-time work to part-time work during the bar study period. Working part-time the entire two months is not ideal, but again, any time off from full-time work will be helpful regarding your bar study. Thus, even part-time work for a lesser amount of time would be helpful. If you decide to shift to a part-time schedule, remember that you still need to get in the equivalent of eight to ten hours a day and six to seven days a week of preparatory work during the bar exam study period. This might mean you will have to start preparing for the bar exam before your commercial program begins and it may mean that you will have to sometimes study longer into the evenings and longer on the weekends. Make sure to approach your employer early regarding this request. You want to make sure you and your employer are on the same page as to the hours and days you will work well in advance of the bar prep period. Also, please note that when arranging a part-time schedule, it is crucial that co-workers are also on-board with your new hours so that they will know not to call you about assignments or projects during that time.

c. Consider Leaving Your Current Job Situation

If neither a leave of absence nor part-time work is realistic, consider leaving your current employment and finding a new position after the bar exam. This will take significant preparation on your part as you must also decide how you will finance your bar study period. While some students find working

---

BOX NOTE 2-3

Negotiating With Your Employer: Possible Approaches

Negotiation techniques usually encourage employees to ask for the top level of what they want but then be willing to settle for somewhat less. If feasible, start off asking for the full two months off prior to the bar exam. Stress how you plan on using that time, painting a picture for the employer as to how much work goes into preparing for the bar exam. Next, if your employer is open to your input, suggest how your job duties can be reallocated to existing employees or postponed. If your employer is not willing to give you the full two months off, discuss other scenarios with less time off. If your employer is unwilling to give you any time off, you must seriously consider if working through your bar exam preparation period is something you want to commit to.

during the bar exam preparation period gives them some peace of mind, some regret it later if they fail the bar and need to retake it.

3. Family Members and Loved Ones

That your graduation day is near is not only a cause of celebration for you, it is also cause for celebration for your family members and loved ones. They too are waiting for the day when you return from study and back to a more normal way of life. They can't wait for you to be able to join them in functions that you may not have been able to participate in due to the demands of law study. Spouses and loved ones may be chomping at the bit for you to resume your responsibility for duties they took over for you so that you could devote time to study. Friends have already made plans for holiday or summer outings that include you. This is the perfect time to disabuse them of all those notions.

You may be graduating from law school, but you are by no means finished. You still need their support. You still need their help with your obligations. You still need them to understand that you cannot become a practicing attorney without their full support during the eight to ten weeks after law school and before the bar exam. So, celebrate your graduation with them. But, before you start studying for the bar exam, make sure you talk with family members and other significant people in your life about the time you will have to spend on bar preparation. Make sure they understand what a "bar exam" is and the study time you will need to pass the bar exam (as stated earlier: eight to ten hours a day, six to seven days a week for eight to ten weeks). Make them your partners so they can help you carve out that time. But, also make sure you schedule some "down" time to spend with the important people in your life. That time is important battery recharging time and can help both you and your loved ones weather this important time in your professional life. Chapter 4 will help you create a study schedule that will incorporate all aspects of bar study. Share it with your loved ones so that you are all on the same page.

4. Study Space

Finding a place to study during bar preparation is something you should do before you begin your commercial bar exam study course. You may need to test out several locations before you find one that is right for you. An optimum place to study should have several common denominators related to conducive study:

a. It should have a comfortable chair and a decent sized desk you can spread your study materials on.
b. If you prefer studying lying down, make sure you have some type of hard surface to spread your materials out on.
c. If you prefer studying standing up, there should be some type of surface that will allow you to rest your materials, and it should allow you to reach them easily.

    d. Your space should have some modicum of privacy and a bathroom fairly nearby.

    e. It should be a place you can concentrate in and where you are not distracted. It should also not be in easy reach of distractions.

    f. It doesn't have to be just one space. You can have a collection of spaces you visit at different points during your bar preparation time. For some, varying the study location can actually improve productivity and retention.[1] This is so because having different study spaces and/or study positions helps to reduce the possibility of going off task which might occur when you find yourself within the same four walls day after day.

B. DETERMINING (OR RE-DETERMINING) HOW YOU LEARN

In addition to establishing a healthy study environment, you must also perform a critical assessment of how you learn. The first step in doing this is determining your learning style—how you best absorb or take in information when it is presented to you and also how you process information. You can use an online learning style inventory such as VARK.[2] A learning style inventory will help you figure out how you obtain, sort, and process information. Knowing your learning style will help you pick the optimum commercial bar exam study course. It will also help you to understand what the optimum method for processing that information is no matter what form it is presented to you in. The key here is to understand who you are as a learner and how it is you best absorb and then process information. Even if you have already determined your learning style, re-evaluate it. You may have a different learning preference. In re-evaluating how you learn, you may find that your preference for absorbing and processing information may change depending on the subject matter or the particular task you are faced with. Keep in mind that the goal in learning your preference is not to look for or respond only to materials presented in the way you best absorb and process, but rather to empower you in knowing how you should process the information regardless of the form it is presented in. See Exercise 2-2 for exercises regarding this point.

    This is the first step in determining how you will process the information you receive from your bar course during the bar study period. We'll discuss the next step—processing the information—in more detail in Chapter 3.

---

1. Benedict Carey, *Forget What You Know About Good Study Habits*, N.Y. TIMES (Sep. 6, 2010), https://www.nytimes.com/2010/09/07/health/views/07mind.html. Additionally, time spent on online social networks can negatively impact academic performance. *See* Jomon Paul et al., *Effect of Online Social Networking on Student Academic Performance*, 28(6) COMPUTERS IN HUMAN BEHAVIOR, 2117-2127 (2012). As time spent on social networking sites increases, the academic performance of the students is seen to deteriorate. *Id.*

2. *The Vark Questionnaire: How Do I Learn Best?*, VARK, http://vark-learn.com/the-vark-questionnaire/ (last visited April 20, 2018). Other learning style inventories include, but are not limited to, the North Carolina State University Inventory and the Paragon Learning Style Inventory. Deb Peterson, *Collection of Learning Styles Tests and Inventories*, ThoughtCo. (March 8, 2017), https://www.thoughtco.com/learning-styles-tests-and-inventories-31468.

EXERCISE 2-2

HOW DO YOU LEARN INFORMATION?

Think about the professors you had in law school. Which of those professors were easy to understand? What made them easy to understand? Look at the following depictions of how information can be presented in class. Circle the one that best represents situations where you understand the information almost immediately after the professor presents it.

A.
1_____ 2
2_____ 3
3_____ 4
4_____ 5
5_____ 6
6_____ 7

B.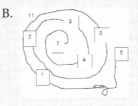

C.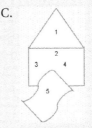

Linear presentation—professor connects each concept for students.	Circular presentation—professor introduces many concepts along a common theme but leaves to the students the ultimate task of determining the intra-relationship among the concepts and building the structure.	Visual presentation—professor presents information using diagrams and drawings to show students connections among topics.

Now, consider courses where the professor presented the material in a way different from what you circled. In those instances, your task was to convert that material into a form more akin to what you circled. This is what you may do with the notes you generate during bar study.

C. ASSESSING YOUR SKILLS

Another important and critical step in preparing yourself for bar study is assessing your study skills. Studying for a bar exam is different in some ways than studying for a law school exam. In law school, you prepare for class by reading cases and legislative or regulatory enactments. You use your class time to delve deeper into the reading by hearing your professor's remarks on it and paying attention to your professor's questions and how your professor reacts to answers to those questions. After class, you review your notes and ultimately draft a product (an outline) that represents a succinct and accurate representation of the course content including a hierarchy of analysis and any exam tips or strategies your professor provided. You use this tool to memorize the law, issue spot, and construct methods of analysis according to topics. This sounds like a big task when considering that students typically go through all these steps for most of the courses they take in one semester. And many of you would agree that it is a huge task even though most of you get approximately four months to complete it.

Bar study is different. The biggest difference is that you have eight to ten weeks to assimilate many, many more subjects than what you typically deal with in one semester.

But here's the good news. Most, if not all, of your first-year courses were bar tested topics. Most of your upper division required courses were bar tested topics. So, already, you at least have a familiarity with the topic. Review your work on Exercise 2-1 to determine your level of familiarity. In addition, while bar study is different because of the increase in number of topics and reduced time when compared to your law school work, your commercial bar course will provide study materials for you that have already been chunked and categorized. Therefore, you do not have to read several cases to learn what the rule is for a topic. The commercial course will give it to you.

As mentioned above, the commercial course is designed to re-teach and teach in some instances the information to you in a way that will prepare you for the bar exam. To that end, the commercial materials come with thousands of questions and many tips and strategies for answering questions on specific topics and on test taking in general. Thus, the approximately eight to ten week study period, if you prepare for it, will be adequate time to become prepared for your bar exam in most cases.

In addition, you have already learned or been exposed to many of the skills necessary for bar exam success during the course of your law school study. In law school, you learned very quickly that you would need to organize your life so you could study multiple topics and practice questions in a relatively short study period. You also learned that you would need to systematize the material so that you could memorize from it. You practiced writing essays so that your thoughts were expressed concisely and clearly. On your final exams, you demonstrated an ability to spot issues, provide the appropriate law, and apply it to the facts. You demonstrated your skill at structuring your writing so that your reader would be confident that you understand how the interrelated parts of the law work. You also showed that you could analyze multiple-choice questions and choices to reach the correct answer in a timely manner. Thus, what is similar between your law school exam preparation and bar exam preparation are the basic foundational legal analytic skills needed for success. To assess where you are with these skills now, think about your study strengths and weaknesses using the worksheet in Exercise 2-3 below.

Your instructor can help you interpret the results.

EXERCISE 2-3

ASSESSING YOUR STUDY SKILLS

Your Acquired Skills

1. Do you feel you understand the IRAC structure? ☐ Yes ☐ No
2. When reading an exam question, are able to spot all of the issues? ☐ Yes ☐ No
3. When answering an exam question, are you able to utilize the IRAC structure? ☐ Yes ☐ No

Study Strategies

1. Please select the answer that best describes the first time you review your class notes. Please select only one answer.
   - ☐ Directly following the class period
   - ☐ At the end of the week
   - ☐ At the conclusion of the class when you begin studying for exams
   - ☐ You never review your notes again
   - ☐ At the conclusion of all your classes for the day
   - ☐ At the end of the month
   - ☐ You don't take notes

2. When you begin studying for an exam which of the following strategies do you utilize? Please select all that apply.
   - ☐ Studying in a group
   - ☐ Studying alone
   - ☐ Discussing concepts/ideas with peers
   - ☐ Seeking help from professors/advisors when you have a question
   - ☐ Studying with commercial study aids
   - ☐ Reviewing notes
   - ☐ Preparing an outline
   - ☐ Rereading cases
   - ☐ Reviewing commercial Outlines

3. Please select the answer that best describes the amount of time you spend preparing for an exam (this includes actual class time, class preparation time and outlining, study groups, visiting professor during office hours, etc.),
   - ☐ 0 - 200 hours ☐ 201 - 400 hours ☐ 401 - 600 hours

4. How often do you consult professors regarding questions or to discuss ideas? Please select only one.
   - ☐ Never
   - ☐ Only when meetings are required
   - ☐ Once a semester
   - ☐ 2-3 times a semester
   - ☐ 3-5 times a semester
   - ☐ 5-10 times a semester
   - ☐ More than 10 times a semester

Processing

1. Do you prepare outlines, flashcards, or other study materials for all or most of your courses?   ☐ Yes ☐ No
2. If you prepare outlines, flashcards or other study materials, how often do you work on them?

   ☐ Following each class period   ☐ Near the end of the semester
   ☐ At the end of each week   ☐ Just prior to the exam
   ☐ At the end of each month

3. Does processing (outlining, flashcarding, or other type of study technique help you organize your thoughts while you are studying for the exam?   ☐ Yes ☐ No

Exam Taking Strategies (This applies to both essay and multiple-choice questions)

1. When starting an exam, do you allocate the appropriate amount of time to each question?   ☐ Yes ☐ No
2. If you allocate time limits for each question, do you adhere to them?   ☐ Yes ☐ No
3. Do you read the call of the question first (before you read the question hypothetical)?   ☐ Yes ☐ No
4. Do you outline your answer before you begin to write it?   ☐ Yes ☐ No
5. Do you organize your writing using IRAC?   ☐ Yes ☐ No

D. EVALUATING YOUR SUBSTANTIVE KNOWLEDGE OF BAR TESTED SUBJECTS

There are some students who have taken a course in law school for every topic potentially tested on the bar exam. As stated earlier, much of your first year and upper division required courses covered bar tested topics. But, there are many of you who will experience a topic for the first time during bar review. Before starting your bar preparation, inventory the courses you have taken and assess how well you did in the courses. If there are courses on your list you have not taken, did not do well in, or do not feel confident about, make time to review the bar subjects related to those courses during your last year of law school and prior to beginning your bar study period.

Begin by reviewing the board of law examiners' website for the state you plan to take the bar in. These websites usually have a link to the state's rules on bar admission and bar tested topics. Your law school website may also contain links to such information. Once you have a list of potentially tested bar topics, review it to determine which courses you took in law school that would cover the topics. As you list the topics, assess your level of comfort with the topic. Your level of comfort will determine the method you use and the time you devote to reviewing a topic pre-bar study.

You have many options for reviewing the bar exam topics on your list. Contact the commercial bar course provider you have signed up with. The provider may be willing to send your books early or give you online access to bar subject outlines. You might also request an audio version of the material. This is especially helpful if you have any learning preferences associated with auditory learning. Also, students who have long commutes typically make use of audio versions of materials for some aspect of their studies.

> **BOX NOTE 2-4**
>
> ### *Bar Topic and Course Name Differences*
>
> Once you know which subjects you haven't been exposed to, briefly look over commercial bar preparation materials to make sure that the material is indeed unfamiliar to you. Sometimes subjects may go by slightly different names and you may have studied a subject but not realize it. Create a list for yourself. This will ensure you know what you don't know.

E. CHOOSING THE COMMERCIAL BAR EXAM STUDY COURSE THAT'S RIGHT FOR YOU

We've already covered much of this information in the earlier sections on paying for a commercial course and assessing your learning style. Use this section for a brief recap of what you learned there and for additional information. When assessing what commercial bar review program is right for you, consider the following:

1. **Learning style.**
   As stated earlier in this chapter, understanding your learning style will help you pick the best commercial course for you. For example, if you learn information visually and/or aurally, a commercial course provides flowcharts as well as live and/or recorded lectures may be a nice fit for your learning style(s).
2. **Absorption environment.**
   Assess the environments in which you best absorb information. Do you feel more comfortable surrounded by people or studying on your own? Does it help you to be at a live or taped lecture or is it easier to learn looking at an online video?
   Once you have decided what kind environment works best for you, you will then have to discover what kind of program each commercial course offers. What type of written and on-line materials are you supplied with? How does the provider impart information?
3. **Financial cost of the courses.**
   Once you have researched the various commercial courses, research the cost of each of those courses. Earlier in this chapter you reviewed your financial situation for the time surrounding the bar exam study period. Now, make sure you revisit that information and review it in terms of the commercial course you are interested in. Make sure that the commercial course is a financial fit as well as a learning style and absorption environment fit.

4. **Performance in law school.**

Finally, when choosing a commercial bar exam study course, review your performance during your time in law school. What kind of course were you the most successful in? What type of course caused you the most problems? If you had problems absorbing and processing information in law school, think about which commercial course would best help avoid or alleviate some of those problems.

F. CONCLUSION

This chapter covers what you should do prior to the beginning of your bar exam studies. Engaging fully with the checklists and surveys located in this chapter will help you get a clear picture of your past study techniques, study habits, learning style, finances, and the kind of study environment that would work best for you. Having a clear picture of what would create a healthy learning environment before the study period begins will help you engage in your bar studies more fully and complete those studies with more confidence. Take this preparation seriously and you will be well on your way to a successful bar exam study experience.

CHAPTER 2 RECAP

▶ *CREATE THE RIGHT STUDY ATMOSPHERE BY CONSIDERING:*
- Your financial condition
- Whether you should work while you study for the bar exam
- How your loved ones will be impacted
- Your physical study space

▶ *DETERMINE OR RE-DETERMINE HOW YOU LEARN*

▶ *ASSESS YOUR SKILLS*

▶ *EVALUATE YOUR SUBSTANTIVE KNOWLEDGE OF BAR TESTED SUBJECTS*

▶ *CHOOSE A COMMERCIAL BAR EXAM STUDY COURSE BY CONSIDERING:*
- Your learning style
- What physical environments you best absorb information in
- Financial costs of courses
- Your performance in law school

Engaging from the Start:
What to Do about Those Lectures, Commercial Subject Outlines, and Other Bar Materials?

INTRODUCTION

A fully engaged approach allows you to not only absorb the information provided by the commercial bar course, but also provides a process for organizing the material, learning it, memorizing it, using it to respond to questions on the bar exam, and ultimately studying it more intensely to increase your chances of bar exam success.

So, how do you begin the process so that you are engaged from the very beginning of your bar study? How do you engage with the voluminous amount of material and resources provided by your commercial bar course in a way that ensures your success on the biggest closed book exam of your life? You apply the three-step process for engaged learning set out in Chapter 1. This process will help you to better engage your analytical skills from the very start by helping you to effectively use the material and resources provided by your commercial bar course.

This engagement process requires that you first critically preview the information on a given topic. Once you have previewed the information and absorbed it more fully, you are ready to organize and begin the process of learning and memorizing the information. Finally, you need to ensure you have assimilated the information in a way that allows you to recall it under time pressure as you encounter bar exam questions. In other words, you need a tool that will help you stick that information in your head, help it stay there, and help you apply the information to an essay or multiple-choice question.

The three-step engagement process will push you to do more than just read the bar course outlines, attend lectures, or do practice questions. While those tasks are important individually, the three-step engagement process provides a method for bringing all these actions together into a pattern of bar study that will ultimately mean success on the bar exam. Below is a detailed explanation of how you might use the process in this stage of your bar study.

A. STEP 1: CRITICALLY PREVIEW BY REVIEWING THE TOPIC AND WATCHING THE LECTURE

The first step in the engagement process is to critically preview the information before you attend the lecture. This step will prime your brain and get it ready for the subject so you don't go into the lecture cold without any recent background. Critically previewing can be analogized to building a bookshelf. This bookshelf will become the repository for your books—the subject areas you will process in preparation for the bar exam. But, before you can develop, organize, and

---

BOX NOTE 3-1

Can I Skip Step 2 (Organizing by Producing a Product) if I Feel Comfortable with the Subject?

Remember, the goal of this step is to process the information. To do that, you need to engage the lecture material. The best way to begin engaging the material is to assess whether it is organized in a way that will help you memorize and answer questions. You may decide that the lecture notes are organized in a way that comports with your learning style and you can thus study from them as they are. You may decide that the lecture notes work for the most part but you need to add a few examples from the bar outlines. You may decide that you only need to process a portion of the lecture notes. You may decide that you need to rework all the lecture notes for a particular subject.

After making a decision about what to do with your lecture notes, you may find, after working a few questions, that you need to rethink that decision. If you discover that you are having difficulty spotting issues, recalling the law, or addressing a factual situation, this may be a sign that you need to rethink your earlier decision regarding the processing product.

As you decide about what to do with your lecture notes, keep in mind that this decision may change from subject to subject. For example, the lecture notes alone may work for Torts, but you may want to create a chart or flashcards for Civil Procedure. Also, keep in mind that you do not need, nor will you have the time, to rework every set of lecture notes. Thus, use the time immediately after the lecture to determine, based on your knowledge of your learning style, your work on questions, or your experience with studying for and taking exams, what you will do with your lecture notes. And keep in mind that you can always change your mind as you continue to work with the material throughout bar study.

These efforts are part of being actively engaged with the material. Researchers have found that by engaging actively with information, a student has a better chance of adequately processing and remembering it. This level of engagement will thus increase your ability to retain the information and ultimately use it successfully in answering a bar exam question.

See Anzai, Yuichiro; and Simon, Herbert A, *The Theory of Learning by Doing*, Psychological Review (86:2), 1979, 124-140.

ultimately shelve your books, you must have a structure for storage in place. The critical preview step provides that structure.

Review subjects before attending or listening to a lecture on that subject. You can use the commercially prepared outlines supplied by your bar course for this action. As you read the body of the outline, use the outline's table of contents to check off the concepts you feel familiar with. As you do this, note that you will have several more attempts to learn, memorize, and apply the information (remember the other steps in the engagement process). At this stage, you just want to make sure you are familiar with the terms and concepts and that nothing is foreign or unfamiliar. If you cannot check off the concept, resolve to read the outline more closely on only that part before the lecture.

You may prefer a more aural approach to reading the outline. Some bar courses offer audio versions of lectures to facilitate this type of review. As you listen, use the commercial outline table of contents to check off the concepts you are familiar with just as you would if you were reading the outline.

This review can be as much or as little as you need. While you want to use it to build a strong beginning structure, you also want to recognize that you will have several opportunities to more fully engage the material and thus you do not want to overspend your time on this one step. If you are very comfortable with the area of the law (e.g., you scored very high in your Torts class, you used many Civil Procedure and Evidence rules when you took Trial Advocacy, you learned all about creating partnerships in your summer internship, you worked as a teaching assistant for your Contracts professor, etc.), a light reading or listening may suffice. If, however, it is an unfamiliar subject area or one where you did poorly, a more intense reading or listening is probably necessary. If you need to do a more intense preview, familiarize yourself with the major topics according

FIGURE 3-1   SAMPLE AGENCY AND PARTNERSHIP BAR OUTLINE TABLE OF CONTENTS

I.		Agency Relationship	2	
	a.	Assent	2	✓
	b.	On behalf of benefit	2	✗
	c.	Control	3	✓
II.		Agency authority	3	
	a.	Actual	3	✓
	b.	Apparent	3	✓
	c.	Ratification	4	✗
	d.	Estoppel	4	✗
	e.	Inherent Agency Power	5	✗
		i. Election and Waiver	5	✗

to the bar course outline by underlining, writing, or highlighting the associated buzz words or phrases. You may find that repeating those words and phrases aloud as you go along may assist you as well. Also, make note of any steps, processes, or methods for analyzing topics under the particular area. Critical previewing activities such as those discussed in this chapter will prime your brain and ensure that you are prepared for and ready to engage the area of law before you attend your lecture.

Working questions may also provide a good critical preview before you watch or attend the lecture. Doing so could help you to understand how the topic is tested and thus how you might begin to chunk and categorize the information in your lecture notes to align with the questions for that particular subject.

Your critical preview does not end with your pre-lecture review. You continue to "build your bookcase" by attending or watching the lecture, being attentive, and generating the lecture notes that will be the foundation for the next step in the engagement process.

B. STEP 2: ORGANIZE THE LECTURE NOTES BY PRODUCING A PROCESSING PRODUCT

Once you engage in the critical preview, which includes your pre-lecture review and attending or listening to the assigned lecture, the next engagement step requires an organizing activity. You will have to organize those lecture notes into a product that assists you in learning and processing the material. This step is potentially the most time consuming of all the engagement steps. It involves creating a product of your own in a way that will allow you to memorize its content, spot issues, recall appropriate rules, apply them to relevant facts, and reach reasoned conclusions. Thus, this product will represent your effort in organizing the information you received during your lecture in a logical and substantive fashion such that you can answer bar exam questions.

This product can take many different forms—traditional outlines, flashcards, flowcharts, tables, and even the lecture notes as provided by the lecturer. This section will provide suggestions for determining which processing product will work for you and creating that product once you make your decision.

Let's return to the bookcase analogy. Once you have built your bookcase by critically previewing the subject and attending the lecture on that subject, you will need to fill that bookcase with books. The processing products you develop are those "books." They are books that are tailored to your needs. These books or processing products cover each of the substantive areas that are tested on the bar exam. They can be as thin or thick as you need them to be. They comprise your library of information, and your dedication to early and consistent bar study.

1. Choosing a Processing Product

There are many processing products you could create to help you memorize and learn the material. To determine which processing product you should create for each bar exam subject, consider the following questions.

a. How Does My Learning Style Influence What Processing Product I Choose?

First, when deciding which processing product to use, have a good understanding of how you learn. Are you a reader/writer type learner? Are you an aural learner? Do visuals help you to best conceptualize ideas? Do you learn better by doing? Do you use a combination of these styles in processing information?[1]

Determining the answers to these questions will maximize your study time and level of preparation by allowing you to study in the most effective and impactful way. For instance, if you are a visual learner, rewriting the information in a traditional outline may not completely assist you in assimilating it. Remember, your goal is to be an active and engaged learner. Thus, if you are a visual learner, creating a processing product that allows you to visually see parts of rules and their connections to facts is more appropriate for you. A flow or symbols chart for some or all the subject matter would be very effective for a visual learner. Similarly, if you learn best by organizing the material into prose, flowcharts and symbols may mean little to you. Writing the concepts to highlight and draw out the connections is the best course for you.

In Chapter 2, we discussed your learning style in terms of how you absorb and process information. Now, using what you know about your learning style, determine how you process information. This will help you to determine what type of processing product you should choose. Keep in mind that you are not stuck with one style of processing. You may use multiple types throughout the course of your bar study. More specifics on producing different products are included later in this chapter.

In addition to knowing how you learn, you should also have a clear understanding of how well you know the subject when deciding on a processing product. Return to Exercise 2-1 in Chapter 2. Even if you took the course in law school and received a grade of A for your efforts, ask yourself (and be honest in your answer) whether you understand the subject enough to, in a closed book test setting, determine what issue is being tested, recall the appropriate law and analysis, and express your thoughts in a coherent manner under time pressure. In almost every situation, if you ask this question at the beginning of bar study,

---

> **BOX NOTE 3-2**
>
> *Engagement Steps*
> 1. Critically Previewing
> 2. Organizing Activity
> 3. Reaching the Goal or Producing the Product

---

1. VARK, http://vark-learn.com/the-vark-questionnaire/ (last visited April 21, 2018).

the answer will be no. However, as you critically preview the subject matter, watch lectures, and process the material, you will begin to get a sense of how well you are learning the subject presented.

b. Does the Lecturer's Presentation Align with How I Learn?

Next, consider the style of the lecturer's presentation. If you learn best when information is presented with lots of visual diagrams showing connections from one concept to another (think flowchart) and the lecturer presents the information that way, then perhaps it will take less effort to create a processing product that will allow you to memorize the information and answer questions regarding it. You may end up only modifying the lecture notes a bit to turn them into a product suitable for you. This may not be the case if you learn the information best when it is presented in traditional outline format. You will have to expend additional effort to turn that visually diagrammed lecture into traditional outline format.

Even if the lecturer presents the information in a way that aligns with your learning style (how you best absorb and process the information), there may still be specific issues within a subject that require additional effort for you to assimilate. Consider the student who learns information best when it's presented in traditional outline format and who encounters a lecture presented in just that way. While this student may have to expend less effort in processing the subject matter as a whole, there still may be areas within that subject that may need additional processing. For instance, imagine that after listening to the Constitutional Law lecture, you determine that the style in which the lecturer presented the material lines up with the way you process and learn information. You thus decide not to create a processing product but to study directly from the lecture notes. Yet, when you begin to practice and test your understanding of the subject by working

---

BOX NOTE 3-3

How Do I Determine and Resolve Any Issues in Lecture Notes (Regardless of the Processing Product I Decide to Create)?

As you are working through your lecture notes, determine if there are any "soft spots." A soft spot would be any place in the lecture notes that provides a less than clear representation of the rules, sub-rules, rule exceptions, and examples. Also, make sure the materials give adequate examples that clearly demonstrate how the rules are applied to facts.

If you find soft spots and need to supplement your lecture notes, regardless of the processing product you choose, use the subject outline books provided by your commercial bar course vendor. Add whatever information you gain from the outlines.

*A note of caution is warranted:

In processing your notes, whether you stick with your lecture notes or create something new from those notes, you should use the vendor subject outline books only to supplement your soft spots. Do not attempt to consolidate what is in the subject outline books and your lecture notes. The goal here is to use the lecture notes as the base of your processing product and to add information from the outline books only as necessary to shore up any soft spots in those lecture notes.

questions, you discover that various constitutional amendments are proving difficult to assimilate. You mix them up or forget them altogether as you work multiple-choice questions. Thus, even though you have a processing product that aligns with your learning style preference, you may still need additional processing products to help you learn those difficult to assimilate areas of a specific subject. Perhaps making flashcards just for the amendments will help you memorize and understand them better as you are practicing multiple-choice questions.

> **BOX NOTE 3-4**
>
> ### What to Include in Your Processing Product
>
> - Issue Spotting Triggers
> - Clear Statements of Law
> - Examples of Factual Scenarios
> - Bar Exam Strategies
> - Organizing Principles

c. What Else Besides the Law Should My Product Include?

Also, keep in mind that the processing product should be useful to you in developing connections among topics and sub-topics. It should not only contain the law, it should also contain triggers to help you determine what topics are at issue and the order in which you address those topics. Assume you are answering a Contracts question that directs you to determine whether there is an enforceable agreement. To be ready for this question, your processing product would need to tell you more than just the fact that offer, offer termination, acceptance, consideration, and defenses were implicated. It would need to also help you learn in what factual context those concepts would be triggered and in what order you should discuss them once they are triggered. Thus, your processing product should contain not only the law, but examples of how the law is applied and bar exam and issue spotting tips. It should also contain organizing principles—a visually clear and direct structure for analyzing and writing an answer to a given bar exam question.

2. The Different Types of Processing Products

There are several different processing products you can use. Below are some of the basic structures. Remember, you can use these products singly or in combination to create your ideal processing product.

a. Outlines

The outline is the most traditional of all products and represents what many students use in law school to organize course material. Creating an outline is helpful because it forces you to marshal the material in an organized format using a hierarchical structure. This structure is divided into headings and subheadings that distinguishes main topics' points from supporting topics[2] and shows the

---

2. Richard Nordquist, *Outline (Composition)*, ThoughtCo. (Feb. 20, 2018), https://www. thoughtco.com/outline-composition-term-1691364.

FIGURE 3-2   SAMPLE AGENCY AND PARTNERSHIP BAR OUTLINE (PARTIAL)

- ***AGENCY RELATIONSHIP (ABC)*—issue spotting trigger**—look for situations where there is a question as to what type of relationship there is—may be default where there is partnership or employer/ee relationship is not plausible
  - The agency relationship is created when both parties have **assented** to the relationship, the agent is acting on **behalf of and for the benefit** of the principal and there is **control** by the principal over the agent.
    - Assented—Principal and agent agree to be in relationship. (Client (principal) agrees to hire attorney (agent) for representation.)
    - On behalf of—Attorney (agent) acts for the benefit of client (principal).
    - Control—The client (principal) has control over the agent's (attorney) actions—must be more than just negative control—must direct the agent's actions.
      - Example: Client (principal) and attorney (agent) relationship. Sole proprietor (principal) engages a marketing expert (agent).

BAR EXAM TIPS/STRATEGIES: Even if it's short, always discuss agency relationship, unless the facts state that such a relationship exists. If so, then acknowledge and move on!

- ***AGENCY AUTHORITY*—issue spotting trigger/bar exam tip**—once the agency relationship is determined (and even if I think it is not), discuss authority (determine what authority the agent had to act on behalf of the principal).
- ***Types of authority*—actual**
  - Rule—***Actual authority*—**that authority given by the principal to the agent to act on the principal's behalf—can be both express and implied—issue spotting trigger—look for direct communications between the principal and the agent where the principal gives direct instructions to agent regarding tasks
    - **Express**—principal explicitly tells the agent what to do.
    - **Implied**—agent's authority to do those things which would accomplish the the principal's express directives.
  - Examples—Sole proprietor engages marketing expert to advertise products and attract consumers to the brand. Sole proprietor tells marketing expert to develop and execute a marketing plan. Marketing expert exercises implied authority to execute marketing plan by signing television ad contracts.
  - Rule –Apparent authority . . .

BAR EXAM TIPS/STRATEGIES: To determine whether an agent had actual authority, consider both express and implied authority. Look for limiting statements from the principal to the agent. This will typically negate actual authority.

connections among those topics. Most students use letters, numbers, indentations, or other word processing techniques to demonstrate those topic distinctions and connections. You should adopt this type of product if organizing the material into meaningful list and/or prose form assists you in processing and learning it.

FIGURE 3-3   Flashcards

Front of trigger flash card	Back of trigger flash card
AGENCY AUTHORITY	Look for facts surrounding communication with Principle and Agent
ACTUAL AUTHORITY	Always discuss

b. Flashcards

While flashcards are traditionally used as a memorization tool, flashcards can also be used in place of the traditional outline to help you process and learn the material. When using flashcards in this way, remember that the same connections that were necessary in a traditional outline are also necessary here. Flashcards are best used when you feel it would be useful to process those connections in discrete pieces. For instance, if you would like to represent your issue spotting triggers on a flashcard, you will put the triggers on one side of the card and the triggered topics and sub-topics on the other side. In addition, you can also create flashcards that reference rules, sub-rules, exceptions to rules, examples, tips, and organizing principals. This will help you with memorization, but it will also allow you to clearly see the connections between and amongst the topics and sub-topics.

When creating the flashcards, make sure the cards do not contain too much information and are not visually overwhelming. Make each card easy to follow with bullet points and some color coding. If you find yourself writing too much on a given flashcard, it may be a signal that you are trying to cover too much within one topic. If so, create another flashcard to break the concept down further. You want each flashcard to be succinct and easy to digest.

> **BOX NOTE 3-5**
>
> ### Make It "Memorizable"
>
> To make your processing product memorizable, use color and bold. Make the entries clear and direct and use bold or color coding to draw the eye. However, be careful not to overdo the color and bold or it will quickly become unreadable and thus impossible to memorize. Furthermore, create the product so that you can cover up part of it and recite the information without looking.

c. Flowcharts and Tables

Flowcharts can be used when a central issue or idea splits off into smaller branches that maintain a direct connection to that central issue. Tables also help to section information into discrete pieces so that you can categorize and organize the information as you encounter and study it. Similar to flashcards, flowcharts will help you visualize those connections in discrete pieces. To bring out the crucial details in a flowchart, use color and different shapes to represent different issues and ideas.

d. Sticking with the Lecture Notes

As discussed in Chapter 2, your commercial bar course vendor will supply many resources and materials for you to use. You've already learned how and when you should use those materials. If you find that the commercial bar lecture notes are organized in a way that comports with your learning style preference and

FIGURE 3-4 FLOWCHART

CONCEPT/ISSUE	**AGENCY RELATIONSHIP**

ISSUE SPOTTING TRIGGERS	Question may ask about the relationship between the parties. • May be default when partnership or employer/ee relationship does not seem plausible.

RULE	Agency is the relationship that results where both parties have **assented** to the relationship; the agent is acting **on behalf and for the benefit** of the principal; and there is **control** by the principal over the agent. Agency relationship = ABC

ANALYSIS	Assented – Principal and agent agree to be in relationship. (Client (principal) agrees to hire attorney (agent) for representation.) On behalf of – Attorney (agent) acts for the benefit of client (principal). Control – The client (principal) has control over the agent's (attorney) actions –must be more than just negative control – must direct the agent's actions. Examples: Client (principal) and attorney (agent) relationship. Sole proprietor (principal) engages marketing expert (agent).

BAR EXAM TIPS	Even if it's short, always discuss agency relationship, unless the facts state that such a relationship exists. If so, then acknowledge and move on!

are in memorizable form, you may not need to create a new processing product. Instead, you can use the already created lecture notes as they are. Even if you decide you can use the lecture notes as they are, you still may need to supplement certain sections. See Box Note 3-3 for help in deciding when you need to supplement.

3. Active Memorization

Finally, keep in mind, as you go about creating your processing product (whatever it might be), that you are going to use it as a memorization tool. Your processing product should contain the law, examples, and bar exam and issue spotting tips. It should also display organizing principles.

Just by reviewing your notes and determining what processing product you will use, you have already begun to memorize. But, remember that you are

FIGURE 3-5 TABLE

Concept/Issue	Issue-Spotting Triggers	Rule/Definition	Examples	Bar Exam Tips/Strategies
AGENCY RELATIONSHIP	Scenarios about the type of relationship between the parties. May be default where there are two parties but neither a partnership nor an employer/employee relationship are plausible.	Agency is the relationship that results where both parties have *assented* to the relationship; the agent is acting *on behalf and for the benefit* of the principal; and there is *control* by the principal over the agent.	Client (principal) and attorney (agent) relationship. Sole proprietor (principal) engages a marketing expert (agent).	Tip for remembering elements—ABC. Even if it's short, always discuss agency relationship, unless the facts state that such a relationship exists. If so, then acknowledge and move on!
AGENCY AUTHORITY	Once the agency relationship is determined (even if not created and I assume for my argument that it was created), discuss what authority the agent had to act on behalf of the principal.	Agency authority can be actual.	Sole proprietor engages a marketing expert to advertise products and attract consumers to the brand.	To determine whether an agent had actual authority, consider both express and implied authority. Look for limiting statements from the principal to the agent. This will typically negate actual authority
Actual		*Actual*—authority is that authority given by the principal to the agent which authorizes the agent to act on behalf of the principal. Can be express or implied.	Sole proprietor tells marketing expert to develop and execute a marketing plan.	
Express		*Express*—principal explicitly tells the agent what to do.	Marketing expert exercises implied authority to execute marketing plan by signing television ad contracts.	
Implied		*Implied*—agent's authority to do those things that would accomplish the principal's express directives.		

actively engaging in each step of the process. Thus, you will have to actively memorize and do more than just passively read your processing product. To ensure you know the material in a way that will allow you to retrieve it during the biggest closed book exam of your life, you will need to cement your approach through active memorization.

If you have lecture notes, supplemented lecture notes, or have created a processing product independently, go through the processing product and mark a green check next to a particular piece of information you have successfully memorized. Mark any information you have not committed to memory with a red *X*. This creates a very easy visual guide that will quickly show if you know a topic or not. It will also create a database of how many times you have reviewed and attempted to memorize that processing product or set of lecture notes. For instance, if there are checks and *X*s three columns thick, you know you have reviewed that processing product outline three times. Finally, it lets you know what your weak areas are and that you should probably spend extra time memorizing those areas.

If you have created or are in the process of creating flashcards, creating piles is a quick and easy visual guide as to what subject topics you have successfully committed to memory. Create a pile for those cards you consistently get correct (the "I know it" pile). Then, create another pile of the cards you consistently get incorrect (the "I don't know it . . . yet" pile). Right away, you will see what specific subject areas you are struggling with. When you are done with that subject, put the "I don't know it . . . yet" pile on top so you will know to give those cards extra attention the next time you go through that subject. Also, consider putting a check mark on each completed flashcard so that you will have a visual reminder of how many times you have reviewed and attempted to memorize the flashcard's information.

If you are working with a flowchart, covering up each box and reciting the information to yourself without looking at what you have covered is a quick and easy way to determine if you have committed the materials to memory. Like the outline, put a green check by the flowchart box you do know and a red *X* by the box you don't. You should also attempt to reproduce a skeletal version of the flowchart (without looking) so that you are certain you have memorized the connections amongst topics and the order in which you should present them in response to a question.

To commit these different processing products to memory, consider using mnemonic and acronym techniques. For instance, memorizing the planets in the solar system, which we all had to do in 4th grade, is usually done with a mnemonic—My (Mars) Very

---

BOX NOTE 3-6

Other Memorization Techniques

There are several other techniques to assist in your memorization and you will already have put many of them to use in processing your lecture notes.

These include:

- Grouping or Chunking
- Word/Place/Thing Association
- Visualization
- Listing

Banikowski, Alison K., Strategies to Enhance Brain Research, Focus on Exceptional Children, 0015511X, Oct. 99, Vol. 32, Issue 2.

FIGURE 3-6

BOX NOTE 3-7

If I Start Memorizing Too Early, Won't I Forget?

Remember that you are already memorizing by working through engagement steps 1 and 2.

Your commercial bar course has already chunked and arranged the material so that the categories and connections among the topic are sorted. Thus, in many instances, as you encounter and continually expose yourself to the material, you are remembering it.

But this won't work for everyone and it won't work on everything. Thus, active memorization is required so that you are constantly assessing what you know and what you do not know during the course of bar study. Active memorization will force you to find some tool or technique to make sure you remember those things that have not "stuck" after reading your processing product or lecture notes. But you cannot actively memorize at the last minute. You must do it throughout bar study. If are consistently categorizing information and establishing connections among the information, you likely will not forget it over the course of bar study.

(Venus) Educated (Earth) Mother (Mercury) Just (Jupiter) Served (Saturn) Us (Uranus) Nine (Neptune) Pickles (Pluto).[3] Also, remember how the acronym H.O.M.E.S. helped us remember the Great Lakes—H (Huron) O (Ontario) M (Michigan) E (Erie) S (Superior)?[4] Even as adults we can still remember this information. That is the power of the mnemonic and acronym techniques.

You can employ the same techniques for bar study. Note that not all the bar exam study content lends itself to these techniques, but in many instances, it can aid in your memorization. For example, to have a valid will, there must be (M) mental capacity, (I) intent, a (S) signature, (T) testamentary age and (A)

---

3. *See Mnemonics for the Order of the Planets Orbiting the Sun*, MNEMONIC-DEVICE, https://www.mnemonic-device.com/astronomy/mnemonic-device-to-remember-the-planets-orbiting-the-sun/ (last visited April 21, 2018). While Pluto is no longer a recognized planet, the power of the mnemonic used to remember it remains! *See generally* Paul Rincon, *Why is Pluto No Longer a Planet?*, BBC News (July 13, 2015), http://www.bbc.com/news/science-environment-33462184.

4. *Mnemonic Device for the Five Great Lakes*, JRANK PSYCHOLOGY ENCYCLOPEDIA, http://psychology.jrank.org/pages/426/Mnemonic-Strategies.html (last visited April 21, 2018).

attestation. The first letter of each of these requirements spells M.I.S.T.A. You may forget a requirement, but it is less likely that you will forget the acronym. Additionally, you could form a mnemonic phrase with the first letters of each requirement—Making It Stick Takes Acumen. The phrase, "making it stick" may force you to think of validity as well as help you to remember the elements. The goal is that you create something that helps you to remember. But, be engaged in your use of these techniques. If they do not work for you or do not help you to remember, abandon them for techniques that do.

You do not have to finish your processing the product to start memorizing the material. In fact, some subjects have such voluminous content, that it may be more efficient to divide it into several parts. If that is the case, you can process and memorize each part separately.

This active memorization will be done according to your schedule (covered in Chapter 4), which will indicate to you what topics you will cover on each day. Set aside time, every day, to go over your completed or mostly completed processing product for the day's topic or topics and make sure you are committing the material to memory. If your days are too full with attending or viewing lectures, processing your notes and working problems, use the weekends to commit the material to memory. It is crucial to the process that you not wait until the last weeks of bar study to engage in active memorization. You must do so throughout the bar study period.

C. STEP 3: REACH YOUR GOAL BY PUTTING THE PROCESSING PRODUCT TO WORK

The final step in the three-step engagement process is reaching your goal. That goal could include answering a certain percentage of multiple-choice questions correctly or providing the appropriate analysis for an essay question. The primary way you will reach your goal is to put your processing products to work consistently throughout the bar study period. Remember the bookcase analogy. The bookcase was built by critically previewing the subject before attending the lecture. That bookcase was further strengthened when you attended or listened to the lecture. You then stocked that bookcase with the products you created as you processed or organized the material generated from those lectures. Now your "library" is ready for use. The books you have created, your processing product or lecture notes, should be your primary study aids for the subjects potentially tested on the bar exam. So, now it's time to put your library to use and move yourself further along the road to bar exam success!

This final step involves using or practicing with the information. Processing and memorizing the material is very important but developing your ability to apply that material to a fact pattern is equally as crucial. In other words, your processing of a subject is not complete until you do practice essays or multiple-choice questions on that subject (if it is a multiple-choice subject) to determine if your process, up to this point, is working.

During the study process, you will use the essays and multiple-choice questions as a tool to help you learn the material and not only as "simulation" for the bar exam. Using the questions as learning tools helps you to verify that you have chosen the correct processing product and memorization technique. Doing questions early and often helps you to simultaneously uncover and correct any deficiencies in your process.

If it is a large subject, complete your processing product in stages. Do essays or multiple choice questions that relate to the subject topics you have processed. Once the essay or multiple-choice questions have been completed, review the detailed model answers. Make sure you have spotted the correct issues, recalled the appropriate rules, engaged in the appropriate analysis, used appropriate buzz words and phrases, and ordered your discussion in a logical way. Review your processing product. Make sure it is organized to help you achieve these goals. If it is not, and you find there are pieces missing from it, supplement your processing product with what you have discovered from the model answers.

Even if you have not finished the processing product on the subject or have not completely committed it to memory, work practice questions. Remember that reaching your goal requires that you create a processing product that helps you to develop your working knowledge of the law by exposing you to the ways bar exam questions are asked and the answers are structured. Working problems will help you to ensure that you have created a processing product that will train you to spot issues, choose correct rules, and write succinct well-reasoned analyses on the actual bar exam. Thus, you **MUST** work problems *as* you develop your processing product and throughout the learning process.

D. CONCLUSION

The three steps that lead to engaged learning are presented and practiced sequentially, but they are also recursive. They represent a cycle of learning that you will engage in during your bar study period. Critically previewing subjects before you watch the lecture and watching or attending the lecture will help you create a structure for ultimately assimilating the material. Organizing the lecture material by choosing and developing your processing products will allow you to continue engagement by building your knowledge base. And finally, you will reach your goal by consistently working problems to test the efficiency of your processing products and your memorization techniques. You will continue this engagement cycle throughout your study period.

Getting used to these steps to become and stay engaged in your bar study may take some time if you do not typically approach your studies in such a methodical fashion. Bar students frequently see the merit in this type of study but question the time commitment given the usual eight to ten week bar study period. To make this work, you will need to schedule your time so that you can successfully complete all three steps on a recurring basis. The best way to visualize this process is to think about a cycle where each step flows to the next and then back again moving in a circular pattern. As you begin bar study by utilizing the three-step cycle of critically previewing the material, organizing and processing the material by producing a product, and reaching your goal by putting that product to work, you are essentially setting yourself up for a pattern of processing and learning the information that will maximize your chance for success on the bar exam.

CHAPTER 3 RECAP

▶ *CRITICALLY PREVIEWING*
  - Reviewing commercial bar prep outline, listening to an audio summary of the subject or working questions prior to attending/watching lecture
  - Attending commercial bar prep lecture

▶ *ORGANIZING THE LECTURE NOTES BY PRODUCING A PROCESSING PRODUCT*
  - Processing notes from bar class
  - Choosing the product (outline, flashcards or flowchart) or product combination that aligns with your learning style
  - Developing a product that will assist you in active memorization

▶ *REACHING YOUR GOAL BY PUTTING THE PROCESSING PRODUCT TO WORK*
  - Working questions to verify you have chosen the correct product(s) and to determine if your process is working

PART II

ORGANIZING ACTIVITIES

CHAPTER 4   Creating the Bar Exam Study Schedule
CHAPTER 5   MPT
CHAPTER 6   MEE—Essays
CHAPTER 7   MBE—Multiple Choice
CHAPTER 8   FINAL DAYS—Review

Creating a Bar Exam Study Schedule: This Is Not Gone with the Wind and You Are Not Scarlett O'Hara!

INTRODUCTION

Let us explain. In the movie, *Gone with The Wind*, the main character, Scarlett O'Hara, has a habit of putting off tough decisions and contemplating difficult thoughts.[1] At one point in the movie, Scarlett says, "I can't think about that right now. If I do, I'll go crazy. I'll think about that tomorrow." Well, again, bar study is not *Gone with The Wind* and you are not Scarlett O'Hara.[2]

The point here is that with such a short study period, there is not time to put off for tomorrow what you should do today. Each day, your commercial bar preparation course will introduce a new subject or portion of a subject. You will be expected to do many things, including attend or watch lectures, organize the notes produced from those lectures, work problems, read sample answers for those worked problems, and memorize. In addition to all these bar related expectations, you will also need to manage your personal life.

Your bar exam study schedule will be key here. It will help you to structure and manage your study time so that you can maximize it during the bar study period. Put another way, if you schedule your time during the bar study period and do so with specificity, you reduce the risk that you will waste time and increase your chances of completing the necessary tasks. Thus, you should attempt to list everything you will do during the bar study period—from study time to free time. See Box Note 4-1 for a list of scheduling categories.

In Chapter 1, we introduced the three engagement steps you want to use as you prepare for the bar exam and explained them more in the context of bar

---

1. *See Gone with the Wind*, Dir. Victor Fleming. Per. Vivian Leigh as Scarlett O'Hara. MGM Studios, 1939.
2. *Id.*

study in Chapter 3. We will continue to expand upon them in the succeeding chapters where we discuss your preparation for the bar exam essay, multiple-choice, and practice test. But, before we can help you develop strategies and practices for each part of the bar exam, we will help you draft a realistic and practical schedule for developing these strategies through the three-step engagement process. See Figure 4-1 on pages 45-46, for a sample schedule.

BOX NOTE 4-1

Scheduling Categories

- Reviewing commercial bar prep outline, listening to an audio summary, or working questions prior to attending/watching commercial bar prep lecture
- Attending/watching commercial bar prep lecture
- Processing (outlining, flashcarding, flowcharting, other processing or any combination) notes from commercial bar class
- Working Essay questions (say which one(s))
- Reading answers to Essay questions
- Working MC questions (say how many, but keep it manageable)
- Reading answers to MC questions—all answers!
- Reviewing/changing outline, flashcards, flowcharts, etc. in case working the questions reveals a lack of understanding of a subject area or topic
- Memorizing material
- Working MPTs—consistently—don't save until the end
- Reading answers to MPTs
- Personal time
- Breaks
- Breakfast
- Lunch
- Dinner
- Travel time (to/from bar class) or study place if applicable
- Exercise
- Anything else you may need to do during the bar study period

---

BOX NOTE 4-2

But My Commercial Bar Prep Course Already Provides a Schedule

You may be thinking to yourself that you will already have a schedule—the one provided by the commercial bar course you just plunked down major dollars for. You may be wondering why on earth you would make a schedule when the experts have already made one for you. Those thoughts are understandable and not in conflict with what we are saying here. Keep in mind that the schedule made by your commercial bar course provider is a general one that is made based on best practices for absorbing and processing material. But, it is not specific to you.

Some commercial schedules may also describe your daily tasks in ways that are too general for your specific needs or study habits. The goal of this chapter is to ensure that you have a working knowledge of all that you should do as you engage in bar study and to supplement or change the commercial schedule if it does not meet your specific needs. This chapter also seeks to paint a clear picture of how you will accomplish these tasks on a given day and over the course of bar study so that you walk into your bar exam confident that you have done all you can to pass.

A. CRITICAL PREVIEW—BUILDING YOUR KNOWLEDGE BASE

Your first task when making your schedule is to make time to critically preview. Have you ever sat in class without completing the assigned readings? If you have, you know that this often makes it difficult for you to follow along with the instructor's lecture. When you critically preview some form of the substantive material, you in essence prime your brain to receive the expanded form of the information.

> **BOX NOTE 4-3**
>
> *Critical Preview:*
>
> Building your Knowledge Base
> - Reviewing commercial bar prep outline, listening to an audio summary, or working questions prior to attending/watching lecture
> - Attending commercial bar prep lecture

Just as we noted in Chapter 3 with the book shelf example, when you critically preview or prime your brain to receive the information, you create a solid foundation for receiving and holding the additional information you will encounter.

Critical preview activities will include reviewing the subject matter material prior to the lecture on that topic. You can do this by reading the table of contents and/or outlines provided by your commercial bar preparation company. What you preview and how much of it will depend on your level of comfort with the subject. You might also listen to an audio preview of the material. Choosing an oral preview tool can be helpful if you take long drives, have to do household chores, or have an oral absorption learning preference. The critical preview can also include working bar questions prior to watching or attending the lecture. Your commercial bar course schedule may or may not carve out time for you to review the material prior to watching the lecture. Make sure you build that time in.

Your critical preview also includes attending or watching the actual commercial lecture and taking notes using the pre-made note outlines provided by your commercial bar preparation course. While your general commercial bar course schedule will indicate that you should attend or watch the lecture, modern technology allows you to essentially watch the lecture online whenever you want. We encourage you, however, to choose the time when you will attend or watch lectures and to be consistent. This will ensure that you actually watch your lectures and thus make it difficult for this important task to fall through the cracks.

B. ORGANIZING ACTIVITY—EXPANDING YOUR KNOWLEDGE BASE

One of the most important things you will do during your bar study is to engage in your organizing activity. Here is where you build your knowledge base. Remember the example illustrations from Chapter 3. First, you build your book case with your critical preview, then you fill your book case with the products you produce from your organizing activities. Your schedule must include time for you to process your lecture notes and produce any processing product you deem necessary. See Chapter 3, Part B to review information regarding choosing your processing product. Your organizing activity also includes working problems. You must work essays, multiple-choice questions, and practice tests throughout your bar study. Make sure your schedule includes time to work the questions. A common refrain among students is that they don't have time to work problems or that they'll work them closer to their bar exam. Similarly, when we counsel students who have failed their bar exam, they often tell us that they only worked a relatively small number of questions over the course of bar study. Students typically cite the heavy workload associated with watching lectures, processing those lecture notes, and memorizing as being too time consuming to also work large amounts of questions. Students also report being afraid to work questions for fear of confirming that they do not know the subject well.

Think about when you worked practice questions during law school to prepare for exams. Did you work them throughout the semester every time you completed a topic or did you wait until the final weeks before the exam? If you did the latter, commit to reversing that behavior. Working questions throughout bar study is not just about testing what you have learned. It's also about processing what you've learned up to a point. You **NEED** to work the questions throughout bar study to help you organize the information and eventually memorize it so that you will be prepared to answer questions on the bar exam.

When you schedule your practice problems, make sure you schedule time to work questions and read the answers—the answers to the questions you answered incorrectly and correctly. You should also schedule time to revise your processing products or add to your lecture notes based on what you read while reviewing the answers. You want the work you did on those questions to live on in your processing product as that becomes your primary tool for learning and memorizing the information.

BOX NOTE 4-4

Organizing Actvity:

Expanding Your Knowledge Base

- Processing (reviewing, outlining, flashcarding, flowcharting, other processing, or any combination) notes from bar class
- Working Essay questions (say which one(s))– every day
- Reading answers to Essay questions
- Working multiple-choice questions (say how many, but keep it manageable)- every day
- Reading answers to all MC questions

- Reviewing/changing outline, flashcards, flowcharts, etc., in case working the questions reveals a lack of understanding of a subject area or topic
- Memorizing material
- Working MPTs—consistently—Don't save until the end!
- Reading answers to MPTs

FIGURE 4-1 SAMPLE SCHEDULE

It's OK to wake up later on the weekends or days when you have a lighter load. But, remember that time if you find yourself looking for additional space in your schedule to work more problems, process your lecture notes, or memorize a subject you are having difficulty with.

This schedule is just a sample. The point here is to see the system employed. Times, actual days, and exact activities may be different from person to person.

Do at least one MPT per week (if your jurisdiction uses this test form). Increase your practice time if you experience difficulty with writing or timing.

Monday Torts I	Tuesday Torts II	Wednesday Torts III	Thursday Family Law	Friday Conflicts of Law	Sat MEMORIZE	Sun MEMORIZE
7:30-9:00 Dress Exercise Breakfast Travel to bar lecture/study place	7:30-9:00 Dress Exercise Breakfast Travel to bar lecture/study place	7:30-9:00 Dress Exercise Breakfast Travel to bar lecture/study place	7:30-9:00 Dress Exercise Breakfast Travel to bar lecture/study place	7:30-9:00 Dress Exercise Breakfast Travel to bar lecture/study place	Sleep in personal matters	Sleep in personal matters
9:00 – 12:00 Attend/Watch Bar Lecture	9:00 – 12:00 Attend/Watch Bar Lecture	9:00 – 12:00 Attend/Watch Bar Lecture	9:00 – 12:00 Attend/Watch Bar Lecture	9:00 – 12:00 Attend/Watch Bar Lecture	10:00-12:15 1 MPT/ read answer	10:00-12:30 Memorize Conflicts
						12:30-1:30 Conflicts essay #2/ read answers/updat e pp if necessary
12:00 – 2:00 Lunch Travel from bar lecture/study place break	12:00 – 2:00 Lunch Travel from bar lecture/study place break	12:00 – 2:00 Lunch Travel from bar lecture/study place break	12:00 – 2:00 Lunch Travel from bar lecture/study place break	12:00 – 2:00 Lunch Travel from bar lecture/study place break	12:15 – 1:00 Lunch	1:30 – 2:15 Lunch

Breaks are important, but make sure they are reasonable and earned. For instance, a 30- minute break after only studying for one hour seems excessive. A 10-minute break after each hour may help you to rest and then stay on task so that you use your time effectively.

Also, watching bar lectures can be brutal. Thus, if you need a couple of hours to decompress after a lecture, take it. Breaks help to maximize your productivity for the rest of the day. Just don't go overboard.

Monday Torts I	Tuesday Torts II	Wednesday Torts III	Thursday Family Law	Friday Conflicts of Law	Sat MEMORIZE	Sun MEMORIZE
11:30 – 2:00 Lunch Travel from bar lecture/study place break	11:30 – 2:00 Lunch Travel from bar lecture/study place break	1:00 – 2:00 Lunch Travel from bar lecture/study place break	11:30 – 2:00 Lunch Travel from bar lecture/study place break	11:00 – 2:00 Lunch Travel from bar lecture/study place break	12:15 – 1:00 Lunch	1:50 – 2:15 Lunch
2:00 – 6:00 Read Notes & outline/process Torts I Torts essay #11 read answers/update pp if necessary	2:00 – 6:00 Read Notes & outline/process Torts II Torts essay #12 read answers/update pp if necessary	2:00 – 6:00 Read Notes & outline/process Torts III Torts essay #13 read answers/update pp if necessary	2:00 – 6:00 Read Notes & outline/process Family Law FL Essay #1 read answers/update pp if necessary	2:00 – 6:00 Read Notes & outline/process Conflicts of Law Conflicts Essay #1 read answers/update pp if necessary	1:00 – 4:00 Memorize Torts	1:35 – 2:35 Torts essay #14/ read answers/update pp if necessary
					4:00 – 5:30 MBE-25 Torts read answers/u pdate pp if necessary	2:40 – 7:30 Memorize Family Law FL Essay #2 read answers/update pp if necessary
6:00 – 7:30 Dinner/ Family Time Personal Time	6:00 – 7:30 Dinner/ Family Time Personal Time	6:00 – 7:30 Dinner/ Family Time Personal Time	6:00 – 7:30 Dinner/ Family Time Personal Time	6:00 – 7:30 Dinner/ Family Time Personal Time		
7:30 – 9:00 MBE-25 Torts and read answers/update pp if necessary	7:30 – 9:00 MBE-25 Torts and read answers/update pp if necessary	7:30 – 9:00 MBE-25 Torts and read answers/update pp if necessary	7:30 – 9:00 MBE-25 Torts and read answers/update pp if necessary	7:30 – 9:00 MBE-25 Torts and read answers/update pp if necessary		
9:00 Review course outline for tomorrow's lecture	9:00 Review course outline for tomorrow's lecture	9:00 Review course outline for tomorrow's lecture	9:00 Review course outline for tomorrow's lecture			7:30 Review course outline for tomorrow's lecture

After attending the lecture, the notes are then reviewed/ organized into a system that renders the material ready for memorization.

Just as it is important to do essay questions and multiple-choice questions during the week, it is also important to do them while you are memorizing.

C. REACHING THE GOAL—PRODUCING A REALISTIC AND WORKABLE BAR STUDY SCHEDULE

In writing a bar study schedule, your goal is to produce a daily guide that will allow you to complete all the tasks necessary to learn and memorize the substantive material so that you can be prepared to take the biggest closed book exam of your career. Accomplishing that goal will require organization and consistent practice. The ABA suggests that law students spend at least two hours outside of class time preparing for every hour spent in class.[3] That amounts to approximately 720 hours spent over the course of one semester based on a 16-hour course load. These are more than just suggested hours of preparation. What they represent is a suggestion about the time and dedication required to assimilate legal material in preparation for a law exam. We recommend a similar time commitment to bar study—approximately 500 to 600 hours over the course of an eight to ten week bar study period.[4] That bar preparation should be multifaceted and should consist of many of the categories listed in Box Note 4-1. Make sure you are on track to accomplish at approximately 500-600 hours of study. If you are not, review the study categories listed in Box Note 4-1. Make sure they are all represented on your schedule. Also, review the amount of time you are allotting for question work, keeping in mind how many minutes you will have to complete similar tasks while taking the bar exam.

> **BOX NOTE 4-5**
>
> *Reaching the Goal:*
>
> Producing a Realistic and Workable Bar Study Schedule
> - Able to memorize material
> - Able to demonstrate knowledge of material in essay writing and multiple-choice question answering
> - Able to execute techniques that allow you to answer essay, MC, and MPTs adequately and in the allotted time

EXERCISE 4-1

CREATE A ONE WEEK BAR STUDY SCHEDULE

Assume your bar study covers the following subjects during the week:
- Monday—Torts I
- Tuesday—Torts II
- Wednesday—Criminal Law
- Thursday—Criminal Procedure
- Friday—Agency

---

3. American Bar Association Standards, Rules of Procedure for Approval of Law Schools 2017-18, Chapter 3, Program of Legal Education, Determination of Credit Hours for Coursework, Standard 310(b)(1), https://www.americanbar.org/content/dam/aba/publications/misc/legal_education/Standards/2017-2018ABAStandardsforApprovalofLawSchools/2017_2018_standards_chapter3.authcheckdam.pdf.

4. While professors may provide students with overall time guides for bar study, the actual time spent may vary depending on the status of the bar exam applicant—first time taker, repeat taker, or multiple bar exam taker. Thus, depending on the student and the student's bar taking circumstance, the overall time needed for study could be more or less than the 500 to 600 hour range.

D. CONCLUSION

Every entry you make on your schedule is like a promise you are making to yourself to do the very best you can to be prepared for and pass your bar exam. And while you will be flexible and adjust when necessary, this schedule will be your guide to your days and nights of bar study. It will also be a set of written promises you can share with your loved ones so that they help you keep your promises or at least not stand in your way. So, resist the urge to be general in describing your activities. Avoid descriptions such as "review torts" or "study family law." Replace those with phrases such as "work 30 torts multiple-choice questions" and "read the answer explanations for each question and work two family law essays."

When your promises are specific, they are harder to break. For instance, how many times have you said you would study a subject for three hours? Were you really on task for three hours? Most of us would not be. We would take calls, send texts, surf the net, check social media, and maybe even make a video or two. We might do all this and still feel somewhat gratified that we had "studied" the subject. However, if you build a schedule with specificity and with appropriate breaks, it's harder to go off task or be distracted. That's the overall goal of the schedule—to ensure that you make promises to yourself about bar study and that you actually keep them!

CHAPTER 4 RECAP

▶ *CRITICAL PREVIEW—BUILDING A KNOWLEDGE BASE*
- Reviewing commercial bar prep outline or work questions prior to attending/watching lecture
- Attending/watching commercial bar prep lecture

▶ *ORGANIZING ACTIVITY—EXPANDING THE KNOWLEDGE BASE*
- Processing (outlining, flashcarding, flowcharting, other processing, or any combination) notes from bar class
- Working Essay questions (say which one(s))—every day
- Reading answers to Essay questions
- Working MC questions (say how many, but keep it manageable)—every day
- Reading answers to all MC questions (even the ones you get right!)
- Reviewing/changing outline, flashcards, flowcharts, etc., in case working the questions reveals a lack of understanding of a subject area or topic
- Memorizing material
- Working MPTs—consistently—don't save until the end
- Reading answers to MPTs

▶ *REACHING A GOAL—PRODUCING A REALISTIC AND WORKABLE BAR STUDY SCHDULE*
- Able to memorize material
- Able to demonstrate knowledge of material in essay writing and multiple-choice question answering
- Able to execute techniques that allow you to answer Essay, MC, and MPTs adequately and in the allotted time

The MPT:[1] A Winner of a Test

INTRODUCTION

Here's why the Multistate Performance Test (or MPT) is likely the best test form you can hope for on the bar exam. The MPT is a "closed universe" test. This means you don't have to learn any rules and you don't have to memorize anything. By way of example, this type of test is very similar to the "closed memo" assignment many of you had in your first-year legal writing class. There, you were given a hypothetical and one or more cases or statutes. You were tasked with incorporating the case law and the facts from the hypothetical into a memo format. Similarly, the MPT is a packet of information that consists of a File (which contains documents setting out the facts related to the matter) and a Library (which contains various forms of legal authority that may be relevant to the matter).

At the beginning of the File portion of the MPT, there is almost always a memo addressed to you, the applicant, detailing the task you are to perform and the product you are to produce. This memo is typically referred to as the *file* or *task memoranda*. Remember, this is a closed book exercise. Thus, the MPT will contain everything you need to complete the task set out in the file memo. That means that every fact and legal authority you need has already been provided to you. You may be asked to write on a topic you did well in while in law school. Or you may recognize an MPT task as being very similar to a task you completed while working as a legal intern. You might even think the templates your legal writing professor provided for writing briefs and memoranda are better than what your MPT packet provides. While your previous experiences should comfort

---

1. All MPT references and materials are printed here pursuant to a licensing agreement with the National Conference of Bar Examiners (NCBE).

FIGURE 5-1

THE
MPT®
MULTISTATE PERFORMANCE TEST

FILE
In re Tamara Shea

This portion of the MPT packet typically contain a memo (which explains your task and provides an outline for the MPT product you are to produce). In addition, the file will contain additional documents that supply more detailed facts regarding the case. These documents typically include:

Transcripts
Letters
Meeting notes
Agreements
Stipulated facts
Newspaper articles
Depositions
Police reports
<u>and</u> more ...

LIBRARY
In re Tamara Shea

This portion of the MPT packet contains the law you will use in analyzing the topic presented to you in the file memo and made relevant by the file facts. It can typically contain any or all of the following:

Statutes
Regulations
Ordinances
Cases

and even empower you in not being asked to do something completely foreign, *resist* the urge to use any facts, legal authority, or organizational schemes you may have encountered in those experiences. Use only what has been provided in the packet and organize your product precisely as you have been directed. To assist you in this, the test drafters include legal authorities from fictitious jurisdictions in the file portion of the MPT.

Your MPT can require that you create one of various documents. Past MPTs have required students to draft an office memorandum, client letter, brief, opinion letter, contract, a will, articles of incorporation, and many other document types. While you may be familiar with some of these documents and not others, do not fret. The MPT tests your ability to

> "...(1) sort detailed factual materials and separate relevant from irrelevant facts; (2) analyze statutory, case, and administrative materials for applicable principles of law; (3) apply the relevant law to the relevant facts in a manner likely to resolve a client's problem; (4) identify and resolve ethical dilemmas, when present; (5) communicate effectively in writing; and (6) complete a lawyering task within time constraints."[2]

Thus, regardless of the task, you will be able to complete it and produce the required document. Remember that the MPT drafters will give you instructions. For those documents that typical law students may not have experienced during their course of law study, the MPT drafters tend to give additional special instructions so that you can focus on displaying the abilities described above. In

---

2. National Conference of Bar Examiners, http://www.ncbex.org/exams/mpt/preparing/.

any event, you should plan to practice MPTs and make sure you review all the different documents you may be required to produce. This will hopefully reduce or prevent all together any "shell shock" at being tasked with doing something you've never done or seen before.

You will typically have 90 minutes to complete one MPT during the bar exam period. Uniform Bar Exam (UBE) states require that you complete two MPTs. [3] The National Conference of Bar Examiners (NCBE) – the organization that drafts the MPT – advises that you divide the 90-minute allotment equally between time for reading and outlining and time for writing the required MPT product.[4] In other words, according to the NCBE's advice, you should spend 45 minutes reading and outlining and the other 45 minutes writing your final MPT product.[5]

As we mentioned earlier, practice is key. First, you will need to incorporate MPT practice into your bar study schedule. Use this course to determine where you stand with MPTs. Do you feel comfortable with them? Are you able to pick out the relevant facts and legal authority? Are you able to complete the task and produce the product required? Are you able to do all of this within the allotted time? Your answers to these questions will determine the amount of practice you need to be prepared for the MPT. Creating a schedule that incorporates taking many practice MPTs is the best way to become familiar and comfortable with the strategies and techniques necessary to score maximum points. Your commercial bar review course will direct you to practice MPTs. We encourage you to personally assess your MPT strengths and weaknesses starting with the MPT work you do in this course. If you feel you need more practice than what your commercial bar course advises, then practice more! Initially, you may create a schedule where you do one MPT per week during the course of bar study. You might even do more if you find that the MPT is a struggle for you. Review Chapter 4, where we discuss how best to integrate MPT practice into your study schedule.

We will use the three-step engagement process to dissect the MPT, expose you to different strategies for taking this type of test, and help you to develop strategies for completing the MPT within the allotted time. Remember, the MPT is a winner! If you don't believe us already, you'll certainly be convinced by the end of this chapter.

A. CRITICALLY PREVIEWING

The first step in writing an MPT is to critically preview the material contained within the packet. As you have read in earlier chapters, this is the first step

---

3. Applicants taking a bar exam in a UBE state or a state that requires more than one MPT will have 90 minutes for each MPT.

4. *See* http://www.ncbex.org/pdfviewer/?file=%2Fdmsdocument%2F191.

5. http://www.ncbex.org/pdfviewer/?file=%2Fdmsdocument%2F191.

you will take in doing most things in preparation for the bar exam. When critically previewing the MPT, think of this stage as an opportunity to prime your brain to receive the information in the packet. You may be overwhelmed by the sheer amount of material when you first encounter an MPT. But don't worry. Approaching the MPT in steps, as advised below, will help you to conquer the material.

Your commercial bar course provider will certainly suggest a method for this stage of the process. We offer a few methods here as well. You may get some indication of a preference from your bar prep instructor as to which section of the MPT you should read first. However, that order must fit with your learning style(s) in terms of how you absorb and process information. See Chapter 2 to get a better understanding of how you learn (how you absorb and process information).

BOX NOTE 5-1

The MPT Critical Preview

We strongly recommend that you use this class to determine and practice the critical preview strategy that works for you.

Some students mention that simply reading the library first is best for them. This may work but use caution here. Students who employ this option have a tendency to write case briefs for all the cases they encounter in the library. This may not be entirely useful as the library may contain cases and portions of cases that are not applicable. Reading the file memo first and then the library gives you some assurance that when you encounter the cases, you will be able to better determine what information from them is relevant.

Don't overspend your time on this part of the engagement process. You will have two more opportunities as you preform the remainder of the engagement steps (when you read more slowly while simultaneously outlining and when you actually produce the product) to consider and analyze the material. Thus, the critical preview should only take a small portion of your time – no more than ten of the 45 minutes allotted for this part of the process.

There are many ways to approach the critical preview in this time frame. Some students prefer to give the entire MPT packet a light read while highlighting or underlining important information. The purpose of critically previewing by doing a light read is to help you get a sense of the facts and the law and what you are being asked to do. Frankly, however, many students find it very difficult to perform a light read during the critical preview stage. And it is clear why. After three or more years of reading cases and statutes very carefully and slowly, it is difficult to become a reader who just quickly reads. Law students, by nature of their legal training, want to read slowly and methodically with intent to capture the big picture as well as the nuances associated with understanding the law and how it works.

If you are in the category of students who find it difficult to critically preview by giving the entire packet a light read, consider doing a light read of portions of the MPT packet. For instance, lightly read the task memo and the library only. Reading the task memo will give you direction in terms of the case background and the task before you. Reading the law will help you to start to see how it will impact the case. This will provide you with a solid foundation before you read the entire packet slowly and complete your outline in the second step.

The important thing to remember about critically previewing the MPT is that you are NOT, at the critical preview stage, doing any deep earnest reading. Instead, you are giving the material a light read. Remember that the goal of the critical preview is to prime your brain to receive the information. Think of this as similar to reading the call of the question when working an essay or a multiple-choice question. The same concept applies to critically previewing MPTs, although the comparison is not exact because the MPT contains much more information than an essay or multiple-choice question. It is normal for students to perceive difficulty in ascertaining what the exact nature of the task is when working an MPT. The critical preview, by introducing you to the information in the MPT packet, provides a method by which you can quickly encounter the information and start the process of categorizing it.

B. ORGANIZING ACTIVITY

Once you have completed the first step, the critical preview process, the next step is to engage in the organizing activity. Here, you will create an outline of the final MPT product. This is an important second step in the three-step engagement method. This step will ask you to continue "processing" the information and then to organize the information in outline form. First, you will setup your outline using the information provided in the task memo regarding the final product specified there. You will also use the information from the file and the library to complete your outline. Since this is a closed universe test, you will not need any outside information. You will have approximately 35 minutes to complete this step of the process.

1. What Is an Outline?

Before we continue describing this step, let's review what an outline is in the context of this stage of completing the MPT. For this second step, keep in mind that you are creating only an "outline." You will not fully write out your final answer until step three. At this stage, use abbreviations, words, or short phrases to represent the information you intend to include in your final product. This will help set the stage for a more complete answer. It is in your own best interest to be succinct here as you don't want to waste those 35 minutes trying to craft perfect sentences. Instead, spend that time pinpointing the important facts and relevant law.

2. Don't Skip This Step!

This second step is a very important step in which many do not want to engage. Most students would prefer to go directly to producing the final product. The impulse is natural particularly when you are sitting in a room of test takers and you hear typing after only a few minutes of testing time have elapsed. Most students want to get right to the ultimate task and do not want to waste a lot of time on outlining. This is a dangerous position and one that is not recommended. Outlining is crucial as it creates an orderly and useful guide that will help direct how the final product is produced. By creating the outline, you obtain a clear idea of what the final product is to look like. In addition, it allows you an additional opportunity to engage with the material and understand what is being asked of you by the bar examiners.

3. Start with the Task Memo

Once you have completed the critical preview, read the entire packet more carefully and slowly. Your goal in doing this is to organize the material in a way that resembles how you will write the final product. This is not the light read you did at the critical preview stage. This is more in-depth reading. To begin this second step, review the task memo for the specifics as to what you should write about and how you should write about it.

a. Tone

In some instances, the task memo will give you a sense of the tone you should achieve in producing the required MPT product. For instance, the task memo may instruct you to write a client letter that is persuasive, but that seeks to conciliate. This means you should set out your case in a persuasive manner, but you should also use the facts and the law to seek opportunities for compromises

FIGURE 5-2

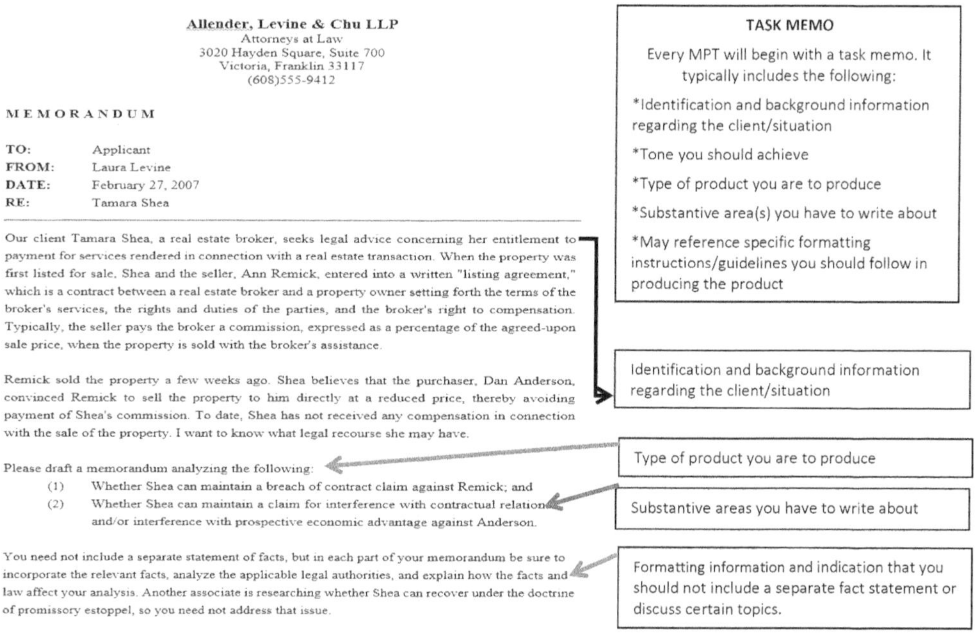

54

between the parties. On the other hand, your task memo may instruct you to write a brief that clearly demonstrates legal support for your client's position and that a finding otherwise is inappropriate. This means that you should persuasively and strenuously argue for your client's position showing how the law, as applied to the facts, supports it.

b. Fact Statements

You will not always have to write a fact statement or include a section that only has facts when producing your MPT product. In many instances, you will include the facts in your application or analysis sections when you apply the law. If you do write a fact statement or section, make sure you have been specifically instructed to do so. For example, you may be asked to provide a brief explanation or introduction of the case. If you have been instructed to write a fact statement or include a fact section and have lots of facts at your disposal, use the law to create categories of facts. For instance, if discussing negligence, write a fact statement or section categorized around the negligence elements. This will help you to stay organized and not get bogged down in irrelevant facts.

c. Legal Analysis

The task memo will instruct you regarding the topics you should analyze. The level of specificity your task memo will have regarding this will vary. In some instances, your task memo will be very specific as to what you should discuss. In others, it may provide broader instructions leading you to a specific area of law without pinpointing the precise topic. In any event, the information in the file and the law in the library will contain all that you need to perform the required legal analysis.

If the task memo instructs you to show, argue, prove, dispute, evidence, provide legal authority in support of, or something similar with regard to a topic, use IRAC or some form of it to comply. These words and phrases are cues that you should perform legal analysis, and in most instances, legal analysis is presented in IRAC form. For instance, if the task memo instructs you to use legal authority to argue persuasively that a party's actions constitute negligence, this means you should IRAC negligence (using smaller iracs for each element if they are relevant).

d. What Not to Discuss

The task memo may also tell you what you should not discuss. This is particularly important to note because if you have been instructed not to discuss something, it means that MPT graders will not be able to award points based on your analysis of those topics. Also, if you spend time writing about something you were instructed not to write about, you will not have time to write about the topics you have been instructed to discuss. This usually comes up in situations where you are instructed not to discuss an element or related concept associated with a topic. That means the file and library may contain information pertaining to this forbidden topic. You thus want to make special note of what you are not to discuss if it is explicitly stated in the task memo. In this way, you can be vigilant about adhering to this directive as you read the remainder of the MPT packet.

e. Special Instructions Beyond the Task Memo

In addition to the instructions contained within the task memo, you will be instructed, on occasion, to review an additional set of instructions. When you have additional instructions, be sure you address whatever the task memo has instructed you to do in the context of the additional instructions. For instance, the task memo may instruct you to write a brief that briefly explains the relevant case facts and uses legal authority to argue persuasively that a party's actions constitute negligence. The task memo may also instruct you to use the "firm's" brief template which, requires that every brief have the following sections: Introduction, Should be Argument, and Conclusion. This may seem like two conflicting sets of instructions, but they do not conflict at all. One set is substantive while the other is more technical in identifying the form in which you should present your substantive information. In a situation like this, the drafters may intend for you to include your brief explanation of the relevant facts in the Introduction and your discussion of negligence (in IRAC form) in the Argument section.

4. Use the Task Memo to Create Headings for Your Outline

Use the task memo to create the foundation of your outline. The task memo should set out the different topics and concepts you must analyze in the final document. Each should be set off by an underlined heading for ease of viewing. Also, use numbers, especially if they have been used in setting out the tasks. By creating this rough outline, you are ensuring that you will have a roadmap to

FIGURE 5-3

Task memo instructions:	Special instructions:	Organization that combines the task memo and special instructions:
• Briefly explain the relevant facts of the case.	• Use the "firm's" brief template.	• Introduction ○ briefly explain the relevant facts of the case

• Use legal authority to argue persuasively that a party's actions constitutes negligence.	• The brief template indicates that every brief should have the following sections:
	  ○ Introduction
	  ○ Argument
	  ○ Conclusion
		• Argument
		  ○ Negligence
		    ▪ IRAC
		
		• Conclusion

help you fill in your outline as you read the rest of the MPT packet. The rough outline will also set the framework for your finished MPT product.

5. Turn to the Other Parts of the Packet

Once you have reviewed the Task Memo and understand what is required of you, the next step is to review the remaining sections of the MPT packet. As you read each section, use the information to fill in the outline foundation you just created. Remember to use abbreviations or phrases to fill in the outline. You will have time to write it out fully later. At this stage, you only want to process the information so that you get the full picture of the task before you. It may even help to note page numbers in your outline from the MPT packet where important information appears.

Within the file portion of the MPT, look for important factual information that pertains to the rules you will discuss. You will have an idea about this because you are familiar with the law after your critical preview from step one. Pay attention to any names, dates, times, or money amounts that may be important.

Within the library portion of the MPT, find the law that is relevant to your task. Statutes, regulations (including ethical requirements), and ordinances may be important. Keep in mind that in each of these examples, the entire rule or only portions of it may be relevant. In addition, make note of the rules that are set out by case law. There may even be a "case within a case" that helps to illuminate a rule.

FIGURE 5-4

Allender, Levine & Chu LLP
Attorneys at Law
3020 Hayden Square, Suite 700
Victoria, Franklin 33117
(608)555-9412

MEMORANDUM

TO: Applicant
FROM: Laura Levine
DATE: February 27, 2007
RE: Tamara Shea

Our client Tamara Shea, a real estate broker, seeks legal advice concerning her entitlement to payment for services rendered in connection with a real estate transaction. When the property was first listed for sale, Shea and the seller, Ann Remick, entered into a written "listing agreement," which is a contract between a real estate broker and a property owner setting forth the terms of the broker's services, the rights and duties of the parties, and the broker's right to compensation. Typically, the seller pays the broker a commission, expressed as a percentage of the agreed-upon sale price, when the property is sold with the broker's assistance.

Remick sold the property a few weeks ago. Shea believes that the purchaser, Dan Anderson, convinced Remick to sell the property to him directly at a reduced price, thereby avoiding payment of Shea's commission. To date, Shea has not received any compensation in connection with the sale of the property. I want to know what legal recourse she may have.

Please draft a memorandum analyzing the following:

1. Whether Shea can maintain a breach of contract claim against Remick; and
2. Whether Shea can maintain a claim for interference with contractual relations and/or interference with prospective economic advantage against Anderson.

OUTLINE OF PRODUCT USING PROMPTS FROM THE FILE MEMO

1. Breach of Contract against Remick
   R Rule
   A Application
   C Conclusion

2. a. Interference with contract relations against Anderson
      R Rule
      A Application
      C Conclusion

   b. Interference with prospective economic advantage against Anderson
      R Rule
      A Application
      C Conclusion

Creating headings using the substantive topics is encouraged, but labeling your IRACs may or may not be appropriate.

FIGURE 5-5

Shea Realty
Victoria's Premier Real Estate Company
420 Tenth Street
Victoria, FR 33117
333.555.0602
www.SheaRealty.com

January 10, 2007

Ms. Ann Remick
5632 Birdie Lane
Diamond Springs, Franklin 33017

Re: Briarwood Parcel

Dear Ann:

This will confirm that our Listing Agreement dated November 10, 2006, is extended for a period of 30 days, effective as of January 9, 2007, through and including February 7, 2007.

I look forward to continuing to assist you in selling your Briarwood property. Please countersign and return this letter to me at your earliest convenience.

Sincerely,

Tamara Shea

Tamara Shea
Licensed Real Estate Broker

I hereby consent to the Listing Agreement extension set forth above.

Seller: _____   Date: _____
         Ann Remick

A letter from the file portion of the MPT packet provides important facts in determining whether the first part of the rule for interference with contractual relations is met — whether there was an existing agreement.

FIGURE 5-6

the defendant's knowledge of the existence of the relationship, (3) intentional *and* improper acts on the part of the defendant designed to disrupt the relationship, (4) actual disruption of the relationship, and (5) economic harm to the plaintiff proximately caused by the defendant's acts.

As stated above, the tort of interference with prospective economic advantage is not dependent on compliance with the statute of frauds. The wrong complained of in this cause of action is that CRC interfered in Mather's advantageous relationship with Bowen. Specifically, Mather alleged that she had an economic relationship with Bowen containing the probability of future economic benefit (i.e., payment of her broker's commission); that CRC had knowledge of the relationship, as evidenced by the commission provision contained in CRC's lease offer; that CRC intentionally excluded Mather from the lease negotiations, knowing and intending that such conduct would disrupt the relationship between Mather and Bowen; that CRC secured the lease at a lower price than it would have if Mather's commission had been paid; and that Mather was therefore damaged in an amount at least equal to the commission. These allegations are sufficient to state a cause of action for interference with prospective economic advantage. *See, e.g., Howard v. Youngman* (Franklin Ct. App. 1985) (defendant real estate broker's economic interest in getting a higher commission if seller sold home to a different buyer did not give broker legal right to interfere with ongoing negotiations for sale of home).

Turning to Mather's second claim against CRC, to state a cause of action for interference with contractual relations, a plaintiff must allege: (1) a valid and enforceable contract between the plaintiff and a third party, (2) the defendant's knowledge of the existence of the contractual relationship, (3) intentional *and* improper acts on the part of the defendant designed to disrupt the relationship, (4) actual disruption of the relationship, (5) economic harm to the plaintiff proximately caused by the defendant's acts.

CRC moved to dismiss this cause of action solely on the ground that there was no valid and existing contract between Mather and Bowen. Because the brochure and registration form were sufficient to satisfy the statute of frauds, we hold that Mather properly pleaded a claim for interference with contractual relations against CRC.

Accordingly, the trial court's judgment of dismissal is reversed and the case is remanded for further proceedings.

This portion of the case, which appears in the library of the MPT packet, sets out the rule for part 2b of the analysis — interference with contractual relations.

Remember that the task memo specifically told you to discuss this. You have thus known since your critical preview stage that this would be an important rule. In addition, you knew exactly where to find it. Because you already have this knowledge, you are in an even better position to analyze this case and the rule from in t in light of the facts.

6. Where to Write Your Outline

If you are typing your answer, it is often a good idea to type your outline on your computer so you can use it as a template that will guide you in creating the final product. Whether you are typing or not, you may prefer to handwrite your outline on scratch paper or a blank page of the MPT packet. Whatever method you use for writing your MPT outline, make sure you practice it consistently during your bar exam study period.

C. PRODUCING THE MPT PRODUCT

The final step in the three-step engagement process is to "produce the required product." Completing the first two steps (critical preview and organizing activity) gives you two chances at processing the material and positions you to produce a clear and complete final MPT product. By this point, you will have read through the packet and become familiar with what type of document you are being tasked with creating and the specific requirements for creating it. This third step allows you to process the material one last time. It's at this stage where you will have yet another chance to review your tone, organization, and law and fact selection.

Make sure to use the outline you spent a total of 45 minutes (half of your MPT time) creating as you begin to write your MPT product. The NCBE advises that you spend 45 minutes reading and outlining and the other 45 minutes writing.[6] That's an indication that the first 45 minutes are critical to what you produce. Thus, stay calm and focused as you move to the second half of the test by using your outline to guide you through the writing process.

Because you have the information in place in your outline, you can now expand that document to create your final MPT product. Go through each section in your outline in a systematic fashion, adding and fleshing out the important details. As for the law, make sure you use the appropriate terminology and "buzzwords." In addition, make sure that anything you quote from the Library section is properly sourced. When discussing the facts from the File section, make sure you are correct in the dates, times, and party names. This is the stage at which you will make a final determination about the organization and content of your final product based on what the task memo instructed you to do and what the applicable law and facts require.

Be sure to pace yourself and avoid "overwriting" in the first part of the document leaving yourself with little time to provide the correct level of depth in the latter parts of the document.

---

6. *See* http://www.ncbex.org/pdfviewer/?file=%2Fdmsdocument%2F191.

CONCLUSION

This three-step engagement process will be extremely valuable in helping you understand the work that goes into producing a successful MPT product. In addition to following the three-step engagement process as you work MPTs, there are two pieces of advice we would leave you with before wrapping up this chapter – practice your strategy under timed pressure during your bar study period and finish the MPT during your actual bar exam. Make time for regular MPT practice in your study schedule (see Chapter 4). This consistent practice will help to cement your strategy for working MPTs and will give you confidence on test day. Additionally, having a working and practiced strategy will also ensure that you finish the MPT during your bar exam.

CHAPTER 5 RECAP

▶ *CRITICAL PREVIEW – BUILDING A KNOWLEDGE BASE – 10 MINUTES*
  - *Lightly read the entire MPT packet*
  - *Lightly read only the task memo and library portions of the MPT packet*

▶ *ORGANIZING ACTIVITY – EXPANDING THE KNOWLEDGE BASE – 38 MINUTES*
  - *Read the entire MPT packet slowly*
  - *Use the task memo to create a foundational outline*
  - *Use the remainder of the information in the file and library portions of the MPT to fill in the remainder of the outline.*

▶ *REACHING A GOAL – PRODUCING AN MPT PRODUCT – 45 MINUTES*
  - *Use your outline to write the final version of the MPT product*

PRACTICE YOUR MPT STRATEGY CONSISTENTLY THROUGHOUT BAR STUDY AND MAKE SURE YOU ARE ABLE TO FINISH THE MPT AND PRODUCE THE APPROPRIATE PRODUCT WITHIN THE ALLOTTED 90 MINUTES.

MPTs

FILE
Whitford v. Newberry Middle School District

The Gogh Law Offices
647 Aiden Place
Newberry, Franklin 33616

MEMORANDUM

TO: Applicant
FROM: Sandy Gogh
RE: *Whitford v. Newberry Middle School District*
DATE: February 28, 2002

I was very pleased with the way you handled the evidentiary phase of the motion for preliminary injunction in *Annie Whitford v. Newberry Middle School District*. You will be making the closing argument tomorrow afternoon. Before then, I'd like you to write out your closing argument to prepare for your presentation in court and let me review it.

The court has instructed you to focus your argument on the likelihood of Annie's success on the merits, which you know is a prerequisite for issuance a preliminary injunction. The judge has already found irreparable injury, so there is no need for you to argue that point.

The closing argument should revolve around the facts that you brought out at the hearing. The School District refused to allow Annie to try out for her school's boys-only volleyball team. Since the District receives federal financial assistance, this refusal violated Annie's rights under Title IX of the Education Amendments of 1972. The refusal deprived her of an equal opportunity, based on gender, to participate in interscholastic athletics.

In the argument, you should tell a persuasive story about why Annie should prevail, highlight the salient facts of that story, and show how the evidence supports the factors that are enumerated in the statute, regulations, and case law. It is also important that you preempt the District's position by showing how the District's evidence fails to support its case and, in fact, supports Annie's. The structure of the argument—i.e., an introduction, main argument, and conclusion—is important. It should be persuasive, organized, well-reasoned, and compelling. You should end it with a clear statement of the relief you are seeking.

1   UNITED STATES DISTRICT COURT
2   CENTRAL DISTRICT OF FRANKLIN
3 Annie Whitford, a minor, by   )
4 her best friends and natural   )
5 guardians Pearl Whitford and George   )
6 Whitford,   )
7   Plaintiff   )   Case Number 02-CV-1068
8 v.   )
9 Newberry Middle School District,   )
10   Defendant   )

---

12   TRANSCRIPT OF HEARING ON PLAINTIFF'S
13   MOTION FOR PRELIMINARY INJUNCTION
14   February 27, 2002

16 THE COURT: Okay counsel, let's begin. You may proceed.

18 APPLICANT: In this case, plaintiff Annie Whitford is a 12-year-old student in the
19   seventh grade at Newberry Middle School. She seeks an order requiring the
20   Newberry Middle School District to let her try out for the interscholastic
21   volleyball team at Newberry Middle School. Newberry Middle School is
22   covered by Title IX of the Education Amendments of 1972, which pro-
23   hibits gender discrimination in school athletic programs. Annie wanted
24   to try out for her school's all-male volleyball team and was informed by
25   the coach that she could not because a District rule prohibits females from
26   playing with or against male students in contact sports.

27 THE COURT: Is that policy in writing?

28 APPLICANT: It's attached to my motion, Your Honor. Let me read it into the
29   record: "Boys and girls shall not be permitted to participate in interscho-
30   lastic athletic games as mixed teams, nor shall boys' teams and girls' teams
31   participate against each other in interscholastic athletic contests when the
32   sports involved are contact sports or sports in which the purpose or major
33   activity involves physical contact, including football, baseball, basketball,
34   volleyball, wrestling, and ice hockey."

36 THE COURT: Mr. Perdue, is this a fair summary of the problem?

37 PERDUE (Counsel for School District): Yes, Your Honor.

39 THE COURT: Call your first witness, counsel.

40 THE PLAINTIFF, Annie Whitford, WAS SWORN AND IDENTIFIED.

42 APPLICANT: Good morning, Annie. I am going to ask you a few questions, okay?

43 WHITFORD: Okay.

1	Q:	When did you start playing volleyball?
2	A:	When I was about seven years old, in the second grade.
3	Q:	Have you been playing ever since?
4	A:	Yes, constantly. I've played on teams through the YMCA, the Parks and
5		Recreation Department, and the U.S. Volleyball League Juniors Club.
6		I've gone to volleyball camps for the last five summers.
7	Q:	Were there boys on these teams?
8	A:	Yes, they were all co-ed.
9	Q:	I notice you're wearing a T-shirt today that has something to do with
10		volleyball.
11	A:	Yeah, it's my lucky T-shirt. It's the one I got as a special award when my
12		team won the silver medal at the National Junior Olympics this year in New
13		Orleans. I play the position of middle blocker, so the T-shirt says, "Annie
14		Whitford, Middle Blocker, Attacker of the Unwary, She Yields to No One."
15	Q:	Have you received other awards?
16	A:	Yes, I've gotten awards when my teams have won tournaments, and
17		also as the team's Most Valuable Player.
18	Q:	Do you know the win-loss statistics of your teams?
19	A:	Counting it all up, the teams I've played on have won 97 matches and
20		lost only seven. We've taken at least 20 titles.
21	Q:	Annie, what does volleyball mean to you?
22	A:	Volleyball is my life. I play it every day. If I'm not practicing or playi.
23		ng on teams, I'm working on my serves, passes, and spikes against the
24		wall of the gym or behind the school. My goal is to get a scholarship
25		to a college with a great women's volleyball team, like the University
26		of Franklin or Stanford. My parents sure couldn't afford those schools
27		otherwise. Maybe I'll even play in the Olympics one day. In fact, even
28		before that, I've got a real good chance of getting a volleyball scholar-
29		ship to Prescott next year. It's, like, the top prep school in the state and
30		has got a great volleyball program.
31	Q:	When did you first attend Newberry Middle School?
32	A:	Just this year when my family moved here from out of state.
33	Q:	Why do you want to play on the boys' volleyball team?
34	A:	For one, seventh grade is the first chance you get to play interscholastic
35		volleyball. Also, it's not like there is even a girls' team for me to try out
36		for. Even if there were, I've played with boys on all of my past teams
37		and I've watched the Newberry Middle School volley- ball team play. I
38		think that playing with the boys will give me the competition I need to
39		develop my skills.
40	Q:	Annie, suppose the judge decided you should be able to try out, but she
41		waited six months before she made that decision. Would that be okay?
42	A:	Well, I don't want to be impolite, but, like, what would be the point? The
43		season starts in two weeks and only lasts three months. I mean, Prescott
44		scouts and even some colleges wouldn't be able to see me play.
45		

APPLICANT: I have nothing further for this witness.

THE COURT: Cross-examination?

PERDUE: Yes. Thank you, Your Honor.

Q: Annie, have you ever been hurt playing volleyball?
A: Well, just twice. In a tournament game last year, I was hit in the face by a ball. I got a bruised eye and a bloody nose.
Q: Was that ball hit by a boy?
A: Yeah.
Q: Any other injuries?
A: At last summer's volleyball camp, a boy on the other team bumped me at the net and caused me to come down off balance. I came down on my right ankle and sprained it.
Q: So, your injury was caused by coming into physical contact with a boy, isn't that right?
A: Yeah, but he did it intentionally and he got called for a foul because you're not supposed to do that. But you really try hard not to do stuff like that because your team could get penalized.
Q: And, lots of times, when you're scrambling to get the ball, you and your teammates collide, isn't that true?
A: Not lots of times, but sometimes.
Q: Thank you, Annie. Nothing further, Your Honor. THE COURT: Next?

APPLICANT: The plaintiff calls Karin Wallenstein.
        THE WITNESS, Karin Wallenstein, WAS SWORN AND IDENTIFIED.

APPLICANT: Ms. Wallenstein, in what positions are you employed at Newberry Middle School?

WALLENSTEIN: I'm the Director of Physical Education and the volleyball coach.

Q: Were you previously employed in school athletics?
A: Yes, after graduating from college, I taught physical education courses for seventh and eighth graders for about six years. After that, I was at different times an assistant coach for the women's volleyball teams at Franklin Community College and Franklin State.
Q: Do you also play volleyball?
A: I play on the "Bruisers" adult co-ed team through the U.S. Volleyball League. I've played since high school.
Q: How many interscholastic sports teams are there at Newberry Middle School?
A: There are 10.
Q: What are they?
A: There are six boys' teams-football, basketball, baseball, ice hockey, volleyball, and wrestling. There are four girls' teams-cross-country, basketball, swimming, and tennis.

1	Q:	Are there any co-ed interscholastic teams?

1   Q: Are there any co-ed interscholastic teams?
2   A: No.
3   Q: Is there a budget for interscholastic athletics at Newberry?
4   A: Yes, it pays for things like coaches' salaries, facilities upkeep, equip-
5   ment and uniform purchases, athlete transportation, and publicity.
6   Q: What percentage of the athletic budget is spent on the boys' teams?
7   A: I'd say approximately 70%.
8   Q: Did you allow Annie Whitford to try out for the school volleyball team?
9   A: Ultimately, no.
10   Q: Why?
11   A: This is a little embarrassing. Being new to Newberry, I didn't even know
12   that the District had a rule barring girls from the volleyball team. I had
13   seen Annie play during P. E. class and she is by far the best player we
14   have in the school—boy or girl. I told her I hoped she would try out.
15   Q: Did any other female students ask to try out?
16   A: No, but not for lack of interest.
17   Q: What do you mean?
18   A: Unlike me, they knew the rule. Before tryouts I asked some of the girls
19   who played well in class if they were going to try out. They told me it was
20   no use, that, although some of them love to play volleyball, they had
21   given up a long time ago trying to get the school to start a girls' team, or
22   to allow a co-ed team. Once I found out about the rule barring girls, I
23   had to tell Annie she couldn't try out for the team.
24   Q: How much, if any, physical contact takes place between players during
25   a game of volleyball?
26   A: We follow U.S. Volleyball League rules, which say volleyball is a non-
27   contact sport. The main activity of the game is hitting the ball back and
28   forth over the net and trying to land the ball in the opponent's court
29   without its being returned successfully. Intentional or threatened phys-
30   ical contact between players can cause the player who acts intention-
31   ally or threatens another—and her team—to be penalized, including
32   expulsion from the match.
33   Q: Thank you, Coach Wallenstein.
34
35 THE COURT: Cross-examination?
36 PERDUE: Thank you, Your Honor. Ms. Wallenstein, isn't it true that volleyball
37 players wear protective padding when they play?
38
39 WALLENSTEIN: Most players wear kneepads, and I have seen a few players wear
40   elbow pads.
41   Q: In a game of volleyball, the six members of one team play on one side
42   of the net and the six members of the opposing team play on the other
43   side, correct?
44   A: Yes, that's correct.
45   Q: And, in the course of running for the ball, team members collide with
       each other, don't they?

1	A:	Not normally, if each player covers her area, but it can happen occasionally.
2	Q:	And sometimes a player in the front line collides at the net with a player
3		from the other team, right?
4	A:	Sometimes.
5	Q:	For example, when trying to spike a ball over the net, a player jumps up
6		to hit the ball, right?
7	A:	Yes.
8	Q:	And that player raises her arm over her head and attempts to slap the
9		ball hard over the net.
10	A:	Yes.
11	Q:	And in trying to make that play, she may physically strike a player on the
12		other team who may be trying to block or pass the ball, right?
13	A:	In my experience, rarely.
14	Q:	Well, isn't it considered a very good play when a player spikes a ball
15		hard over the net? A: Yes.
16	Q:	And a hard, fast hit over the net that the other team can't respond to is
17		even called a "kill," right?
18	A:	Yes, but certainly not with the aim of "killing" anyone.
19	Q:	In the course of your impressive career as a college coach, how many
20		injuries to players have you observed as a result of physical contact
21		between players?
22	A:	Some.
23	Q:	Because a good player is going to use all her power, speed, and strength
24		to get that volleyball over the net, right?
25	A:	Come on, Mr. Perdue, we are talking about 12-year-old boys and girls.
26	Q:	Ms. Wallenstein, please answer my question.
27	A:	I guess so.

28
29 PERDUE: I have no further questions of this witness.

30 THE COURT: Redirect?

31
32 APPLICANT: Briefly, Your Honor. Ms. Wallenstein, do volleyball rules require
33 players to wear knee or elbow pads?

34 WALLENSTEIN: No.

35
36 Q: How about mouth protectors or shin guards?
A: Neither.
37 Q: Do the rules prohibit players from wearing jewelry?
A: The rules don't but good sense does.
38

39 APPLICANT: Nothing further, Your Honor, and the plaintiff rests.
40 THE COURT: Mr. Perdue?
41 PERDUE: Your Honor, the District calls its only witness, Grace Huang.
42 THE WITNESS, Grace Huang, WAS SWORN AND IDENTIFIED.
43 PERDUE: Ms. Huang, you have been the Superintendent of the Newberry Middle
44 School District for 10 years?
45 HUANG: Correct.

1	Q:	What, if any, responsibility do you have over the interscholastic athletic
2		programs at the schools in your District?
3	A:	I decide the budget allocations, approve the types and number of inter-
4		scholastic teams and, with help of counsel, monitor compliance with
5		the law.
6	Q:	Were you responsible for the issuance of the rule at issue in this case?
7	A:	Yes.
8	Q:	What are the reasons for this rule?
9	A:	I read Title IX to prohibit co-ed interscholastic teams in contact sports
10		and the District has concluded that volleyball is a contact sport.
11	Q:	Your Honor, I have nothing further for this witness.
12		
13		THE COURT: Cross-examination?
14		APPLICANT: Thank you, Your Honor. Ms. Huang, you have no firsthand experi-
15		ence in school athletics, do you?
16		
17		HUANG: No, not really.
18	Q:	You have never taught seventh grade students, have you?
19	A:	My previous teaching experience was with high school students.
20	Q:	Am I correct that only seventh and eighth grade students may partici-
21		pate in interscholastic athletic activities in the Newberry Middle School
22		District?
23	A:	Yes, that is correct.
24	Q:	How many students are there in the seventh and eighth grades at
25		Newberry Middle School?
26	A:	Approximately 1,000.
27	Q:	How many of the 1,000 students are female?
28	A:	About 600.
29	Q:	That would make about 400 of the students male?
30	A:	Yes.
31	Q:	Of the 600 female students, approximately how many participate in
32		interscholastic athletics?
33	A:	About 100 among the four girls' teams.
34	Q:	And, of the 400 male students, how many play on interscholastic sports
35		teams?
36	A:	About 200.
37	Q:	In the past, female students at Newberry Middle School have requested
38		the formation of a girls' interscholastic volleyball team, am I right?
39	A:	I vaguely recall some parents sending me a letter to that effect.
40	Q:	And their request was denied?
41	A:	That's true.
42	Q:	There are talented volleyball players among the female students at
43		Newberry Middle School, aren't there?
44	A:	I don't really know.
45		

1 Q: I assume you have thought through the reasons why you denied the
2   request for an interscholastic girls' volleyball team?
3 A: Yes, I have.
4 Q: Well, are some of those reasons that you have limited facilities, and that
5   it would be hard to schedule practice and game times if you had both
6   girls' and boys' teams?
7 A: Yes.
8 Q: You might have to hire another coach, and even if you didn't, you'd have
9   to pay Ms. Wallenstein more to take on the extra work?
10 A: Yes.
11 Q: You would have to increase your lockers and other facilities to accom-
12   modate visiting teams.   Is that right?
13 A: Yes.
14 Q: This all would cost a great deal of money, wouldn't it?
15 A: We only have so much money to spend on the athletic programs at each
16   school.
17 Q: I have nothing further for this witness.

18
19 THE COURT: Mr. Perdue, any redirect?

20 PERDUE: No, the District rests.

21 THE COURT: Thank you, counsel. I see it's getting late, so let's reconvene
22   tomorrow afternoon for argument. We will get you a transcript with our
23   new simultaneous transcription equipment. Before we adjourn, however,
24   let me say I think it's pretty clear Annie has established that waiting for
25   a trial doesn't do her any good. If her legal theory is right, she will suffer
26   irreparable harm. You have adequately briefed the issue whether the Title
27   IX regulations comport with constitutional equal protection standards so
28   do not argue that point again. I want you to focus your arguments on the
29   likelihood of plaintiff' s success on the merits.
30
31
32
33
34
35
36
37
38
39
40
41
42
43
44
45

LIBRARY
Whitford v. Newberry Middle School District

Title IX of the Education Amendments of 1972
20 United States Code § 1681

(a) No person in the United States shall, on the basis of gender, be excluded from participation in, be denied the benefits of, or be subjected to discrimination under any education program or activity receiving Federal financial assistance.

34 Code of Federal Regulations § 106.41. Athletics.

(a) General. No person shall, on the basis of gender, be excluded from participation in, be denied the benefits of, be treated differently from another person, or otherwise be discriminated against in any interscholastic athletics offered by a recipient, and no recipient shall provide any such athletics separately on such basis.

(b) Separate teams. Notwithstanding the requirements of paragraph (a) of this section, a recipient may operate or sponsor separate teams in a particular sport for members of each gender where selection for such teams is based upon competitive skill or the activity involved is a contact sport. However, where a recipient operates or sponsors a team in a particular sport for members of one gender but operates or sponsors no such team for members of the other gender, and athletic opportunities for members of that gender have previously been limited, members of the excluded gender must be allowed to try out for the team offered unless the sport involved is a contact sport. For the purposes of this paragraph, contact sports include boxing, wrestling, rugby, ice hockey, football, basketball, and other sports the purpose or major activity of which involves bodily contact.

(c) Equal opportunity. A recipient that operates or sponsors interscholastic, intercollegiate, club or intramural athletics shall provide equal athletic opportunity for members of both genders. In determining whether equal opportunities are available, the following factors will be considered:
  (1) Whether the selection of sports and levels of competition effectively accommodate the interests and abilities of members of both genders;
  (2) Provision of equipment and supplies;
  (3) Scheduling of games and practice time;
  (4) Travel and per diem allowance;
  (5) Opportunity to receive coaching and academic tutoring;
  (6) Assignment and compensation of coaches and tutors;
  (7) Provision of locker rooms, practice and competitive facilities;
  (8) Provision of medical and training facilities and services;
  (9) Provision of housing and dining facilities and services; and
  (10) Publicity.

Unequal aggregate expenditures for members of each gender or unequal expenditures for male and female teams if a recipient operates or sponsors separate teams may be considered in assessing equality of athletic opportunity for members of each gender.

Metcalf v. Homer School District
United States Court of Appeal for the Fifteenth Circuit (1998)

Ryan Metcalf, a male student at Homer High School in Homer, Franklin, alleges that he is unlawfully precluded on the basis of his gen der from playing interscholastic field hockey because he is not allowed to compete for a place on the only field hockey team at his school, which is the girls' team. The district court ruled in favor of Ryan, under Title IX of the Education Amendments of 1972.

The District argues that its policy prohibiting boys from being members of the girls' field hockey team falls within both of the exceptions set forth in 34 C.F.R. § 106.41 (b) concerning the obligations placed upon a recipient when it sponsors a team for members of only one gender and not the other gender. When the sport is a contact sport, the recipient can provide a team for only one gender. When the sport is a non-contact sport, the recipient must provide an opportunity for the excluded gender to try out for the team only when "athletic opportunities for members of that gender have previously been limited." *Id.*

The contact sport exception is the broadest exception under Title IX. Whether field hockey is a contact sport depends on whether it is a sport "the purpose or major activity of which involves bodily contact." *Id.* An expert testifying on plaintiff's behalf stated that "field hockey is technically, and according to the international rules that govern the game, a non-contact sport. Almost all bodily contact or threatened bodily contact between players is a violation or foul. Any physical contact is incidental."

The District offered its own expert, who explained that the major activities of the sport of field hockey involve running up and down the field attempting to score a goal or prevent the other team from doing so. She stated that these activities "inevitably produce and involve bodily contact." She concluded that field hockey is a contact sport because bodily contact regularly occurs throughout the course of any competitive field hockey game.

Both parties agreed that the "purpose" of field hockey, unlike wrestling, boxing or football, does not involve bodily contact. The district court held that "no major activity of field hockey involves bodily contact and it is, therefore, not a contact sport." We disagree.

The district court's inquiry as to the major activity suggests that bodily contact can be deemed a "major activity" of a sport only if it is sanctioned activity. While the fact that the rules penalize bodily contact is an important factor in determining whether the purpose of field hockey involves bodily contact, the regulation does not allow the inquiry to end there. It requires a further inquiry into whether the major activity of field hockey involves bodily contact.

In making this determination, we consider it significant that the rules require mouth protectors and shin guards, prohibit spiked shoes, and prohibit the wearing of jewelry. Such a level of protective rules suggests that bodily contact does in fact occur frequently. Further, even if bodily contact is incidental to the game, it may be an inevitable and frequent occurrence in the game. In sum, both the level of protective rules as well as the inevitability and frequency of bodily contact in the actual game must be analyzed to determine whether the major activities of a sport involve bodily contact.

Applying these factors, we find that field hockey is a contact sport under 34 C.F.R. § 106.41(b), and reverse. Because Ryan's Title IX claim is disposed of by our finding that field hockey is a contact sport, it is not necessary to inquire into whether the athletic opportunities of males at Homer High have previously been limited.

Milley v. Arlington School District
United States Court of Appeal for the Fifteenth Circuit (2000)

Tommi-Jo Milley is an extraordinarily gifted female baseball pitcher. Since "T.J." was seven years old, she has pitched in organized baseball teams in programs run by the Arlington Park District and the Arlington Little League. She has also participated in the U. S. Baseball Association Batter-Up and Elks Club competitions. During this period the teams T.J. played on have won 95% of their games. She has received numerous awards recognizing her abilities. In all of these programs, T.J. played with boys.

In the fall of 1999, T.J., now 11, enrolled in sixth grade at Arlington Junior High School in Des Plaines, Franklin. She was then presented with her first opportunity to play interscholastic baseball. There is only one baseball team at Arlington and that is a boys' baseball team. Defendant in this case, the Arlington School District, denied T.J. per mission to try out for the boys' baseball team. T.J. and her parents filed this action, seeking injunctive relief requiring defendants to permit her to try out for the boys' team. The district court's grant of summary judgment for the plaintiff is now before us on appeal.

Plaintiff challenges her exclusion from the tryouts under Title IX of the Education Amendments of 1972 and the regulations thereunder. 34 C.F.R. § 106.41 subsection (b) requires a recipient of federal funds who sponsors a team in a particular sport only for members of one gender to allow members of the excluded gender to try out for the team if the sport is a non-contact sport and athletic opportunities for members of the excluded gender have previously been limited. The parties stipulate that baseball is not a contact sport. They agree that the sole question on appeal is whether "athletic opportunities . . . have previously been limited" for girls at Arlington.

In interpreting this language, the district court considered the absence of a girls' or a co-ed baseball team at Arlington and held that the District was in violation of Title IX because opportunities for girls in baseball have previously been limited. The court interpreted the regulation's inquiry as sports-specific. We disagree.

The phrase "have previously been limited" must be understood in the context of the entire athletic program. If the district court's construction were adopted, there could never be a situation in a non-contact sport in which a team was limited to a single gender without a corresponding team for the other gender because, by definition, the opportunities in that particular sport would be limited for the excluded gender. It would mean that girls would always be able to argue that they had previously limited athletic opportunities just because certain sports have traditionally been considered boys' sports, such as baseball.

Our view is consistent with subsection (c) of the regulation, which enumerates ten factors that will be considered in determining whether interscholastic programs provide equal athletic opportunity. That subsection further provides, "Unequal aggregate expenditures for members of each gender or unequal expenditures for male and female teams if a recipient operates or sponsors separate teams may be considered in assessing equality of athletic opportunity for members of each gender." Thus, it is clear that the obligation of an educational institution in complying with the requirements of Title IX cannot be measured only by comparing types of teams available to each gender, but instead must turn on whether disparities of a substantial and unjustified nature exist in the benefits, treatment, services, or opportunities afforded male and female athletes in the institution's sports program as a whole.

The district court's grant of summary judgment for the plaintiff is reversed.

FILE
In re Madert

Memorandum

To:	Applicant
From:	Sarah Lindsay
Re:	Allie and Bruce Madert
Date:	February 26, 2002

Our clients, Allie and Bruce Madert, are having a problem with their next-door neighbors, Adrian and Evelyn Doyle. The Doyles are trying to start a rock band. They are constantly practicing alone or with an ever-changing group of other musicians in a shed they converted into a music studio behind their house. The Maderts have repeatedly asked the Doyles to restrain themselves in a variety of ways, but to no avail. When the Maderts mentioned that they might even be forced to take legal action, Adrian Doyle told them to contact his lawyer, George Austin.

In fact, the Maderts are reluctant to file a lawsuit. Before they go that far, they want us to write a letter to George Austin to see if we can convince the Doyles that, unless they make changes to reduce the intrusiveness of their playing to acceptable levels, the Maderts will sue for an injunction and damages.

Draft a letter for my signature to George Austin. The letter should briefly explain the dispute, emphasize the key facts, and use legal authority to argue persuasively that the noise produced by the Doyles' music constitutes a nuisance to our clients and that, if the Maderts sue, a court will likely issue an injunction and award significant damages. Be sure to include in the letter a statement of what relief the Maderts could expect to obtain and constructive suggestions of what steps the Doyles can take to abate the noise so that it is no longer a nuisance.

Austin is a stickler for legal analysis, but a very reasonable and competent lawyer. He is likely to be receptive to solutions that will avoid litigation for his clients if he is persuaded that his clients' case is weak, so don't hesitate to lay out our case to him.

**Transcript of Recorded Interview with
Allie and Bruce Madert
February 25, 2002**

Attorney: Allie, Bruce, how good to see you. What brings you to see me in this setting?

Allie: I can hardly believe it—a problem with our new next-door neighbors. Well, not so new. They moved in about a year ago. Our old neighbor, Cecil, was always friendly, but our lives didn't overlap much. When Adrian and Evelyn Doyle moved in, our neighbors suddenly became a big problem.

Attorney: What kind of problem?

Allie: Let me go back to the beginning. Cecil was a painter, and he spent most of his time in an old shed behind the house, which he used as a studio. When the Doyles bought the house, the first thing they did was get a permit to remodel the shed and bring in contractors to make it fancier—they put in a skylight, made the windows larger, and made other improvements. At first we thought they were trying to create an accessory apartment, which would have been illegal without a zoning variance. They said they were creating a music studio. Adrian plays the bass guitar and Evelyn the drums. They had lived in an apartment before and were excited to have a place where they could just "let go" with their music. I told Evelyn that I was disturbed by noise—especially the bass guitar—and that the shed didn't seem like it would contain the sound. Bruce though I was being kind of rude when I told her about hating the sound of the bass coming through the floor in my college dorm. She assured me that they were looking into ways to absorb the noise. As the renovations went along, I asked specifically about all the glass they were adding—I thought it would exacerbate the problem. Again, Evelyn said they were "dealing with it."

Bruce: I did think Allie was being a little paranoid, but then, during the renovations, they started to practice their instruments in their house late into the night. At midnight you could hear the same six notes on the bass, over and over, not to mention the sharp sounds of the drums.

Allie: I couldn't decide if the practicing or the playing was worse. Other people would go over to the Doyles and they would all play. I don't know how they ever got any jobs, but apparently they did. Sometimes we'd see them loading up their old Chevy with all their equipment and they would say they were headed off to a "gig."

Attorney: Did you ever let them know that the noise was bothering you?

Allie:	Lots. Once after they had been practicing during a weekday evening, I saw Adrian and told him that it was distracting to the kids when they were doing their homework. He said it would be better when the studio was finished and that they would try to keep the noise down. It never seemed any better to me.
Bruce:	Another time, Evelyn came over about five on a Saturday afternoon to say they were having people over that evening and that she hoped it didn't bother us. I felt funny saying that I hoped they didn't go too late. At 2 a.m., when I finally fell asleep, they were still going strong.
Allie:	After one particularly awful Friday night after the studio was finished when they had at least six other musicians there, we put a letter in their mailbox that said we were considering legal action. I brought a copy for you.
Attorney:	Did you get a response?
Bruce:	A vague one. Adrian said that they'd had a "really intense" night and that it was unlikely to happen again. He said that if we had legal problems to contact his lawyer, George Austin. It was so strange. Adrian showed no anger or embarrassment.
Attorney:	So then what happened?
Allie:	Things only got worse. They keep practicing till all hours and having people over to play—anywhere from two to eight of them. If there was any difference in the sound after the studio was completed, it was louder. It was certainly more frequent.
Bruce:	And I never saw any sound insulating material when they were doing the construction. I've looked in the window and can see that the walls are just drywall. They have shades on the windows, but they don't seem specially designed for acoustical qualities. The noise is especially terrible in warm weather. I like to keep the windows open rather than run the air-conditioning. But then I feel like the band is in the living room.
Attorney:	Before I find out what you would like to have happen, I'd like to know more about the neighborhood. Tell me about the Windsor section of town where you live.
Allie:	We love Windsor. When we looked for a house to buy 16 years ago, we looked only there. The area has a strong sense of community, commitment to diversity and acceptance of all sorts of artistic types. A lot of people are ecologically minded. We have our own special recycling programs where we separate our garbage into five categories. You can't cut down a tree on your own property without a special permit. Some of the commuters who try to use our neighborhood to avoid busy streets don't like our speed bumps, but the bumps keep our children safe and keep away the motorcycles and trucks, with their noise and dirty exhaust.

Bruce:	Like Allie says, we have a lot of artistic types in the neighborhood. That's part of what attracted us. We have our own jazz and folk festivals and a local weekly music series outside the library in the summer. One neighborhood group puts on a yearly Shakespeare play using all child actors and another has a neighborhood dance recital. We hold an art festival for local artists in our commercial district. We could go on, but you get the idea.
Allie:	It's ironic that a couple of musicians are causing our trouble. We've had all sorts living around us over the years, and they've always been careful about not disturbing anyone. There are artists' cooperatives and community centers close by where people can go if they want to play loudly or with a group or late at night. They don't charge very much.
Bruce:	I think the difference is that the Doyles are recently married, middle-aged teenagers who are trying to experience a carefree, vaguely rebellious youth they never had. Our kids think they're just pathetic. During the day, they're both computer programmers. At night, they have dreams of starting a rock band.
Attorney:	How do you fit into the Windsor community?
Bruce:	Over the years, we've restored our Victorian, which is in the historic district. Most of the houses have large backyards, but the side yards are only 12 feet wide.
Attorney:	Now let me find out what you would want—other than for the Doyles to move.
Allie:	You're right. I'd throw them a good-bye party, and they could play. But given the work and money they've put into the studio and, by the way, the house, too, I don't see any celebration in my future.
Bruce:	Also, they're not mean people. They're just kind of ridiculous and out-of-it so they do some pretty inconsiderate things. If we can keep from suing them, I'd prefer that option, but we're prepared to spend some money on this if we have to. Also, we don't know if the law is on our side.
Allie:	I'd be happy enough if they kept the noise from reaching our house—the whole year. So I guess they'd have to change the times they play and practice. And, I bet there are alterations they could make to the studio to muffle the noise a lot.
Bruce:	But probably they can't do everything they're now doing out of their studio.
Attorney:	Let me tell you how I'm thinking about proceeding, and you can see if that makes sense to you or if you have other ideas. I think the law is quite favorable in your direction. The law provides a variety of remedies, that is, things we can ask for, both in terms of getting money and getting the Doyles to change. Before spending money on an investigation and hiring a battery of experts, we might be

	able to convince the Doyles, through their lawyer, to make the necessary changes.
Allie:	I don't know if a lawyer can get through to them, but it seems worth a try. I'm not particularly interested in getting money from the Doyles, as long as the noise stops. But I wouldn't mind threatening—it might get their attention.
Bruce:	I agree. Out of curiosity, could we get a court to order them to stop playing their music completely?
Attorney:	Probably, but I'll have to do the research. The legal argument about the scope of the problems they face will have to be strong and convincing. I'll draft something and send it to you to see what you think before I send it to Austin.
Bruce:	Sounds great. We'll wait to hear from you.

209 Westland Road
Oakton, Franklin 33329
December 7, 2001

Adrian and Evelyn Doyle
211 Westland Road
Oakton, Franklin 33329

Dear Adrian and Evelyn,

We are writing to you out of our frustration and unhappiness about the problem created for us by the noise level of your music. We know that you both love music, as we do. We also appreciate your enthusiasm for it. However, you do not seem to understand that the noise level interferes with the lives of our family. Your party last night was only the most recent and egregious example of the way your playing is out of hand. You and your friends continued to play very loudly until after 3:00 a.m. For all we know, you continued even later, but we finally got to sleep a little after 3:00. Laurie fell asleep by midnight, but she had a recital this morning at 8:30 so was much more tired than was good for her. Noah, who fell asleep about 12:30 a.m., had to get up at 7:00 a.m. for his basketball game. We all need our sleep, even on weekends. Although you might not have to wake up on weekend mornings, many of us do, and these late hours spoil what are important times for us.

We are asking you to please stop playing in a way that we can hear. It is intolerable that your music interferes with the regular activities of our lives. If the noise does not stop, we may have to take legal action. We hope that we can work together to solve this problem.

Very truly yours,

Allie and Bruce Madert

Allie and Bruce Madert

NOISE POLLUTION AND CONTROL

University of Franklin Department of Ecological studies 1998

INTRODUCTION

One of the drawbacks of our advanced technology is that we have produced the loudest noises known to humans. The realization that noise is a pollutant has been very slow in coming. Noise is invisible. Defining its impact on people and the environment is more difficult than with other environmental pollutants such as those that affect air or water. In addition, some people just plain like to make noise because of its association with power. It is a common misconception that you can adjust to noise by ignoring it or getting used to it. The ear never closes and is continually responding to sound, even during sleep. Noise can

- cause permanent hearing damage;
- contribute to the development or aggravation of heart and circulatory diseases;
- affect the quantity and quality of sleep;
- interfere with conversation and social interaction;
- disrupt the educational process and hinder the development of language skills in children;
- transform our initial annoyance into more extreme emotional responses and behavior; and
- endanger life and limb by obscuring shouts for help or masking warning signals, thereby delaying or preventing rescue attempts.

Home should be a place for rest and quiet after the labor and cares of each day. Excessive noise in the community deprives most people of access to such a retreat. Community noise problems are varied and include everything from barking dogs to traffic noise.

Univ. of Franklin Dept. of Ecological Studies hllp://www.ufranklin/estudies/report_np.edu

SUGGESTED OPERATIONAL RESTRICTIONS FOR COMMUNITY NOISE REDUCTION

Nuisance Laws: Prohibit loud or raucous behavior, disturbing the peace, and/or making unnecessary noise. This approach may be difficult to enforce, except in controlling noise from animals, radios, televisions, and musical instruments, and this approach needs to be employed in conjunction with another approach such as property-line noise limits.

Property-Line Noise Limits: Effective in controlling noise from stationary sources. Place a decibel level limit on noise at the boundary of the receiving or (less commonly) of the emanating property. Most often the noise limits are stated in terms of the character of the receiving land use (e.g., residential, commercial, etc.), and the time of day.

Source-Distance Noise Limit: Restricts operation of a device that creates a noise disturbance within a specified distance from the source. May be imposed to control noise from radios, televisions, stereos, motor boats, refuse collection vehicles, and recreational vehicles.

Time Limitations: Effective in controlling both stationary and mobile noise sources. Specify hours during which noise is prohibited.

Area Limitations: Specify areas such as noise sensitive zones and places of public entertainment where noise is controlled.

Use Controls: Restrict the operation of the noise sources such as motor vehicle horns, motor vehicles and cycles, and places of public entertainment.

SUGGESTED NOISE CONTROL TECHNIQUES

Use of Buffers: Setbacks can be provided in the form of open space, frontage roads, recreational areas, garages, etc. between the noise source and the receiver. The objective is to achieve attenuation of noise with distance.

Use of Barriers: This includes walls, berms, or other structures intended to provide extra attenuation by blocking noise from the source.

Univ. of Franklin Dept. of Ecological Studies hllp://www.ufranklin/estudies/report_np.edu

Unit Design: Placement of relatively sensitive rooms or fixtures away from the noise source is cost-effective. Garages, bathrooms, and storage areas can serve as internal noise barriers for bedrooms and living rooms.

Building Orientation: Using one building to shield another can reduce noise control costs. Placing yards or patios inside the "L" or "U" of buildings can reduce outdoor noise exposures if these face away from the noise source.

Noise Attenuation by Building Facades: The most obvious example of this technique is the reduction of window area on noise-impacted facades. Practices such as the use of double or staggered-stud walls, acoustical glass (with low air-infiltration window frames), resilient channels, etc., are effective in reducing interior noise levels. Weather stripping and caulking of wall penetrations are essential.

LIBRARY
In re Madert

Meadowbrook Swimming Club v. Albert
Franklin Supreme Court (1938)

This appeal is from a decree for an injunction against the continuance of a noise nuisance. Several years ago Meadowbrook Swimming Club built an amusement park, including a large swimming pool, in the narrow valley of Jones Falls. High hills, which rise on both sides of the valley, have become popular sites for expensive residences. In 1935 Meadowbrook added an outdoor dance floor, with a "shell" platform for the musicians' stand. The club opened the dance floor to the public, engaged modern jazz orchestras to play dance music from nine to twelve, six nights per week, and used amplifiers to enhance the volume of sound.

Immediately, a number of residents, whose houses were located on the hills some 200 feet or more above the dance floor, complained in writing to Meadowbrook. The club made sundry efforts to minimize the alleged nuisance. The club abandoned the amplifiers, limited dancing to four nights a week, sought expert advice, and undertook acoustic experiments. Nevertheless, the blare of the brasses, the beating of the drums, and the thumping of the bass were, and are, so penetrating and loud that witnesses who live on the sides of the hills, who are doubtless normally constituted and of exceptional integrity and intelligence, are unable to sleep, to study, or otherwise lead normal lives in their own homes for four evenings a week during the summer.

Though not a nuisance per se, where a trade or business as carried on interferes with the reasonable and comfortable enjoyment by another of his property, a wrong is done to a neighboring owner for which an action lies at law or equity. It makes no difference that the business was lawful and conducted in the most approved method. The question is whether the nuisance complained of will or does produce unreasonable physical discomfort to persons of ordinary sensibilities, tastes, and habits. However, not every inconvenience will call forth the restraining power of a court. The injury must diminish materially the value of the property as a dwelling and seriously interfere with the ordinary comfort and enjoyment of it.

Noise alone may create a nuisance and be the subject of injunction. In Lloyd v. Parsons, Franklin Court of Appeal (1934), a person who kept on his premises so great a number of domestic animals, fowl, and hogs that their noise deprived the complainant neighbor of the reasonable use and comfortable enjoyment of his adjacent dwelling was properly enjoined from keeping the animals. Any habitual noise, whether produced by domestic animals or by skilled musicians, which is so loud, continuous, insistent, not inherent to the character of the neighborhood and unusual therein, that normal people are so seriously incommoded that they cannot sleep, study, read, converse, or concentrate until it stops, is unreasonable . The decree in this case permanently enjoined Meadowbrook from "the playing of loud music, or the creation of other similar noises" upon its property "in such manner that the noise is transmitted onto the properties of the plaintiffs, so as to deprive them and the members of their families of the reasonable use and comfortable enjoyment" of their respective homes. Meadowbrook argues on appeal that the decree has the effect of an unqualified prohibition against the playing of jazz or other loud music. But such a purpose is not indicated by the decree.

A change of the conditions under which the loud jazz music is played might prevent the disturbance. For example, the club's president suggested that the construction of a roof to cover the open-air dance floor and connect it with the top of the shell might obviate the cause of complaint. The decree leaves Meadowbrook free to adopt any effective method of so reducing the volume of sound transmitted to the homes of the plaintiffs that they will no longer he disturbed.

The form of the decree is not objectionable as insufficiently definite for it specifies the purpose and extent of the restriction that it imposes, while leaving the defendant at liberty to devise and apply promptly an efficient plan for the abatement of the prohibited nuisance.

Decree affirmed, with costs awarded to plaintiffs.

Gorman v. Sabo
Franklin Court of Appeal (1956)

The jury returned a verdict of $3,500 against Mr. and Mrs. Gorman in a suit by their neighbors, Mr. and Mrs. Sabo, based on the willful and malicious beaming into the Sabo home of loud blaring of the Gorman radio. The Gormans appealed.

The jury found the following facts. Mr. and Mrs. Sabo and their four children moved in next door to the Gormans, who also had children. Trouble arose among the children, producing ill feeling on the part of Mrs. Gorman against the Sabo family.

Mrs. Gorman deliberately harassed the Sabo family with the aim of making them move. She turned up the radio to an excessive volume, beaming it directly from a west window of the Gorman house into the east side of the Sabo house. The window was kept open even in cold weather. This continued for hours each day over a period of several years. Mrs. Gorman also ordered her children to beat with sticks and stones on metal furniture and cans at strategic times.

Mrs. Gorman's efforts to get rid of the Sabo family were known to the neighbors, many having seen the radio and heard its noise. Mrs. Gorman told various neighbors that she intended to make the Sabos move, that she would make life miserable for Mrs. Sabo, and that she hoped Mr. Sabo would be struck down.

As a result of the noise, life became miserable for Mr. and Mrs. Sabo. Their children could not take their naps.

It was necessary to move them from their rooms on the side of the house facing the Gormans. On innumerable occasions it was impossible to carry on a conversation in the Sabo home. Mrs. Sabo suffered from an actual illness because of the constant noise. Mr. Sabo became irritable and nervous.

If noise causes physical discomfort and annoyance to those of ordinary sensibilities, tastes and habits, and seriously interferes with the ordinary comfort and enjoyment of their homes and thus diminishes the value of the use of their property, it constitutes a private nuisance, entitling those offended against to damages. Where there is a non-trespassory invasion of rights in real property occupied as a home, consisting of a private nuisance, the measure of damages is the diminution in the value of the use of the property as a home. The elements in the loss of the value of the use include the ordinary use and enjoyment of the home and also sickness or ill health of those in the home caused by the nuisance. A plaintiff is not limited to the recovery of the diminished rental value but may be compensated for any actual inconvenience and physical discomfort that materially affected the comfortable and healthful enjoyment and occupancy of the home.

Damages for illness, pain and discomfort, and annoyance caused by a nuisance are recoverable in addition to, and separate from, damages for diminution in the value of the use or the value of the property. The Sabos produced sufficient evidence of the ill effects suffered by them to entitle them to substantial damages.

Once the right to compensatory or at least nominal damages has been established, punitive damages may also be awarded. The testimony also clearly supports a finding of willfulness and malice on the part of Mrs. Gorman sufficient to justify punitive damages.

Judgment affirmed, with costs awarded to plaintiffs.

Arundel Fish & Game Club v. Carlucci
Franklin Court of Appeal (2000)

This case concerns noise resulting from gunfire on the premises of the rifle and pistol firing range of the Arundel Fish & Game Club (the Club), which was established in the early 1950s. The issue is whether that noise constituted a common law private nuisance to resident owners of properties adjoining the Club. The District Court concluded that it did and issued an injunction requiring the Club to design and implement a noise abatement system. This appeal ensued.

When the Club purchased its property, there was relatively little residential development in the area. The real estate surrounding the Club's premises is now predominantly residential.

At trial, the owners of the adjoining residential properties described the noise emanating from the Club's activities. Michael Darrow testified that in 1987 he completed the home that he shares with his family. His house is located approximately 800 feet from the Club'8 land. Darrow related that the gunfire from the Club occurred from 9 a.m. until 9 p.m. seven days a week. He could hear the gun club's activities from any place in his house, including the shower with the water running. He testified that he and his family could not use their yard on the weekends. The noise prevents sleeping, reading, watching television or any other activity that requires concentration.

Five other residents similarly testified to the interference that the noise caused with enjoyment of their residences. The residents related their efforts to persuade the Club to modify its activities. Their complaints to the police also had not resulted in any relief.

The Club first argues that, since it is not subject to the noise restrictions imposed by regulations adopted by the Franklin Department of the Environment, its activities cannot be enjoined as a private nuisance. Under Title 3 of the Franklin Environment Code, which concerns Noise Control, Franklin Environment Code § 3-101 *et seq.*, the Department of the Environment has been charged with promulgating regulations that limit noise. Significantly, the legislature has exempted shooting sports clubs from the reach of noise regulations.

The regulations adopted by the Department of the Environment to control noise pollution are codified in the Franklin Code of regulations (FCR) at 26-01 through 26-59.[1] The maximum permissible noise levels for commercial enterprises operating on residential land, measured at its boundary, are set forth at FCR 26-23(a):

> The maximum allowable noise level for a commercial enterprise in a residential zone shall

---

1. Note that these regulations apply only to commercial and industrial enterprises.

not exceed 65 decibels in the daytime hours nor 55 decibels in the nighttime hours.[2]

Even though the Club qualifies for an exemption from the regulations of the Franklin Department of the Environment, the exemption does not bar residents from seeking equitable relief from a nuisance created by appellant.

In order to provide quantifiable guidelines for the operation of the gun club, the court will use some standards provided by the regulations promulgated by the Franklin Department of the Environment simply for the advisory benefit they provide. In this case, the measurements of the noise levels at the residents' property lines taken by experts retained by the residents varied between 72 and 89 decibels. All are significantly above the levels permitted by the Department of the Environment for commercial enterprises in residential zones. These guidelines can help a court inform its judgment about whether noise levels are unreasonable and can have deleterious effects on those subjected to them and what those levels should be.

Nuisance is usually placed into three classifications: first, those that are nuisances *per se* or by statute; second, those that prejudice public health or comfort such as slaughter houses, livery stables, etc.; third, those that in their nature are not nuisances, but may become so by reason of their locality, surroundings, or the manner in which they may be maintained.

The gun club is a nuisance that falls into the third category. There is ample evidence to justify the court's conclusion that the gunfire on the Club's premises constituted a private nuisance to its residential neighbors.[3]

The Club also relies on the Restatement (Second) of Torts § 822.[4] The Club argues that liability for private nuisance should apply only when the interference is intentional and unreasonable or caused by negligent, reckless, or abnormally dangerous conduct. We agree.

In this case, however, the gun club's activities do violate the standard enunciated in the Restatement and are intentional, as we have defined that term:

---

2. Terms used in the regulations are defined at Franklin Code of Regulations (FCR) 26-02.

* * *

b. 'Daytime hours' means 7 a.m. to 10 p.m., local time.

c. 'Nighttime hours' means 10 p.m. to 7 a.m., local time.

* * *

3. The fact that most of the residents purchased their properties and built their homes on residentially zoned property after the Club had been established did not bar those residents from seeking relief from the nuisance.

4. The Restatement (Second) of Torts § 822 provides:

One is subject to liability for a private nuisance if, but only if, his conduct is a legal cause of an invasion of another's interest in the private use and enjoyment of land, and the invasion is either

(a) Intentional and unreasonable, or

(b) Unintentional and otherwise actionable under the rules controlling liability for negligent or reckless conduct, or for abnormally dangerous conditions or activities.

An intentional invasion of another's interest in the use and enjoyment of land need not be inspired by ill will or malice. An actor who knowingly causes an invasion of this interest in the pursuit of a laudable enterprise without any desire to cause harm also commits an intentional invasion. It is the knowledge that the actor has at the time he or she acts or fails to act that determines whether the invasion resulting from his conduct is intentional or unintentional. When an actor is put on notice concerning the harm of certain activities and continues to engage in them with knowledge of the harm, the actor is liable for creation of a nuisance. *Lawrence v. Simms*, Franklin Supreme Court (1995).

Finally, the gun club argues that the injunction issued by the court was overbroad. We again disagree. The court ordered that within six months the Club design and implement a noise abatement system for all of its facilities so as to reduce the noise to not more than 65 decibels during the daytime and 55 decibels during the nighttime. It further provided that the sound would be measured by devices at locations on the residents' properties from the sides of the residents' houses that faced the Club's premises. It further ordered that during a six-month period the operation of the Club's firing ranges be limited to certain hours calculated to reduce the likelihood of interference with the use and enjoyment of the residents' properties.

Both experts who evaluated the noise emanating from the Club testified that there are effective noise abatement procedures that could be employed by the Club to reduce the noise levels that the residents were enduring on their properties. We perceive no abuse of the court's discretion in so framing the injunction.

Affirmed, with costs awarded to plaintiffs.

FILE
Acme Resources, Inc. v. Black Hawk et al.

Peterson, Michaels & Williams
Attorneys at Law
1530 Lakeside Way
Franklin City, Franklin 33033

MEMORANDUM

To: Applicant
From: Conrad Williams
Date: July 24, 2007
Re: *Black Hawk et al. v. Acme Resources, Inc.* (Black Eagle Tribal Court);
               Acme Resources, Inc. v. Black Hawk et al. (U.S. Dist. Ct. for the
               Dist. of Franklin)

We represent Robert Black Hawk and seven other members of the Black Eagle Indian Tribe (the Tribe) in an action in Black Eagle Tribal Court (Tribal Court) against Acme Resources, Inc. (Acme). Acme's mining activities, specifically the extraction of coal bed methane, have caused our clients' water wells to begin to run dry. In the Tribal Court action we are seeking damages and an injunction ordering Acme to cease its operations on the Black Eagle Indian Reservation.

The coal bed methane underlies private land on the Reservation owned in fee simple by Patrick Mulroney, who is not a member of the Tribe. While Mulroney owns the surface of the land, the underlying minerals are owned by the Tribe. The Tribe granted Acme the right to extract the methane from under Mulroney's land in exchange for a royalty. At the same time, Mulroney granted Acme the right to use his land to build the infrastructure that is necessary for mining.

In response to our complaint in Tribal Court, Acme filed an answer denying liability and also denying the jurisdiction of the Tribal Court. No further proceedings have occurred in Tribal Court. Instead, Acme filed a separate federal action in U.S. District Court for the District of Franklin seeking both a declaratory judgment that the Tribal Court lacks jurisdiction in this matter and an injunction against prosecution of our Tribal Court action. (See attached complaint.)

I plan to respond to Acme's complaint by filing a motion with the federal court: (1) for summary judgment on the ground that the Tribal Court has jurisdiction; or, in the alternative (2) to stay or dismiss Acme's federal action on the ground that the Tribal Court should be permitted to consider its jurisdiction over the matter. (See attached draft motion and affidavits of Robert Black Hawk and Jesse Bellingham, Ph.D.)

Please draft the argument sections of the brief in support of both points. Each distinct point in the argument should be preceded by a subject heading that encapsulates the argument it covers and succinctly summarizes the reasons the court should take the position you are advocating. A heading should be a specific application of a rule of law to the facts of the case and not a bare legal or factual statement of an abstract principle. For example, <u>improper</u>: The Police Did

Not Have Probable Cause to Arrest Defendant. <u>Proper</u>: The Fact That Defendant Was Walking Alone in a High-Crime Area at Night Without Photo Identification Was Insufficient to Establish Probable Cause for His Arrest.

The argument under each heading should analyze applicable legal authority and state persuasively how the facts and the law support our clients' position. Authority supporting our clients' position should be emphasized, but contrary authority should also generally be cited, addressed, and explained or distinguished. Be sure to address the grounds asserted in Acme's complaint; do not reserve arguments for reply or supplemental briefs. No statement of facts is necessary, but be sure to incorporate the relevant facts into your argument.

Transcript of Interview with Robert Black Hawk
May 18, 2007

Williams:	Good afternoon, Mr. Black Hawk. What can I do for you?
Black Hawk:	My neighbors and I are at the end of our ropes. We are all members of the Black Eagle Tribe and we are in bad shape. Our wells are running dry.
Williams:	Do you know why?
Black Hawk:	You bet we do. Two years ago, Acme Resources came onto our Reservation with promises of jobs and riches. Acme wanted to develop a huge coal bed methane field under the Reservation. The easiest access to the field is by way of Patrick Mulroney's land. None of us tribal members wanted it because we had heard of water problems associated with the development of coal bed methane.
Williams:	I know that methane is a primary source of natural gas and that coal bed methane is simply methane found underground in coal seams. How does developing coal bed methane affect your water wells?
Black Hawk:	Well, I read up on this. Both groundwater and methane flow through fractures in the coal seams—in fact, coal seams are often aquifers. To extract the methane, water is pumped out of the coal seam. As the water pressure decreases, the methane separates from the groundwater and can be piped out. Developing coal bed methane involves extracting huge quantities of groundwater to reduce the water pressure enough to release the methane gas in the coal seam. Since my neighbors and I all farm and ranch on land surrounding Mulroney's place, we were worried about our wells running dry because of the drop in water pressure.
Williams:	And your worries came true.
Black Hawk:	No kidding. We're running out of water for our livestock and our crops. We're going to go broke because our land just won't support us without water. A geologist who looked at it says that all wells on the Reservation are likely to be affected eventually. We tried to tell the Tribal Council before it voted on the Acme agreement, but the promises of easy money from Acme carried the day. Under the deal, the Tribe is getting a 20 percent royalty on all methane production.
Williams:	So you want to see what we can do for you?
Black Hawk:	Yes. We really are in a tough spot. Word about the water problem has spread around the Reservation and we believe the vast majority of our fellow tribal members have second thoughts about what the Tribal Council did. We have a Tribal

	Court and the judge is a fair man. He knows the history of our Tribe and tribal ways. We think that if he and a tribal jury could hear about our problems caused by Acme's extraction of the coal bed methane, we could win.
Williams:	Well, I've litigated some in Tribal Court. I know there is no federal statute or treaty addressing the Tribal Court's civil jurisdiction. Your Tribe's constitution and code have some provisions in them about protecting the environment. Maybe that could be a hook for us. I'm somewhat worried about the Tribal Council approving the deal. Can you tell me what your losses have been?
Black Hawk:	We neighbors got together with a farm finance guy from Franklin City. He estimates our losses to date to be $1.5 million, and they aren't done yet.
Williams:	What about this Patrick Mulroney?
Black Hawk:	Well, he's a non-Indian—not a member of our Tribe. Mulroney owns fee land within the Reservation that his family bought from Tribe members about a hundred years ago. Anyway, I'm surprised he went along with the Acme deal because he must be losing his water, too. But he's getting a lot of money from Acme and he's been talking for years about selling and moving somewhere warmer. With the money from the deal, he may not care anymore.
Williams:	Okay. Let's get your neighbors in to discuss filing an action in Tribal Court to see what we can do.
Black Hawk:	Great. I'll get in touch with everybody and call you.

IN THE UNITED STATES DISTRICT COURT
FOR THE DISTRICT OF FRANKLIN

Acme Resources, Inc.,	)	**Case No. CV 103-07**
Plaintiff,	)	
	)	**COMPLAINT**
v.	)	
	)	
Robert Black Hawk, Stewart Marsh, Irene Martin,	)	
James Davis, Mary Gray, Katherine White Horse,	)	
Lester Stewart, and James Black Hawk,	)	
Defendants.	)	

Plaintiff Acme Resources, Inc., alleges:

1. This action involves the federal question of whether the Black Eagle Tribal Court can exercise jurisdiction over Acme Resources, Inc. (Acme), in an action brought by members of the Black Eagle Indian Tribe arising out of a controversy involving the development of coal bed methane underlying fee land owned by Patrick Mulroney, who is not a member of the Tribe.
2. This court has jurisdiction under 28 U.S.C. § 1331.
3. Defendants are all members of the Black Eagle Indian Tribe and brought an action against Acme in Black Eagle Tribal Court seeking damages and an injunction to stop Acme from developing the coal bed methane underlying Mulroney's land.
4. The Black Eagle Tribal Court lacks jurisdiction over Acme in the tribal court action because Acme is not a member of the Tribe. *Montana v. United States* (U.S. 1981).

Wherefore, Acme Resources, Inc., prays the Court enter judgment:

1. Declaring that the Black Eagle Tribal Court lacks jurisdiction over Acme in the tribal court action;
2. Enjoining the defendants from prosecuting the tribal court action; and,
3. Awarding Acme its costs and any other appropriate relief.

Dated: July 9, 2007

Respectfully submitted,

Frank Johnson
Frank Johnson
Franklin Bar #1012
Counsel for Acme Resources, Inc.

Draft

**IN THE UNITED STATES DISTRICT COURT
FOR THE DISTRICT OF FRANKLIN**

Acme Resources, Inc.,	)	Case No. CV 103-07
Plaintiff,	)	
	)	MOTION FOR
v.	)	SUMMARY JUDGMENT,
	)	OR TO STAY OR
Robert Black Hawk, Stewart Marsh, Irene Martin,	)	DISMISS
James Davis, Mary Gray, Katherine White Horse,	)	
Lester Stewart, and James Black Hawk,	)	
Defendants.	)	

The above-named defendants move the Court as follows:

1. To grant the above-named defendants summary judgment on the ground that there exists no genuine issue of material fact that the Black Eagle Tribal Court has jurisdiction over plaintiff Acme Resources, Inc., and the action pending before it under *Montana v. United States* (U.S. 1981), and that the defendants are entitled to judgment as a matter of law; or, in the alternative,

2. To dismiss or stay this action on the ground that Acme has failed to exhaust its remedies in the Black Eagle Tribal Court as required by *National Farmers Union Ins. Cos. v. Crow Tribe* (U.S. 1985).

This motion is supported by the affidavits of Robert Black Hawk and Jesse Bellingham, the pleadings on file, and a brief filed contemporaneously herewith.

Dated: July ____, 2007

Respectfully submitted,

_____

Conrad Williams
Franklin Bar # 1779
Counsel for Defendants

IN THE UNITED STATES DISTRICT COURT
FOR THE DISTRICT OF FRANKLIN

Acme Resources, Inc.,	) Case No. CV 103-07
Plaintiff,	)
	) AFFIDAVIT OF
v.	) ROBERT BLACK HAWK
	) IN SUPPORT OF
Robert Black Hawk, Stewart Marsh, Irene Martin,	) DEFENDANTS' MOTION
James Davis, Mary Gray, Katherine White Horse,	) FOR SUMMARY
Lester Stewart, and James Black Hawk,	) JUDGMENT, OR TO
Defendants.	) STAY OR DISMISS

County of Custer)
) ss:
State of Franklin)

Upon first being duly sworn, Robert Black Hawk says:

1. I am a member of the Black Eagle Tribe, a federally recognized Indian tribe.
2. I farm and ranch a 3,000-acre tract of land on the Black Eagle Reservation.
3. My land abuts land owned in fee simple by Patrick Mulroney. All of Patrick Mulroney's land is within the Black Eagle Reservation. Two years ago, Mulroney granted Acme Resources, Inc., permission to use his land to explore for and develop coal bed methane.
4. The Black Eagle Tribe leased the minerals under Mulroney's land to Acme, and Acme began developing the coal bed methane.
5. Within six months of the commencement of Acme's coal bed methane operation under Mulroney's land, the water wells on my land began to run dry. My neighbors have told me that their wells are also running dry.
6. I cannot economically use my land to grow crops and feed my cattle without water, and there is no other source of water reasonably available to me.

Dated: July 23, 2007

Robert Black Hawk
_____
Robert Black Hawk

Signed before me this 23rd day of July, 2007

Jane Mirren
_____

Jane Mirren
Notary Public

IN THE UNITED STATES DISTRICT COURT
FOR THE DISTRICT OF FRANKLIN

Acme Resources, Inc.,	) Case No. CV 103-07
Plaintiff,	)
	) AFFIDAVIT OF JESSE
v.	) BELLINGHAM, Ph.D.,
	) IN SUPPORT OF
Robert Black Hawk, Stewart Marsh, Irene Martin,	) DEFENDANTS' MOTION
James Davis, Mary Gray, Katherine White Horse,	) FOR SUMMARY
Lester Stewart, and James Black Hawk,	) JUDGMENT, OR TO
Defendants.	) STAY OR DISMISS

County of Custer)

) ss:

State of Franklin)

Upon first being duly sworn, Jesse Bellingham says:

1. I am a geologist and have a Ph.D. in geology from the University of Franklin.
2. I was employed by Beta Resources in its mineral exploration department for twenty years before I began my own forensic geology firm, Bellingham Geologic Consulting.
3. I was engaged by the defendants to conduct a study to determine the cause of the water wells running dry on the Black Eagle Reservation and have completed my study.
4. Coal bed methane development requires the extraction of huge quantities of water from the land. Based on my investigation of (a) the records of the water produced from the defendants' land over the last ten years, (b) geological studies of the area, and (c) my knowledge and experience with coal bed methane development, it is my professional opinion that coal bed methane development activity by Acme Resources, Inc., is causing the defendants' wells to run dry.
5. Due to the nature of the groundwater system underlying the Black Eagle Reservation, my professional opinion is that it is likely all wells on the Reservation will run dry over the next five years if Acme's coal bed methane development continues.

Dated: July 23, 2007

Jesse Billingham

_____

Jesse Bellingham, Ph.D.

Signed before me this 23rd day of July, 2007

Jane Mirren

_____

Jane Mirren
Notary Public

LIBRARY

Acme Resources, Inc. v. Black Hawk et al.

Article IV, Black Eagle Tribal Constitution

Section 1

The land forms part of the soul of the Black Eagle Tribe. The land of the Black Eagle Reservation shall be preserved in a clean and healthful environment for the benefit of the Tribe and future generations. The Tribal Council shall have power to enforce, by appropriate legislation, the provisions of this section.

Black Eagle Tribal Code

§ 23-5   Protection of Reservation Environment

(1) Recognizing that a clean and healthful environment is vital to the economic security of the Black Eagle Tribe, no person shall pollute or otherwise degrade the environment of the Black Eagle Reservation.

(2) Any person harmed by a violation of subsection (1) may bring a civil action in Black Eagle Tribal Court for damages and other appropriate relief against the person responsible for the violation.

AO Architects v. Red Fox et al.
United States Court of Appeals (15th Cir. 2005)

The question in this appeal is whether a tribal court may exercise civil jurisdiction over a nonmember of the tribe in a wrongful death action arising from injuries on nonmember fee land.[1]

The Church of Good Hope, composed of tribal members, owns a parcel of land in fee simple on the Red River Indian Reservation in the State of Columbia. The Church built a meeting hall designed by AO Architects, a firm with offices in Columbia City, Columbia. The Church acted as its own general contractor for the project. AO was not asked to, and did not, supervise the construction. The meeting hall served the Church. However, from time to time the Red River Tribe leased the hall for general tribal meetings in which tribal leaders were elected and other tribe business was conducted.

After a very heavy snowfall in January 2003, the meeting hall's roof collapsed during a general tribal meeting. Five tribe members were killed and many more were injured. The families of those killed brought wrongful death actions in tribal court against AO Architects alleging negligence in the design of the meeting hall roof. Before responding to the complaint filed in tribal court, AO filed a complaint in federal district court claiming that the tribal court did not have jurisdic-

tion over it or the action pending in tribal court. The district court granted a preliminary injunction to AO Architects against further proceedings in the tribal court. The tribe members appealed. For the reasons set forth below, we vacate the preliminary injunction and remand for further proceedings consistent with this opinion.

Standard of Review

Whether a tribal court may exercise civil jurisdiction over a nonmember of the tribe is a federal question. *National Farmers Union Ins. Cos. v. Crow Tribe* (U.S. 1985). We review questions of tribal court jurisdiction and exhaustion of tribal court remedies *de novo*. A district court's order regarding preliminary injunctive relief is reviewed for abuse of discretion.

Governing Law

Analysis of Indian tribal court civil jurisdiction begins with *Montana v. United States* (U.S. 1981). In *Montana*, the United States Supreme Court held that, although the tribe retained power to limit or forbid hunting or fishing by nonmembers on land still owned by or held in trust for the tribe, an Indian tribe could not regulate hunting and fishing by non-Indians on non-Indian-owned fee land within the reservation. In what is often referred to as *Montana*'s "main rule," the Court stated that, absent express authorization by federal statute or treaty, the inherent sovereign powers of an Indian tribe do not, as a general proposition, extend

---

1. The terms "nonmember fee land" and "non-Indian fee lands" refer to reservation land acquired in fee simple by persons who are not members of the tribe.

to the activities of nonmembers of the tribe.

The Court acknowledged, however, that "Indian tribes retain inherent sovereign power to exercise some forms of civil jurisdiction over non-Indians on their reservations, even on non-Indian fee lands." *Id.* The Court set out two instances in which tribes could exercise such sovereignty: (1) "A tribe may regulate, through taxation, licensing, or other means, the activities of nonmembers who enter consensual relationships with the tribe or its members, through commercial dealings, contracts, leases, or other arrangements"; and (2) "A tribe may also retain inherent power to exercise civil authority over the conduct of non-Indians on fee lands within its reservation when that conduct threatens or has some direct effect on the political integrity, the economic security, or the health and welfare of the tribe." *Id.*

In *Strate v. A-1 Contractors* (U.S. 1997), the Court held that a tribal court had no jurisdiction to hear a personal injury lawsuit between non-tribal members arising from a car accident that occurred on a state highway running through a reservation. The road upon which the accident took place, although on tribal land, was subject to a right-of-way held by the State of North Dakota. The Court determined that this right-of-way rendered the stretch of road "equivalent, for non-member governance purposes, to alienated, non-Indian land." The Court declined to comment on the proper forum when an accident occurs on a tribal road within a reservation.

Strate also considered whether either of the two *Montana* exceptions conferring tribal court jurisdiction applied. In determining that the case was not closely related to any consensual relationship between a nonmember and the tribe or a tribe member, the Court noted that the event at issue was a commonplace state highway accident between two non-Indians. Therefore, even though it occurred on a stretch of highway running through the reservation, it was "distinctly non-tribal in nature." *(Cf. Franklin Motor Credit Co. v. Funmaker* (15th Cir. 2005), also finding no consensual relationship under *Montana* because there was no "direct nexus" between the lease entered into by Franklin Motor Credit and the tribe and the subsequent products liability claim against Franklin Motor Credit by a tribe member injured while driving one of the leased vehicles.)

Turning to the second *Montana* exception for activities that directly affect the tribe's political integrity, economic security, or health and welfare, the Court in *Strate* also concluded that the facts did not establish tribal civil jurisdiction. The Court recognized that careless driving on public highways running through the reservation would threaten the safety of tribal members. However, if the assertion of such broad public safety interests were all that *Montana* required for jurisdiction, the exception would swallow the rule. Instead, the exception must be interpreted with its purpose in mind, which was to protect tribal self-government and control of internal relations. "Neither regulatory nor adjudicatory authority over the state highway accident at issue is needed to preserve 'the right of reservation Indians to make their own laws and be ruled by them.'" *Strate* (quoting *Montana*).

Exhaustion of Tribal Remedies

In *National Farmers*, the Supreme Court applied a tribal exhaustion doctrine requiring that a party exhaust its remedies in tribal court before seeking relief in federal court. This doctrine is based on a "policy of supporting tribal self-government and self-determination," and thus a federal court should ordinarily stay its hand "until after the tribal court has had a full opportunity to determine its own jurisdiction." *Id*. In other words, the tribal court should be given the first opportunity to address its jurisdiction and explain the basis (or lack thereof) to the parties. In such cases, the proceedings in federal court are stayed (or dismissed without prejudice) while the tribal court determines whether it has jurisdiction over the matter.

The Supreme Court has emphasized that the exhaustion doctrine is based on comity. The comity doctrine reflects a practice of deference to another court and is not a jurisdictional prerequisite. Thus, where it is clear that a tribal court lacks jurisdiction, the exhaustion doctrine gives way for it would serve no purpose other than delay. *See Strate*. In the present case, tribe members allege that there has been no exhaustion of tribal remedies because AO Architects commenced this federal action without affording the tribal court the opportunity to consider the jurisdictional issues.

Disposition

Here, the accident occurred on non-member fee land, and AO Architects is not a member of the tribe. This would suggest under *Montana*'s main rule that the tribal court would lack jurisdiction. Moreover, on the record before us, it appears that AO Architects did not perform any services on the reservation, and that its contract was with a nonmember of the tribe, the Church of Good Hope.

Yet AO Architects must have known that it was designing a building for use of large gatherings on the reservation, and it may well have known that the facility would be used by the tribe for general meetings involving governance functions. The consequences of AO Architects' actions in designing the building would certainly be felt on the reservation. We are mindful of the two exceptions to *Montana*'s general rule against extending a tribe's civil jurisdiction to nonmembers of the tribe in the absence of express Congressional authorization or any treaty provision granting a tribe jurisdiction.[2] As discussed above, those exceptions are that a tribe may have jurisdiction over (1) nonmembers who enter into consensual relationships with the tribe or its members, or (2) activities that directly affect the tribe's political integrity, economic security, or health and welfare. Either or both of the exceptions may have application here.

The record comes to us on appeal from a preliminary injunction. The proceedings were abbreviated, and we are uncertain on the record before

_____

2. The parties concede that no federal statute or treaty bears on the question before us.

us whether the tribal court would have jurisdiction under either of the *Montana* exceptions and whether AO Architects must first exhaust its tribal court remedies before seeking relief in federal court.

Therefore, we vacate the preliminary injunction and remand to the district court to develop a record and reach a reasoned conclusion on these issues of jurisdiction and exhaustion. We express no opinion on these questions.

Vacated and remanded.

FILE
Logan v. Rios

Dowell, Brown & Pope
Attorneys at Law
944 Metro Square Plaza
Bedford, Franklin 38701

MEMORANDUM

To: Applicant
From: Norman Brown, Supervising Attorney
Re: Logan v. Rios
Date: February 23, 2010

We represent Trina Rios, owner of Trina's Toys, a business in Bedford, Franklin. She has been sued by Karen Logan. Logan claims to have been injured when she slipped and fell while shopping at Trina's Toys. I've attached the complaint. We answered the complaint, denied the key allegations, and raised the affirmative defense of contributory negligence. We have conducted some discovery and investigation.

Under the local rules, we must attend an early dispute resolution (EDR) conference, conducted by an EDR judge. Although we have not completed our discovery, these settlement conferences are conducted early. Local Rule 12 describes the purpose of this conference.

In preparation for the EDR conference, please draft Item 6 of the EDR statement. I will use your draft to prepare the final submission. Item 6 of the EDR statement requires us to candidly "discuss . . . the strengths and weaknesses of" our case in the statement. As directed in Item 6, use the jury instructions to organize your discussion of the claim and affirmative defense. You will need to carefully review the evidence gathered to date and identify and evaluate the proof available for each legal element of the claim and the affirmative defense. Where relevant, provide citations to case law that supports your analysis; you need not provide citations to the factual record.

Do not address the other items required by the statement and do not address Logan's damages; I will prepare the portion of the statement concerning her medical condition, including her pain and suffering and medical costs.

Green County Local Rule 12. Early Dispute Resolution

Before trial, the parties shall participate in Early Dispute Resolution (EDR). EDR promotes direct communication between parties about possible claims, defenses, and supporting evidence, under the supervision of the EDR judge, a neutral evaluator. The EDR conference gives the parties an opportunity to narrow the issues and possibly settle the case with the assistance of the EDR judge. During the conference, the EDR judge may require the parties to assess all claims and defenses with the aim of settling the case. The EDR judge may meet with the parties separately or together. The conference discussion is confidential and will not be admissible at trial.

Five days prior to the EDR conference, each party must submit an EDR statement using Form 12. The EDR statement assists the EDR judge in evaluating each party's case. It may be used solely by the EDR judge, and is confidential, and may not be used at trial or shared with the other party or parties.

Form 12: Early Dispute Resolution Statement

Each party must provide the following information concerning the case:

1. Name of party and trial counsel.
2. Short description of the case.
3. Legal theories presented by the case.
4. Evidentiary issues likely to be raised at trial.
5. Damages sought.
6. A candid discussion of the strengths and weaknesses of the party's claims, counterclaims, and/or defenses and affirmative defenses. Parties are advised to use the jury instructions to identify each element of the claims, counterclaims, and/or defenses and affirmative defenses stated. For each element that must be proven, parties should discuss the specific strengths and weaknesses of the evidence gathered to date relating to that element in light of the jury instructions and any commentary thereto.
7. The approximate number of witnesses to be called and the length of time that the party estimates will be needed for the trial.

STATE OF FRANKLIN
IN THE CIRCUIT COURT OF GREEN COUNTY

Karen Logan,	)	
Plaintiff,	)	
v.	)	
	)	2009-CV-3420
Trina Rios,	)	
doing business as Trina's Toys,	)	COMPLAINT
Defendant	)	

1. Plaintiff Karen Logan, a resident of Green County, Franklin, on January 27, 2009, entered the defendant's premises, Trina's Toys, located at 727 Mill Street, City of Bedford, County of Green, Franklin, during business hours, for the purposes of shopping in the store.
2. Defendant Trina Rios, a resident of Green County, Franklin, owns the building at 727 Mill Street, Bedford, Franklin, and conducts a business there under the name Trina's Toys.
3. On the date mentioned, the defendant had a duty to exercise ordinary care to see that her premises were reasonably safe for persons lawfully on the premises, including the plaintiff.
4. In violation of this duty, the defendant negligently permitted and maintained on the business premises the following unsafe conditions, creating an unreasonable risk of injury to persons lawfully on the premises, including the plaintiff: water accumulating on the floor where customers shopped and failure to warn that water had accumulated on the floor.
5. On January 27, 2009, the plaintiff was injured when she slipped and fell, owing to the unsafe conditions alleged in Paragraph 4.
6. As a proximate result of the negligence of the defendant, the plaintiff suffered an injury to her ankle, which has caused her great pain and suffering, lost wages, and a lost scholarship. The plaintiff has also incurred medical, hospital, and related expenses.

Wherefore the plaintiff requests judgment against the defendant in the sum of $30,000 or more, including costs of suit and such other and further relief as this court deems just and proper.

Dated: July 15, 2009

Barbara Santos

_____

Barbara Santos, attorney for Karen Logan, Plaintiff

I was asked to investigate certain aspects of an incident that occurred at Trina's Toys on January 27, 2009, on which date Karen Logan alleges she fell. Logan claims she hurt her ankle when she slipped and fell in a puddle of water in the store. Logan filed suit against Trina Rios on July 15, 2009. She claims the ankle injury caused her to lose her part-time job at Fresh Grocers and to lose her basketball scholarship at Franklin State University.

I contacted Joe Nguyen, who was Logan's supervisor at Fresh Grocers. Nguyen confirmed that Logan had worked part-time at the office of Fresh Grocers for the six months prior to her alleged fall, working about 15–20 hours a week, and earning $9/hour entering data into a computer. He confirmed that her employment was terminated February 2, 2009, after she failed to report to work for three days and failed to call in. Nguyen said he knew nothing about her falling or having hurt her ankle.

I tried to contact the women's basketball coach at Franklin State University (FSU), but he would not talk to me without a subpoena. However, I read back issues of the FSU student newspaper online. For the 2008–09 academic year, Logan was a second-year basketball player for FSU on scholarship. According to the articles I read, she did not get much playing time. I also found an article that reported that she was dropped from the team a couple of weeks before her visit to Trina's Toys due to "academic difficulties." I did confirm that Logan is currently enrolled at FSU.

Rios's employees Nick Patel and Naomi Feldman confirm that, on the date of the incident, Feldman called Green County Emergency Services and paramedics responded and took Logan to the emergency room. I cannot learn anything more about her medical condition without a medical release signed by Logan.

Patrick Ling

Patrick Ling
December 11, 2009

Excerpts from 1/14/10 Deposition of Karen Logan
EXAMINATION BY NORMAN BROWN, COUNSEL FOR TRINA'S TOYS

Attorney:	Please state your name, address, occupation, and age.
Logan:	Karen Logan, 2044 North Fifth Street, Apt. 23, Bedford, Franklin, student at Franklin State University. I am 20 years old.
Attorney:	Were you at Trina's Toys on January 27, 2009?
Logan:	Yes, my little sister had a birthday coming up and I wanted to get her a gift.
Attorney:	Were there other customers there at the time?
Logan:	A mom and her little boy, a toddler, who kept getting in and out of his stroller, and some other people.
Attorney:	What time did you arrive at the store that day?
Logan:	Around 11:30 in the morning. I was just looking around, walking up and down some aisles, and then I fell.
Attorney:	Where were you when you fell?
Logan:	I had just turned into the games and puzzles aisle and down I went.
Attorney:	As you turned into the aisle, what were you doing?
Logan:	Well, I had just been playing Wii bowling at a Wii display at the end of the aisle.
Attorney:	Tell me more about that. What is a "Wii"?
Logan:	A Wii is a video gaming system. You hold a controller and move as if you were really bowling; the action shows up on the video screen. There was a sign inviting people to "test your Wii bowling skills." So I did. When I finished, I started walking down the aisle where the games were so that I could check them out.
Attorney:	Did you look at the floor as you proceeded down the aisle?
Logan:	No, I was looking at the games on the shelves.
Attorney:	Was there anything blocking your view of the floor?
Logan:	No, but why would I look at the floor? I was looking at the games.
Attorney:	Was there any problem with the lighting in the aisle where you fell?
Logan:	I don't think so. The whole store was brightly lit.
Attorney:	Had you been in this aisle prior to falling?
Logan:	No, I was at the end of the aisle Wii bowling. I then walked down the game aisle, took a few steps, and fell.
Attorney:	Tell me how you fell.
Logan:	I took a few steps into the aisle, saw the games ahead, started toward them, and then I felt my right foot sort of slide, and then twist around, and then it just slipped out from under me, and that's when I landed in the puddle.
Attorney:	Do you know what caused you to fall?
Logan:	Yeah, there was water on the floor.
Attorney:	How much water was there?

Logan:	I fell into a puddle of water, a couple of feet long, just a trail of water.
Attorney:	How wide was the trail of water?
Logan:	Several inches, maybe a foot.
Attorney:	How deep was the water?
Logan:	Oh, pretty thin. The floor there was level. There was just a thin puddle of water.
Attorney:	What happened after you fell?
Logan:	I took a minute to catch my breath. I felt sort of jolted. Then my right ankle began to hurt, really badly. I had been sitting there for a minute or so, when a customer asked if I was okay. I said, "No, I fell and I'm hurt." I started to get up, but she said I should wait and she would get help. I took off my shoes while I sat there.
Attorney:	Did she get help?
Logan:	A store employee came up and asked if I was okay. I said, "No, I fell and I'm hurt." He helped me get up and get to a chair near the front of the store. He brought my shoes and backpack to me—I had taken off my pack after I fell.
Attorney:	Describe the shoes you were wearing. Were they high heels?
Logan:	They were backless sandals with heels not more than three inches high. I had just gotten them the week before the accident.
Attorney:	What kind of sole and heel were on the sandals—leather, rubber, what?
Logan:	Leather, I'm pretty sure.
Attorney:	What do you mean by backless?
Logan:	You just slide your feet into the sandals; there is no strap around the heel.
Attorney:	Had you ever worn the shoes before?
Logan:	Yes, at least three times. They're very comfortable. Everyone wears them.
Attorney:	Had it been raining or snowing that day?
Logan:	No. I remember it was mild. And it was sunny.
Attorney:	Do you know how the water got on the floor?
Logan:	No.
Attorney:	Were you carrying a water bottle on the date you fell?
Logan:	Yeah, I always carry one. I had it in the mesh pocket of my backpack.
Attorney:	How much water did the bottle contain?
Logan:	It was the size I usually buy at the grocery store, a 16-ounce bottle.
Attorney:	When you left your apartment, was the water bottle full?
Logan:	Yes. I just grabbed an unopened bottle as I left my apartment.

Attorney:	Did you drink any water from the bottle before you arrived at Trina's Toys?
Logan:	Maybe. I don't remember.
Attorney:	Did you spill water on the floor in the aisle where you fell?
Logan:	Of course not. The bottle was in a pocket in my backpack. I told you that.
Attorney:	Do you know how the water got on the floor in the aisle where you fell?
Logan:	Someone spilled something, but I don't really know. I know that the little boy who was in and out of the stroller had a sippy cup with him.
Attorney:	A sippy cup?
Logan:	You know, a cup with a lid for toddlers. It has a slot in the lid so the toddler can drink but won't spill all over. It's a step between a baby bottle and a regular cup.
Attorney:	But you didn't see the little boy spill or drop the sippy cup?
Logan:	I wasn't paying too much attention to him.
Attorney:	Regarding your water bottle, was it still in your backpack after you fell?
Logan:	Absolutely.
Attorney:	Did you see anyone—including the little boy—spill where you fell?
Logan:	Not that I saw, but I wasn't watching people to make sure they didn't spill.
Attorney:	By the way, did you use your cell phone while in the store?
Logan:	I called a friend right after I bowled on the Wii to tell him what my score was.
Attorney:	Were you talking on the phone when you fell?
Logan:	No; I hung up just as I started down the aisle.

*   *   *   *

Attorney:	You said you lost wages as a result of your ankle injury?
Logan:	Yes, I had been working 20 hours a week at Fresh Grocers, entering data on the computer. I had been there for six months at the time of the accident.
Attorney:	Do you still work there?
Logan:	No, they told me I could not work anymore because I fell and was hurt.
Attorney:	How did the fall affect your being able to work there?
Logan:	I don't know. I missed a couple days of work and then I came with my ankle all wrapped up and I was on crutches. They said I could not work there anymore.
Attorney:	Did your work at Fresh Grocers require you to stand?
Logan:	No, I sat at a computer.

Attorney:	You said you missed a couple days of work. Did you contact your supervisor at Fresh Grocers to let him know that you would be absent?
Logan:	No, I was in pain and was overwhelmed by school and getting used to crutches.

*   *   *   *

Attorney:	Is it your claim that you lost your basketball scholarship because of this injury?
Logan:	Yes, it is. The coach said I wasn't contributing to the team anymore. The season was well under way and I couldn't practice due to the injury, and that obviously affected my playing. So this fall and the injury made me lose my scholarship.
Attorney:	When did you learn that you lost the scholarship?
Logan:	I don't remember the exact day.
Attorney:	Did the coach give any reason for your losing the scholarship other than that you weren't contributing to the team anymore?
Logan:	Not that I recall. I was really upset.
Attorney:	Didn't the coach tell you your grades were the reason you lost the scholarship?
Logan:	I don't remember him saying anything about my grades.
Attorney:	Well, how were your grades last year?
Logan:	They were good until this injury caused me to miss a lot of my classes.

Excerpts from 1/15/10 Deposition of Nick Patel
EXAMINATION BY BARBARA SANTOS, COUNSEL FOR KAREN LOGAN

Attorney:	Please tell me your name, address, and occupation.
Patel:	Nicholas Patel, but I go by Nick. I live in Bedford, 835 Jefferson Street. I work part-time at Trina's Toys and I go to school at Franklin State University.
Attorney:	Were you working at Trina's Toys on January 27, 2009, the day Ms. Logan fell?
Patel:	Yes; I clean up, stock shelves, and wait on customers.
Attorney:	What were your duties regarding cleaning the store at the time Ms. Logan fell?
Patel:	Every evening after we close, I sweep and mop the entire floor. In the morning, before we open, I dust and wipe down the counter area. Then I clean anything else my boss tells me to. So, on the night of January 26, 2009, the night before Ms. Logan fell, I swept and mopped the floor.
Attorney:	Did you see Ms. Logan fall?
Patel:	No, I heard a customer say that someone had fallen and needed help, so I went to see what had happened.
Attorney:	What did you see?
Patel:	I saw a girl, about my age, sitting on the floor in aisle 3, with her shoes off, rubbing her right foot and saying she was hurt. I later found out she was Karen Logan. There was a water bottle next to her on the floor. Also, I saw her cell phone and her shoes on the floor right next to her.
Attorney:	Did you see any water?
Patel:	Yes, she was sitting in a puddle of water.
Attorney:	Describe the water.
Patel:	It was a thin puddle, about a couple feet long.
Attorney:	Are you sure it was water?
Patel:	Well, it certainly looked like it. I cleaned it up later, and it cleaned up just like water—no color or odor.
Attorney:	When was the last time you were in aisle 3 before you saw Ms. Logan?
Patel:	I was in aisle 3 a couple of times that morning, restocking games. She fell around noon; I guess I had been there just before we opened at 10 a.m. I don't remember being in aisle 3 after we opened. I mainly stayed at the counter. We had a steady stream of customers in and out of the store.
Attorney:	How often are you supposed to patrol all the aisles?
Patel:	Once every hour.
Attorney:	Did you do so at 11 a.m.?
Patel:	No.

Attorney:	Why not?
Patel:	My girlfriend called me and I guess I just forgot. And we were busy.
Attorney:	Did you see any water on the floor when you were in aisle 3 around 10 a.m.?
Patel:	No.
Attorney:	Are there any sources of water in the store? Any squirt guns or water-related games?
Patel:	No, not in the main part of the store where customers are. There's a bathroom in the back. And the squirt guns are not filled with water. Besides, we only sell them in summer.
Attorney:	Any water leaks in the store's ceiling?
Patel:	No.
Attorney:	Do you know how the water got on the floor?
Patel:	I think Ms. Logan spilled it. I saw a water bottle next to her on the floor. It was empty. I put it in her backpack when I helped her up—I could tell the bottle was empty.
Attorney:	Did you or anyone else see her spill water?
Patel:	I didn't see her spill, and I don't know of anyone else who saw her spill, either.
Attorney:	So you have no reason to conclude that she spilled her water other than that you saw the water bottle?
Patel:	No, I guess not.
Attorney:	How many other customers were there in the store between 10 a.m. and noon?
Patel:	I don't know; a handful. Only one, two or three at a time, but there was a constant flow of customers. One would leave and another come in. I stayed busy at the counter. Maybe 10 or 12 customers altogether.
Attorney:	It's a toy store, so is it fair to say there were children in the store during that time?
Patel:	Yes, there are always kids in the store.
Attorney:	So it is possible that a child spilled something in the store?
Patel:	I suppose so, but I doubt it.
Attorney:	Was there any warning sign in aisle 3, indicating that there was water on the floor?
Patel:	No. We didn't know there was any water there, so how could we put out a sign?
Attorney:	Does the store have any warning cones or signs to put out?
Patel:	No. We don't have spills like that.
Attorney:	Had anyone told you or any employee that there was water on the floor?
Patel:	No. If they had, I would have checked it out and cleaned it up.
Attorney:	Are you aware of anyone else having fallen in the store?

Patel:	No.
Attorney:	Do you have any other knowledge of what might have caused Ms. Logan to fall other than the water on the floor?
Patel:	Well, she had been wearing these shoes—sandals, sort of, with high heels—that looked pretty hard to walk on—not too steady. And she had a backpack and it weighed a ton—I had to pick it up and take it to her. So maybe she lost her balance because of the sandals and the backpack and then fell. Or maybe she just twisted her ankle on those sandals and then she spilled some water so we would think she fell on the water. Or maybe she spilled some water and fell on it.
Attorney:	Did you see Ms. Logan fall?
Patel:	No, I just saw her after she fell.
Attorney:	Do you know if anyone saw her fall?
Patel:	Not that I'm aware of.
Attorney:	Did she tell you why she fell?
Patel:	She said she slipped on the water and then she pointed to the water.
Attorney:	Do you have any reason to believe she was lying?
Patel:	No. I just don't know where the water came from.
Attorney:	What products are displayed in aisle 3?
Patel:	That's the aisle with puzzles, games, and video games.
Attorney:	Are there any overhead displays?
Patel:	No, but we try to display the puzzles and games so that they are attractive to customers. We had a computer-animated display of games right in the middle of the aisle near where I found Ms. Logan. At the head of the games aisle we had a Wii on display for customers to play some of the Wii sports video games.
Attorney:	Were there any displays sticking out from the shelves?
Patel:	No. Not that I remember—not in that aisle.
Attorney:	What is the composition of the floor in aisle 3—carpet, tile, what?
Patel:	It is tile. It is easy to clean up. I mop it up every evening and so I know it is real level there. We even make sure we use a cleaner that does not make the floor slippery. The boss, Trina, wants to be sure kids don't slip and fall.
Attorney:	Is it fair to say that if wet, the tile floor would be slippery?
Patel:	I suppose so.
Attorney:	Describe the lighting in aisle 3.
Patel:	Overhead lights. We want the customers to be able to see the toys without any trouble, so it is pretty bright.
Attorney:	Were there any other employees on duty that day?
Patel:	Yes, the boss, Trina, was in the back storeroom all morning checking inventory. Naomi Feldman and I were at the counter.

* * * *

LIBRARY
Logan v. Rios

FRANKLIN SUPREME COURT APPROVED JURY INSTRUCTIONS

Excerpts from Jury Instruction 35: Premises Liability with Contributory Negligence Claimed

The plaintiff seeks to recover damages for an injury that occurred while on the defendant's premises. In order to recover damages, the plaintiff has the burden of proving by a preponderance of the credible evidence that

1. There was a condition on the defendant's property which presented an unreasonable risk of harm to people on the property.
2. The defendant knew or in the exercise of ordinary care should have known of both the condition and the risk.
3. The defendant could reasonably expect that people on the property would not discover such danger and the defendant failed to warn of the unreasonable risk of harm to people on the property.

If you find that the defendant had or should have had notice of a condition that presented an unreasonable risk of harm and failed to use ordinary care to prevent harm under the circumstances, then the defendant was negligent.

*   *   *   *

If you find that the plaintiff has proved that the defendant was negligent, then you should consider the defendant's affirmative defense of contributory negligence. In order to defeat the plaintiff's claim, the defendant must prove by a preponderance of the credible evidence that

> The plaintiff was guilty of negligence that was a direct and proximate cause of the occurrence and the resulting injuries and damages, if any, sustained by him or her, in that the plaintiff [*insert the ways in which the plaintiff was negligent here*].

If the defendant proves all of these items by a preponderance of the credible evidence, your verdict should be for the defendant.

*   *   *   *

Commentary (Duty of Owner of Land): The Franklin Supreme Court has eliminated the distinction between licensees and invitees.

The Court has ruled that the owner of a premises, though not an insurer of his customers' safety, owes his customers the duty to exercise reasonable care to maintain his premises in a reasonably safe condition for use by his customers. In determining what constitutes reasonable care, one issue is the length of time an unsafe condition has existed. In *Owens v. Coffee Corner*

(Fr. Ct. App. 2007), the premises owner was liable for coffee that had "just spilled" because it was reasonably foreseeable that coffee-shop customers would spill coffee. On the other hand, the owner of a camera shop was not liable for soda that had "just spilled," because it was not reasonably foreseeable that soda spills would occur in a camera shop, where no refreshments were available. *Chad v. Bill's Camera Shop* (Fr. Ct. App. 2006). In *Rollins v. Maryville Mini-Golf Park* (Fr. Ct. App. 2002), the owner of a mini golf and recreation park was liable when a ketchup spill went unnoticed for an hour because the park had a snack bar, the owner knew that children frequently spilled food items, and the owner had an hour to discover and remove the spill that created the unreasonable risk.

A business owner is not liable for harm caused by a condition on his premises that is open and obvious, nor must the owner warn of conditions that are open and obvious. *Townsend v. Upwater* (Fr. Sup. Ct. 2000). Whether a condition is open and obvious may present a question of fact for the trier of fact to determine. The test to determine if a condition is open and obvious is objective. The court does not consider whether the plaintiff actually saw the alleged condition and the risk posed but whether an average user with ordinary intelligence would have been able to discover the risk presented upon casual inspection. *Roth v. Fiedler* (Fr. Sup. Ct. 1987).

There is one exception to the "open and obvious" rule: the "distraction exception" set forth in *Ward v. ShopMart Corp.* (Fr. Sup. Ct. 1991). The distraction exception applies when the owner has reason to suspect that guests or workers may not appreciate the danger or obvious nature of the condition because they are distracted or preoccupied. In *Ward*, carrying a large mirror distracted the plaintiff, preventing him from seeing a concrete post located in a doorway. Although ordinarily a post in the middle of a doorway would be an open and obvious condition, the distraction exception applied because it was foreseeable that customers would be leaving the store carrying large, unwieldy packages. In *Gardner v. Wendt* (Fr. Sup. Ct. 2000), the distraction exception applied when the plaintiff had failed to look at the floor he was walking on and fell over a box left in the aisle because he was distracted by holiday decorations. The box in the aisle was an open and obvious condition. The Court reasoned, however, that where the owner has created a distraction, such as blinking lights or a mobile suspended from the ceiling, the owner has reason to suspect that individuals on the premises might not appreciate the danger or obvious nature of an unsafe condition. In such cases, the owner has a duty of reasonable care.

The distraction exception does not apply, however, where those claiming injury created the distraction. In *Brown v. City of De Forest* (Fr. Ct. App. 2005), the plaintiff could not recover where she had tripped on an uneven sidewalk while chasing after a runaway child. She admitted that her attention was diverted from the sidewalk by her concern for the child. The court held that the distraction exception did not apply because the distraction was the result of the plaintiff's concern for the child and her own inattentiveness to where she was going, and the city could not be held responsible.

Commentary (Contributory Negligence): If the jury determines that the plaintiff's contributory negligence is a proximate cause of the injury claimed, the jury must find for the defendant and against the plaintiff. The term "contributory negligence" means negligence on the part of the plaintiff that proximately caused the alleged injury. Contributory negligence is a complete bar to recovery.

Commentary (Burden of Proof): Proof by a preponderance of the credible evidence means that the jury must be persuaded, considering the evidence, that the proposition on which the party has the burden is more probable than not. The jury must evaluate the quality of the evidence, including witness testimony, and the weight to be given it.

Commentary (Proximate Cause): Proximate cause means a cause that, in the natural or ordinary course of events, was a substantial factor in producing the plaintiff's injury.

FILE
In re Al Merton

Locher, Lawson & Klein, P.A. Attorneys and Counselors at Law
6714 Tulsa Cove Munster,
Franklin 33448

To: Applicant
From: Catherine Locher
Date: July 30, 2002
Subject: Al Merton's Will

Al Merton came in earlier today to talk about updating his will. I've attached a transcript of my interview with him. I've also charted his family tree insofar as it is relevant to our task.

Mr. Merton is going to have heart surgery tomorrow. He is apprehensive and wants us to draft a new will in accordance with the wishes he expressed when I interviewed him. He will come in and sign the will later today.

Eventually, we may need to draft additional documents necessary to carry out Mr. Merton's testamentary scheme, but the main thing now is to get the will done in time for Mr. Merton to execute it before his surgery. I would like you to complete the following tasks:

1.   Draft the introductory clauses and all dispositive clauses for Mr. Merton's new will. Follow our firm's Will Drafting Guidelines and set forth the clauses in separately labeled paragraphs, using the headings set forth in the guidelines. Do not concern yourself with the definitional and boilerplate clauses.

2.   I'm particularly concerned about how you deal with Stuart Merton and the gifts of the corporate stock. Once you draft the provisions regarding those issues, please explain why you drafted them the way you did.

Another associate is researching the tax implications, so you need not concern yourself with them.

Locher, Lawson & Klein, P.A.

MEMORANDUM   September 8, 1995

To: All Attorneys
From: Robert Lawson
Re: Will Drafting Guidelines

Over the years, this firm has used a variety of formats in drafting wills. Effective immediately, all wills drafted by this firm should follow this format:

PART ONE: Introduction.

1. Set forth the first of the introductory clauses with a statement declaring it to be the testator's will and the name and domicile of the testator.
2. Include an appropriate clause regarding the revocation of prior testamentary instruments.
3. Include a clause naming the testator's immediate family members and identifying their relationship to the testator (parents, siblings, spouse, children, grandchildren, nephews, and nieces).

PART TWO: Dispositive Clauses (to be set forth in separate subdivisions or subparagraphs by class of bequest.) See the attached excerpt from *Walker's Treatise on Wills* for the definitions of the different classes of bequests. Bequests should be set forth in the following order, using the appropriate heading:

1. Specific bequests
    a. Real property
    b. Tangible personal property
    c. Other specific bequests
    d. Any other clauses stating conditions that might affect the disposition of specific bequests
2. General bequests
3. Demonstrative bequests
4. Residuary bequests

PART THREE: Definitional Clauses. Clauses relating to how words and phrases used in the will should be interpreted.

PART FOUR: Boilerplate Clauses. Clauses relating to the naming of fiduciaries and their administrative and management authority, payment of debts and expenses, tax clauses, attestation clauses, and self-proving will affidavits.

Attachment A Will
Drafting Guidelines

WALKER'S TREATISE ON WILLS

<u>CLASSIFICATION OF BEQUESTS:</u>

Section 500. All bequests under wills are classified as either (1) specific, (2) general, (3) demonstrative, or (4) residuary.

Section 501. A *specific* bequest is a bequest of a specific asset.

Section 502. A *general* bequest (typically a gift of money) is a bequest payable out of general estate assets or to be acquired for a beneficiary out of general estate assets.

Section 503. A *demonstrative* bequest is a bequest of a specific sum of money payable from a designated account. To the extent that the designated account is insufficient to satisfy the bequest, the balance is paid from the general funds of the estate.

Section 504. A *residuary* bequest is a bequest that is neither general, specific, nor demonstrative and includes bequests that purport to dispose of the whole of the remaining estate.

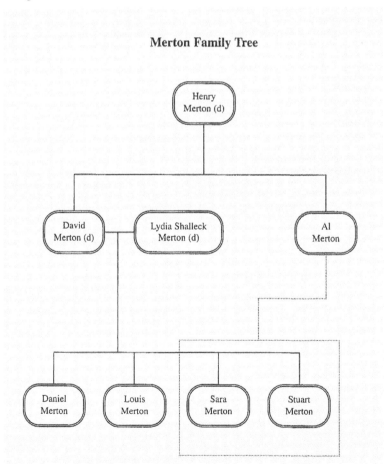

Merton Family Tree

Transcript of Interview with Al Merton
July 30, 2002

* * * *

Q: What brings you here today?

A: Tomorrow I will have open heart surgery and I'm thinking some about death. The surgery is very risky, plus I lost my father last year.

Q: Sounds like a scary time for you.

A: I can't think about anything else. My will is more than 20 years old and so much has happened since it was drafted, I'm sure that it needs to be revised. When my father passed away, I inherited his office supply business, and I need to figure out how to deal with it in case I die. I know I've left everything to the last minute. I just couldn't force myself to deal with this task.

Q: Did you bring your old will with you?

A: Yes. I also brought my father's.

Q: Tell me more.

A: When my brother David and his wife died three years ago in an auto accident, I became responsible for their two youngest children, the twins, Sara and Stuart. At the time their parents died, the twins were 17 years old.

Q: What do you mean you were responsible for them?

A: Well, there was no one else to take care of them so I adopted the twins. I was reluctant to adopt Stuart because he has always been trouble. About a year ago, he left home and I only hear from him when he wants money. David also had two older children, Daniel, who is 27 and has become very wealthy in the software business, and Louis, who is 25 and somewhat irresponsible. There was no point in adopting them.

Q: Tell me about the business you inherited from your father.

A: At least 40 years ago, my father, Henry Merton, inherited from his own father Merton Office Supply and the Lincoln Street land and building where the business is located. Dad incorporated the business, but he retained ownership of the Lincoln Street Property in his individual capacity. The rental income he received from the corporation for the Lincoln Street Property supported him when he retired.

Dad had two children, David and me. I earned a Ph.D. in business strategy and joined the faculty of Franklin College 30 years ago. My brother began working at Merton Office Supply 26 years ago, shortly after earning his B.B.A. in marketing.

Q: And David is the brother who died?

A: Yes. David and his wife Lydia died three years ago without a will. Although their debts effectively wiped out most of their assets, they left a trust holding $75,000 in life insurance proceeds for each child. Each child began receiving the income at age 18 and will receive the principal at age 25. Daniel and Louis have already received their $75,000.

Q: Do you have children of your own?

A: Nope, I never married or had kids. My students at the college keep me young.

Q: Can you tell me about your resources?

A: Well, there is Dad's business, Merton Office Supply Corporation. I brought an appraisal that was done in the year after Dad died. I think it is very accurate. There is a net profit of around $100,000 on sales of $3 million.

Q: I want to learn a lot more about the business, but tell me what else you own.

A: I inherited the Lincoln Street land and building that are leased to the office supply corporation. I also have a savings account of about $50,000 and a stock portfolio worth a little more than $2.5 million. I also own my house in Highland, worth around $450,000.

Q: Now can you tell me about the business?

A: Dad would have left the business to my brother David because he worked there for his whole life and ran it after Dad retired, but that was not to be. I inherited it from Dad and have been running it, but I really want to go back to teaching and the important pro bono work I was doing in Franklin College's small business program. Since David died, Sara has become more interested in the business and has worked there after school and in the summers. Neither of David's two older kids ever had any interest in the business. Sara really seems to have a head for it and is majoring in business in college. She will graduate at the end of this semester. I am reluctant to sell the business as long as she has an interest in running it, and it really may be that her interest in it is a way of dealing with the death of her father when she was so young. The older boys just want me to sell it. Indeed, I have an unsolicited offer of $900,000 for the Lincoln Street Property already.

Q: So let me see if I understand. There are twins, age 20, one of whom is interested in the business and the other of whom is not. There are two older boys—one is wealthy and the other?

A: Ahh, Louis. Louis has yet to graduate from college after six years and can't seem to focus. He just switched to his fourth major and his grades are terrible. He took part of the insurance money and bought a fancy car. I don't think he will ever amount to very much, and I am sure he will want a lot of money if he can get it without hard work.

Q: What about Sara's twin, Stuart?

A: It is heartbreaking, but I have given up. He hung around with a bad crowd, and I know they were into drugs and motorcycles. I tried but couldn't reach him, and now he is out of contact. I think that if I left him anything it would only exacerbate his worst behaviors, and so I can't in good conscience give him anything in my will.

Q: So you want to permanently disinherit him?

A: Yes, but if he turns around, then I may change my mind. Besides, he'll get his share of the proceeds from his parents' life insurance.

Q: And have you thought about what you want to do with your assets?

A: I am torn. My father wanted the business to continue in the family. I want to go back to teaching. Only one of the kids, Sara, could conceivably carry on the business. Louis and Stuart would sell it and waste the money, and Daniel doesn't need another penny. Also, the college has been my home for the last 30 years and I want to support it. I also need to protect Sara until she can support herself and, if she really wants to run the business, I need to give her a chance. To do that, the assets of the business plus the Lincoln Street Property must be kept intact, but it would be unfair to leave the whole thing to Sara and cut out the others completely.

Q: So . . . ?

A: I need some advice about how to do it. I want to give the three kids other than Stuart an equal share of the business but be sure that Sara has the power to make the decisions she will need to make in order to be successful. I would like her to be able to have all of the votes and for the three of them to share in the profits, but if either Louis or Daniel won't agree to give her the power, then that person's shares should go to Sara.

Q: There is such a thing as a voting trust, and I think it might be useful here. We can't create a voting trust in a will, but we can attach enough conditions to the gifts of the corporate stock to Sara, Daniel, and Louis to lay the groundwork for the trust. We can formalize the voting trust later.

A: That's fine. That's exactly what I want you to do. Sara's going to need at least 15 years to make a success of the business.

Q: Do you know if the articles of incorporation of Merton Office Supply say anything about voting trusts?

A: I just looked at them yesterday, and they say nothing at all about voting trusts.

Q: Okay. What would you like to do with the rest of the property?

A: I want to leave Franklin College $1 million in assets to endow the small business program and name it for my dad—The Henry Merton Small Business Assistance Program.

Q: There is still a sizable amount left. What would you like to do with it?

A: Well, I want to pay whatever taxes I owe. Then, I want to leave Sara some money so she can finish college—say $25,000, which should be paid first out of whatever is left in my savings account. Then, I want to leave Sara, Louis, and Daniel $100,000 each. If there is anything left, I want to leave it to the Franklin College Faculty Development Fund.

Q: Is there anything else?

A: Well, both the land and the building that comprise the Lincoln Street Property are absolutely essential to the successful operation of Merton Office Supply. Is there some way to make sure they remain linked?

Q: Well, the simplest thing would be to give the Lincoln Street Property to the corporation.

A: That sounds okay.

Q: All right. Anything else?

A: No, I think that covers it.

Q: In light of how you are feeling about your surgery, we will put a priority on revising your will so that you can sign it before you go to the hospital. In the long run, you will need to have a more sophisticated estate plan that includes tax planning, but for now let us get to work and get this done. Can you come back late this afternoon, and we will have it ready?

A: Okay. I'll be back later.

Last Will and Testament
Henry Merton

I, Henry Merton, a resident of Griffin County, Franklin, do make, publish and declare this my last will and testament. I revoke all wills and codicils previously made by me. I am widowed and have two adult sons, Al and David, and two grandchildren, Daniel and Louis.

Article One. I bequeath my real property to my son David. If my son David predeceases me, I bequeath my real property to my son Al. If both sons predecease me, I bequeath my real property to Franklin College.

Article Two. I bequeath my stock in Merton Office Supply Corporation to my son David. If my son David predeceases me, I bequeath said stock to my son Al. If both sons predecease me, I bequeath said stock to Franklin College.

Article Three. I bequeath the sum of $10,000 to my secretary Mary Jones if she survives me.

Article Four. I leave all the rest, residue, and remainder of my estate in equal shares to my sons David and Al or to the survivor of them.

Article Five. I appoint my son David to serve as my personal representative. If he is unable or unwilling to serve as personal representative, I appoint Franklin State Bank to serve. I direct my personal representative to pay as soon as practicable all of the following sums: all debts owed by me at my death; the expenses of my last illness; the expenses of my funeral; any unpaid charitable pledges, whether or not these are enforceable; and the costs of administering my estate.

Date: _____ July 21, 1978 _____   Signed: _____

Witnesses: _Liza Marchant_

Anna Miller

Charlie Adams

Last Will and Testament
Al Merton

Introduction

A. I am Al Merton, a resident of Griffin County, Franklin. This is my last will and testament.
B. I revoke all wills and codicils previously made by me.
C. My father is Henry Merton. I have one brother, David, and two nephews, Daniel and Louis.

Article One. I bequeath all my real property to Franklin College.

Article Two. I bequeath all other property owned by me at my death to those individuals who would inherit my property under the laws of Franklin if I died intestate.

Article Three. I appoint my brother David to serve as my personal representative. If my brother David is unable or unwilling to serve as my personal representative, I appoint Franklin State Bank as my personal representative. I direct my personal representative to pay, as soon as practicable, all of the following sums: all debts owed by me at my death; the expenses of my last illness; the expenses of my funeral; any unpaid charitable pledges, whether or not these are enforceable; and the costs of administering my estate. My personal representative shall have the power to sell property as needed for the payment of debts and expenses and to distribute property to those individuals who take under Article Two.

Date: <u>September 19, 1980</u>

Witnesses: _Jennifer McFarlane_

TR Gabriel

Mary Miller

Al Merton
Al Merton

Appraisal of Merton Office Supply Corporation
by Expert Appraisals LLC October 24, 2001

Executive Summary

Merton Office Supply Corporation (MOSC) has operated at the same Lincoln Street location since its founding as an unincorporated business in 1917. Henry Merton, the second owner, incorporated the company in 1946 and, until his death, owned all 150 of the issued and outstanding shares of stock. He retained individual ownership of the Lincoln Street land and the building on that land. Henry's executor valued the MOSC stock at $800,000 and the land and the building (i.e., the Lincoln Street Property) at $1,000,000. On Henry's death, his son, Al Merton, inherited Henry's corporate stock and the Lincoln Street Property. Al now owns all 150 shares.

MOSC has not responded well to the challenges posed by large chains and the Internet. Because Henry did not expand into larger quarters, open additional stores, or even join a buying cooperative, MOSC foregoes economies of scale with respect to inventory buying, insurance rates, and other costs. The existence of competitors limits its ability to increase prices.

Last year's $100,000 profit on sales of $3 million would have been wiped out if Al Merton had received a salary as his father and brother had before him. Neither his brother David nor his father Henry received a salary reflecting anywhere near the amount of effort required to run this business.

MOSC's assets consist only of the inventory, the lease on the Lincoln Street Property, and the corporate name. Potential purchasers of the stock would discount the price offered unless they could be guaranteed a long-term lease option on the Lincoln Street Property. Without that guarantee, Al Merton would be fortunate to receive even $800,000 for his stock. With the guarantee of a long-term lease, the value of the stock would be $1.1 million. If he sold the business and the land and invested in no-risk certificates of deposit, Al Merton could easily earn 5% per year on the sale proceeds. Unless he is willing to undertake significant expansion activities, MOSC's value will not grow at even that conservative rate.

144

LIBRARY
In re Al Merton

Franklin Probate Code

Article One. Succession
§ 101. Definitions.

* * * *

(e) Lineal Descendant. An adopted person is a lineal descendant of the adopting parent and is not a lineal descendant of his or her biological parents.

* * * *

Article Two. Wills

* * * *

§ 206. Pretermitted Heirs.

(a) Surviving Spouse. If the decedent's will fails to provide for a surviving spouse who marries the decedent after the will is made, the surviving spouse shall receive an amount equal to what he or she would have received if the decedent had died intestate. This provision shall not apply if the surviving spouse waived that share in a valid prenuptial or postnuptial agreement.

(b) Surviving Children. If the decedent's will fails to provide for children born or adopted after the will is made, each omitted child shall receive the share that he or she would have received had the decedent died intestate. This provision shall not apply if language in the will indicates that the omission was intentional.

* * * *

Franklin Corporations Code

* * * *

§ 102. Stockholders' Rights.

(a) Each owner of a corporation's common stock shall be entitled to one vote per share owned when electing the board of directors. No stockholder shall have any right to manage the corporation solely by virtue of his or her status as a stockholder.

(b) One or more stockholders can voluntarily limit their voting rights by transferring those rights to a trustee under a voting trust. No voting trust agreement shall be valid unless it is in writing, deposited with the corporation at its registered office, and subject to inspection by both stockholders and holders of the beneficial interests in the trust. No voting trust shall be established for more than ten years unless the articles of incorporation authorize a longer term.

(c) Dividends or other distributions made with respect to a class of stock shall be made on a per-share basis. All distributions made with respect to shares that are subject to a voting trust shall be made to the beneficial owner. All distributions made with respect to shares held in any other type of trust shall be made to the trustee.

* * * *

Barry v. Allen
Franklin Supreme Court (1992)

This case arises out of Paul Barry's attempts to protect his daughters' disparate interests. Lisa Barry appeals the lower court's determination that a voting trust was void ab initio.

Paul Barry founded Eon Corporation 30 years ago. Eon issued only voting common stock.

Paul had three children, Lisa, Dorothy, and Judy. Only Lisa ever worked for Eon. As Paul contemplated retirement, he considered methods of ensuring that Lisa would retain operating control.

Paul could have bequeathed all of his shares to Lisa. Because the shares represented virtually all of his intangible personal property and because he had no tangible personal or real property, he would have effectively dis-inherited Dorothy and Judy. His attorney suggested using a voting trust for the shares.

When Paul retired, he transferred 150 shares to each daughter and retained 150 shares for himself. Lisa, Dorothy, and Judy transferred their shares into a voting trust. Each signed a trust agreement that provided for voting all of their shares according to Lisa's wishes for the next 15 years and that bound subsequent takers of these shares.

As president, Lisa operated the company successfully. Eon continued to pay the $300 annual per-share dividend that it paid before Paul's retirement. Paul and his daughters each received $45,000 in each of the next five years.

When Paul died, he bequeathed his remaining shares equally to each daughter conditioned upon their agreement to transfer those shares to the voting trust. The shares of any daughter who did not agree would be divided equally between the ones who did. All three daughters agreed. Two years later, Lisa decided that Eon should cease paying such large dividends and instead should use corporate profits to expand the company. The board cut the dividend to $3 per share.

Dorothy and Judy concluded that Lisa was acting in her own interests, rather than those of the entire family. Only the trust prevented them from electing a board that might be more amenable to their wishes.

In the eighth year of the trust, Dorothy and Judy sued to have the voting trust dissolved because it was not limited to a 10-year term, as provided in Franklin Corporations Code § 102(b). The corporation's articles do not specifically mention voting trusts.

Lisa argues that her father's primary goal was preserving her control, which he could have achieved in a number of ways. She claims the trust is valid for at least 10 years because the language in § 102(b) that mandates invalidity does not appear in the sentence limiting the term of such trusts.

This court must decide whether § 102 voids the voting trust ab initio or operates only to limit it to a 10-year term.

Paul could have carried out his plan in several ways. For example, he could have re-capitalized the corporation and transferred voting stock only to Lisa. That action would have avoided the requirements applicable to voting trusts.

Alternatively, he could have bequeathed the remaining stock on the condition that the daughters agree to vote for an amendment of the articles of incorporation to validate the 15-year voting trust. That conditional bequest could also have provided that any daughter who failed to vote for the amendment would be divested of her shares, with a gift over to Lisa. There are few limits on the conditions a testator can place on bequests in a will.

We cannot determine which of Paul's goals vis-a-vis his children governed his actions. Even if we could, we will not validate the voting trust merely because he could have accomplished the same goal using a different means. Paul chose a voting trust, and we must determine its validity under § 102.

At common law, courts invalidated voting trusts because they separated the voting power from the ownership of the stock. Because statutory authorization changes the common law rule, many courts will not enforce a voting trust unless it strictly complies with the statutory language. We interpret the last sentence of § 102(b) as validating voting trusts exceeding 10 years only if the corporate articles authorize a longer term.

We agree with the trial court that the voting trust was void *ab initio*.

We affirm.

In re Estate of Henry K. Tourneau
Franklin Court of Appeal (1920)

This case presents the problem of whether the bequest to the testator's wife of one-fifth of the residuary estate is burdened by the conditions set out in Paragraph Five of the will. This paragraph reads:

Five: With respect to my interests in the corporation known as Tourneau, Inc., and as a condition precedent to turning over my stock interests in such business to my brother and sisters as hereinabove set forth, I direct that such beneficiaries enter into a voting trust agreement in favor of my brother, Pierre S. Tourneau. The voting trust agreement shall give to my brother the full voting rights for a minimum of ten (10) years with respect to the stock interests of all of the beneficiaries. The voting trust agreement shall further provide that, if my brother dies prior to the expiration of the voting trust agreement, the voting trust shall cease, and the stock certificates shall be delivered to the beneficiaries thereof.

Paragraph Five clearly shows the intention of the testator to give his brother the voting rights to the stock in question for the specified period.

The cases cited by the siblings challenging the will under the proposition that the condition precedent is illegal under the Franklin Corporations Code do not involve the right of a testator who owns stock in a corporation to impose conditions precedent upon a bequest of such stock. That the testator has the right to impose conditions is unquestioned. The donee must take the gift with the condition imposed or not at all, so long as the condition does not offend public policy or statutory enactment.[1] We hold, therefore, that the bequest is valid.

---

1. The same result would be reached with a condition subsequent, as long as there was an express gift over to another person if the condition were breached.

MEE:[1] You Write, Therefore You Are . . .[2]

INTRODUCTION

A lawyer. This oft-used Descartes quote serves as the perfect axiom to designate the importance of writing in the legal profession. We have all heard it before. Lawyers write. Whether you intend to be a litigator, transactional attorney, or a policy analyst, conducting the necessary legal analysis and presenting that analysis in writing is the cornerstone of law practice. The direct training associated with legal writing begins in law school where it is introduced, cultivated, and nurtured.

Perhaps to reflect the importance of writing in the legal profession, every jurisdiction uses essays on its bar exam. Some states write and use their own essays while many use essays written by the National Conference of Bar Examiners (NCBE). These NCBE questions are often referred to as the MEE—Multistate Essay Exam. The number of essays (state or MEE) given, the length of time to complete them, and the subjects you are potentially asked to write about may vary from jurisdiction to jurisdiction.

---

1. All MEE references and materials are printed here pursuant to a licensing agreement with the National Conference of Bar Examiners (NCBE).

2. See Descartes, Rene. DISCOURSE METHODS AND MEDITATIONS (1637) (adapted from Descartes' famous phrase, "I think, therefore I am").

FIGURE 6-1

The MEE consists of six 30-minute questions and is a component of the Uniform Bar Examination (UBE). It is administered by user jurisdictions as part of the bar examination on the Tuesday before the last Wednesday in February and July of each year. Areas of law that may be covered on the MEE include the following: Business Associations (Agency and Partnership; Corporations and Limited Liability Companies), Civil Procedure, Conflict of Laws, Constitutional Law, Contracts (including Article 2 [Sales] of the Uniform Commercial Code), Criminal Law and Procedure, Evidence, Family Law, Real Property, Torts, Trusts and Estates (Decedents' Estates; Trusts and Future Interests), and Article 9 (Secured Transactions) of the Uniform Commercial Code. Some questions may include issues in more than one area of law. The particular areas covered vary from exam to exam.

The way you prepare for and write an essay on any bar exam in the country will be similar. This is because most jurisdictions rely on your use of an analytical paradigm you learned in law school — IRAC.

IRAC, more than a formula or template, represents the way lawyers think about and analyze legal issues. It is no surprise then that jurisdictions' boards of law examiners expect you to use IRAC to present your legal analysis in narrative written form when responding to essay prompts on the bar exam. So you have several tasks when preparing for essays on the bar exam. You must know the law; you must be able to apply the law to the given facts; and you must present that writing in IRAC form. Don't be confused or worried if your jurisdiction does not use the phrase IRAC or some variation of it. Most jurisdictions are looking for this paradigm or some form of it to be represented in your writing.

The NCBE gives the following instructions regarding the MEE:

> The purpose of the MEE is to test the examinee's ability to (1) identify legal issues raised by a hypothetical factual situation; (2) separate material which is relevant from that which is not; (3) present a reasoned analysis of the relevant issues in a clear, concise, and well-organized composition; and (4) demonstrate an understanding of the fundamental legal principles relevant to the probable solution of the issues raised by the factual situation.

While this may not sound like your traditional IRAC, most bar examiners will expect that you marshal these components into a clear and concise writing. Your key to achieving that is IRAC.

We will use the three-step engagement process not only to help you execute IRAC when writing your essay answers but also to help you navigate your bar exam essay preparation. The three-step engagement process will allow you to attack each essay question in a very systematic way. This will set you on the right path to ensuring that when writing essays, you answer the specific question asked, use the appropriate law, and apply the law to the appropriate facts from the hypothetical.

Unlike the MPT section, for this portion of the bar exam, the law will not be given to you. Instead, it will be your job to issue spot the hypothetical you are given and to retrieve the applicable rule of law from your memory. Using the processing and memorization techniques set out in Chapter 3 will insure that you have committed the law to memory and that you understand the pattern and structure of analysis associated with each subject and the topics within it.

This chapter will look at each step in the three-step process and show you how each step will help you move closer to your goal of writing a high-scoring essay answer.

A. CRITICALLY PREVIEWING

The first step in preparing for an essay question is to engage in a critical preview. This step ensures that you will have a general understanding of the question being asked in the essay (often called the "call of the question"). Reading the call of the question first can give you a great deal of useful information about what subject(s) and specific subject topics you are being tested on.

This brief review will allow you to focus on understanding as much as you can as to what's being asked of you by the question call. This understanding will help you to engage the facts more in the second step — the Organizing Activity.

Don't shoot for the moon on the first step. Remember that the critical preview process is only the first step. You will get two more passes at processing the material when you read and outline the essay fact pattern and when you write the answer. Think of the benefits. If you take the time to critically preview, you will likely get a sense, if not an outright confirmation, of the subject you are being tested on. That allows you to push all the other bar tested subjects out of your mind as you are reading the question. Better still is the situation where the critical preview stage reveals the specific subject topic you are being tested on. Again, this knowledge will allow you to read the fact pattern with only those subjects in mind. In this way, you will be thinking of the specific rules and analysis structure associated with the subject or specific subject topic. This is a very effective way to begin your work on an essay question.

FIGURE 6-2

ESSAY

Sunrise Lodge is a corporation that develops and operates luxury resort hotels. Sunrise recently began constructing a hotel in East Beach, a beach town on the Atlantic coast of the United States. Sunrise hoped to give the East Beach hotel a local flavor by using local sources for materials.

Sunrise hired Adam to be its interior design agent on the East Beach project. The contract between them, which was for a one-year term, included the following language:

Adam has the discretion to make selections for interior floor and wall coverings, works of art, furniture, plumbing fixtures, and lighting fixtures for East Beach hotel, provided that (a) the cost of such purchases does not exceed the budgeted amounts listed in Exhibit A, (b) all purchases will be made from local vendors, and (c) the items selected are within the quantity and style guidelines described in Exhibit B. Adam shall inform vendors that purchases are for Sunrise East Beach and should arrange for Sunrise to be billed on a 30-day net basis.

The style guidelines in Exhibit B include a comprehensive list of themes and styles typical of an Atlantic fishing village like East Beach, including lighthouses, whitewashed wood, lobster traps, wicker furniture, and sailboats.

After hiring Adam, Sunrise sent a letter to prospective local suppliers on Sunrise stationery signed by the Sunrise president, announcing Adam's appointment as follows:

Sunrise Lodge is delighted to announce the appointment of Adam, a well-known local interior designer, to act on its behalf in the selection of interior floor and wall coverings, works of art, furniture, and plumbing and lighting fixtures for the Sunrise East Beach hotel. We are confident that—working only with local suppliers—Adam will exercise a wonderful creative flair in coming up with just the right look for this exciting project. Know that you deal with Sunrise when you deal with Adam on this project.

During the first months of Adam's one-year term, Adam entered into the following transactions with suppliers who had received Sunrise's letter.

First, Adam contracted with Tahini for the main lobby area of the hotel to be decorated entirely in a Tahitian theme. The items for the Tahitian decor are within the budget and are from a local supplier. However, they are not within the Exhibit B style guidelines.

Second, Adam contracted with Moby for the guest rooms to be decorated using authentic themes from the Atlantic seaboard region as required by Exhibit B. The decor selections are within budget and are from local suppliers, but the Sunrise officials do not like the design.

Sunrise has refused to pay either vendor and has terminated Adam's contract.

1. On what agency principles, if any, is Sunrise liable to Tahini and Moby on their respective contracts? Explain.

2. Is Adam liable to Sunrise as a result of the contracts with Tahini and Moby? Explain.

3. May Sunrise terminate Adam's agency before the end of their one-year contract term without incurring liability to Adam? Explain.

Thanks to the phrase "agency principles," we know immediately that this is an agency question (broad subject being tested).

Question one gives additional clues regarding the subject specific topics: From your Agency study, think of how a principle can be liable for contracts made by agents. Typically, when an agent acts with actual or apparent authority, the principal will be bound. There can be other types of authority to bind the principal, but you will almost always discuss those two. Thus, at least those two will be part of your discussion.

Regarding Question two, you probably need more information as to who these mentioned parties are at the critical preview stage. But, the question still tells you that agency authority may still be at issue.

Question three is very direct. After reading it, you know with certainty that you will have to discuss agency relationship termination. Thus, for that question, everything you know about agency termination should come to mind. You can push everything else out.

Bar essays do not come with substantive labels. Your first task in writing an answer to the question is to correctly identify what subject and then specific subject topics you are being asked to write about. In most cases, critically previewing the essay by reading its question call should give you a good sense of what you are being asked to write about. MEE essays often contain pointed question calls.

B. ORGANIZING ACTIVITY — READING THE FACTS AND CREATING AN ANSWER OUTLINE

This second step is a crucial step in writing a strong answer to an essay question. Once you have completed the critical preview step, the next step is to read the facts from the question thoroughly and to organize those facts, along with the law you have determined to be applicable, into an answer outline. Here, you will

---

BOX NOTE 6-1

Alternative Critical Preview Strategy

Instead of only reading the question call, you may find it more effective to skim the entire question (facts and question call(s)). If you choose this critical preview strategy, keep in mind that you are only skimming to understand what subjects and specific subject topics you are to write about. You will be able to read the question again more slowly to understand the facts and how the law should be applied to them.

While most MEE essays contain a pointed question call, some essays may not. You may encounter question calls that tell you to

"Discuss" or that ask you to "Determine how the court should rule on party's claims" or "Determine what rights a party has." Reading the call of the question in these instances may not help to advance your analysis. A skimming critical preview strategy may be the remedy for this.

Consider other alternatives if you determine neither reading the call of the question nor skimming work for you. In doing so, keep in mind what you are seeking to achieve. Lastly, make sure you practice your chosen strategy so you are certain it will meet your needs.

---

get yet another chance to process the information. There are different ways to organize your answer depending on the subject of the question.

1. Visual Organization

When organizing your essay answer, pay attention to whether the question was presented to you in numbered or lettered parts. If so, make sure you organize your answer to correspond to the numbers or letters the bar examiners provided with each question. This will ensure that the bar grader is clear as to which part of your analysis is in response to the specific question asked. If the question has two parts, then the grader can see from the instant she encounters your essay that you are following the requirement to answer two separate parts.

Make sure that you do not bunch all your writing together. How many times have you encountered a case that had a page long paragraph with no breaks in it? You, of course, read it but the presentation isn't exactly welcoming especially since you know you will have to read this material closely and discern precisely what the writer is attempting to communicate. While we are sure bar graders are thrilled to read every one of your essay words, let's try to make the presentation as visually appealing as possible, just in case they are not their normal cheery selves while reading your work. Thus, make new paragraphs for each issue and also where it makes sense logically.

Create headings where appropriate. You can create headings for each issue or sub-issue. For instance, if you have a hearsay question which requires you to write about hearsay, hearsay exceptions and non-hearsay, you might label each discussion so the grader can easily see where your discussion on each issue is.

2. Substantive Organization

As you continue to spot issues while reading the question facts, make sure you are accounting for the proper substantive organization. For instance, if you had to address whether there was a valid contract, you would not discuss acceptance before offer. In an Agency question that asked you to determine liability, you would not address agency authority without first addressing whether there was an agency relationship in the first place, unless the facts make it clear there was such a relationship. If so, you would note that the agency relationship aspect is satisfied from the facts. But, you would still note it first, before discussing agency authority.

Headings can also be helpful substantively. If you provide them, your grader may be able to read down the headings. This will show that you not only have spotted the issues, but that you have also correctly organized the issues in a way that represents not just your knowledge of the law, but your knowledge of how the law works.

Just as the question call can create visual organization; it can also help with substantive organization. If you are faced with an essay question that does not have a specific question call, another way to create headings is to start thinking about the rule that will govern your answer. For instance, if the major rule has sub-parts in the form of elements, consider creating your headings and thus your answer organization by the sub-parts of the major rule. In doing so, you will ensure that every element is covered, and that you have added the appropriate details concerning the law and facts.

BOX NOTE 6-2

Other Organizational Concerns

As you read your essay question and begin to organize it, you may find that different organizational schemes work better for different subjects.

For instance, a Torts question which may have several parties potentially committing many Torts may direct you to discuss the potential Tort claims against each party. You can organize your essay by party or by Tort. For instance, if you organized by party, the structure of your writing could look like the following:

Amy	Ben	Carl
Battery	Assault	False Imprisonment
False Imprisonment	Battery	

If you organized by Tort, it might look like the following:

Assault	Battery	False Imprisonment
Ben	Amy	Amy
	Ben	Carl

3. Sketching in the Law and Facts and Reaching a Conclusion

As you continue reading the facts, you will continue to spot issues. As issues come to mind, think about the law; begin to fill in the rest of your outline by writing in the law and the facts that relate to the issues you spotted. Most of us will make notes as we read by writing the issues we spot and the rules they make us think of in the margins. It is also not uncommon to underline and circle key words as you read the essay question. For some bar studiers and certain questions, this may be enough of an organizing activity. For other studiers and questions, a more detailed, but still abbreviated, outline may be more appropriate. Once you have sketched in the law and facts, determine whether the elements have been met or the standard has been proven. This will be your conclusion. A simple check or plus can indicate yes while an x or minus can indicate no.

In any event, whatever method you use to organize your answer, remember that this is yet another step in a three-step engagement process. You will get to process this information again when you begin to write. This is critical because you only have time to write an outline (in whatever form) and write an answer for each essay question once. You do not have time to write the answer twice. In other words, when outlining, outline. Do not write. In your outline, use abbreviations, phrases, mnemonics, or whatever shortened form you will be able to understand. Try to limit this phase of your essay writing process, including the critical preview stage, to 10 minutes if you have a 30-minute essay. If you are faced with an essay with different timing requirements, dedicate approximately a third of the time in total to your critical preview and organizing actives steps.

See Figure 6-3 below for examples of how your outline might look at this point.

FIGURE 6-3

Issue	Rule	Facts	Conclusion
Battery	-	-	+
	Unlawful force	P punched D in face & wrestled D to ground	+
	Person of another	Acts committed against P's person – face punch and wrestling to ground	+
	Cause bod injury	P –cut on lip and bruise on leg after P punched and wrestled	+

Torts Essay Question:

D saw her roommate, P, walking on University's campus one day and noticed that P was wearing her couture one-of-a-kind designer red sweater. D told P several times not to borrow her clothes without permission. D was so angry when she saw P wearing her sweater that she ran up to her and told her that she would punch her in the nose if she did not take her sweater off. When Kimber refused, D punched her in the face, wrestled her to the ground, and took the sweater off of her. The punch from D cut P's lip and P's leg was bruised when she fell after D wrestled her to the ground.

Discuss any torts D may be liable for.

Answer Outline

Remember to abbreviate and shorten where appropriate.

You would likely have to handwrite this outline form. You can also choose to type it vertically on your computer. If you type, you can fill in your outline once you get to the writing stage.

Margin notes
Batt –
unlawful force – punch/wrest
per of anoth - acts committed against P's person – face punch & wrest to ground

Margin notes
Batt –
cause bod inj – P – cut on lip/bruise on leg

At this point, we hope you have noticed a crucial point about outlining your answer. Your outlines, margin notes, or whatever organizing activity you use should be done with IRAC in mind. After all, if this is the way legal readers think and process information, then you want to present your answer in that way — so that it lines up with your bar grader's thinking. This should not be a daunting task for you at this point because you will have processed (flashcarded, flowcharted, outlined, etc.) each subject using IRAC as a principal form of organization. See Chapter 3 for a review of how IRAC is represented in each processing product form.

C. REACHING YOUR GOAL — PRODUCING A CLEAR, CONCISE, AND CORRECT ESSAY ANSWER

The final step in the three-step engagement process is to reach your goal of producing a clear, concise, and correct essay answer. Completing the first two steps of the engagement process gives you invaluable information on the relevant facts and the relevant parts and sub-parts of the law that will help in the production of the finished essay. The final step requires you to use your outline to flesh out, in full sentences, a cohesive answer that is responsive to the essay question. IRAC, or some form of it, is the best way to achieve this goal.

1. Using CRAC, CIRAC, or IRAC to Produce Your Final Essay Answer

Individual bar exam jurisdictions may have a preferred way for you to write your essay answers. In any event, it is usually some form of IRAC. As you know, the acronym IRAC stands for Issue, Rule, Application, and Conclusion. IRAC ensures that for every issue you spot, you have the applicable law, facts relevant to that law, and the conclusion regarding the application of that law to the relevant facts set out in a format that legal readers understand and are comfortable with. Do not get too hung up in slight differences (IRAC, CRAC, CIRAC, etc.). Regardless of the exact form, note that bar graders (who are typically lawyers) want you to identify an issue, supply a rule that addresses that issue, apply the law to those facts, and reach a reasoned conclusion — typically in that order. Whether you start with a conclusion statement or an issue statement or include both, as you long as you write about each issue with the above in mind, you increase your chances of reaching your goal of a successful essay answer.

a. Issue or Beginning Conclusion

Because MEE essay question calls tend to be pointed, bar examinees often repeat or mimic the question call in IRAC sentence — the issue or conclusion statement. In many instances, this is acceptable. But, consider focusing your issue/conclusion statement to move beyond the question call. This would alert the bar grader that you have spotted not just the macro issue (that was given to you in the question call), but the precise issue you are to write about. You may not be able to achieve this on every essay, so don't get too bogged down with it. If, when studying for and taking the bar exam, you can't discern the precise issue and you have a pointed call of the question, mimic it and move on to the other parts of the analysis. But consider honing this skill. Figure 6-4 illustrates the benefits of using the specific issue or beginning conclusion statement.

FIGURE 6-4

Question call asks, "What rights does SOS have against TAMU?"

ISSUE

Try to focus this statement so that it lets the grader know that you have spotted the appropriate issue

- OK — The issue is whether SOS has rights against TAMU.
  - Doesn't show how you extrapolated the precise issue from the general question. It does not advance your discussion.
- BETTER — The issue is what kind of damages are available when a contract for services is breached.
- BEST — The issue is whether SOS can recover expectation, consequential, or incidental damages from TAMU.

---

b. Rule

The rule should always follow your issue or beginning conclusion statement. If your issue is a question, then your reader expects an answer. For legal readers, that answer comes in the form of a legal principal that will resolve the issue. If you start with a conclusion, then think of it as a declarative statement about a situation's outcome. Similarly, your legal reader will want proof that your statement is correct. That proof will begin with an applicable rule statement. The legal reader wants these answers or proofs immediately. Do not make the legal reader (the bar grader) wait. Include your rule statements immediately after your issue or beginning conclusion statements.

To include the correct rule statement, you will need to know the law. There is no way around it. When you are processing and memorizing, keep this in mind. More specifically, process and memorize in a way that will position you to think of the correct rule when you see certain facts. Thus, when you process your lecture notes, make sure they include not just rules, but also factual situations depicting how the rule would be relevant (issue spotting triggers) and factual examples that demonstrate how the rule should be applied. Also, make it clear in your processing product how answers should be structured. For instance, your Agency processing product should clearly indicate that you must establish an agency relationship before you can establish whether there was agency authority. Thus, when you memorize, you'll be doing more than just memorizing the rule. You will be memorizing the facts that make certain issues relevant, the appropriate rules for those issues, and the pattern and structure of analysis associated with those issues, facts, and rules.

FIGURE 6-5

State an overall rule

RULE: When a contract for services is breached, expectancy, consequential, and incidental damages are available.

— Each of these damage types has its own rule. After stating the main rule above, provide the rule for each type of damage. You may add these rules with the overall main rule or write them separately as part of mini iracs.*

Mini iracs work best when you have a main rule with sub-parts that have their own rules.

Example of mini IRAC structure using one part of the rule

RULE: When a contract for services is breached, expectancy, consequential, and incidental damages are available.
mini issue: expectancy
mini rule:
mini application:
mini conclusion:

c. Application

The application is typically where points for your essay are concentrated. The other steps are important because it's hard to put together a proper application section if your issue and the rule are incorrect. However, the application section shows the bar grader not only that you know the applicable rule but that you also know how it works.

When writing your application sections, be sure to signal to your reader that you are moving from your rule section to your application section. Writing the word *Here* or phrase *In this case* at the beginning of your application section should accomplish this. Use your rule as a guide to organizing your application. For instance, if your rule has three parts to it, apply those parts in the same order you set them out in your rule statement.

Some of the most common pitfalls bar examinees face when writing application sections are restating facts without any applicable reference to the law, restating the law without reference to any facts, or being conclusory. There really should be nothing new in an application section. The facts will have been provided by the bar examiners in the form of your essay. You will have provided the rules in your rule section. The application should be a combination of the two. Thus, just restating the facts (that were already given to you) or just restating your rule (that you will have just set out above) is not application. If you are having these troubles, consider asking yourself why. If you are asking about *facts*, you will say, "Because [insert rule or rule part]." If you are asking about rules, you will say, "Because, [insert relevant facts]." We like to call this the power of WHY and the resultant power of BECAUSE. Conclusory statements can plague bar essay writing as well. If you find you are doing this, ask the same "why" question to unpack what has brought you to that conclusion. Your answer will typically involve law, facts, and hopefully some combination of the two.

If you are having trouble with this portion of the IRAC, consider the following very basic formula. Application = Rule/rule part + because (or because type word) + facts relevant to the rule or rule part. While you do not have to adhere to this precisely when writing your application, practice using the formula to make sure you stay on track and avoid the pitfalls. See the illustration in Figure 6-6.

FIGURE 6-6

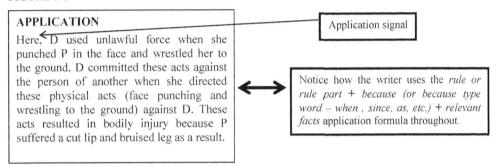

d. Conclusion

The very last step in writing your essay answer is to make sure you come to a conclusion. You should have a conclusion for each of your issues. In addition, if you are following the CRAC or CIRAC format make sure that the beginning conclusion and the ending conclusion are consistent with each other (i.e., make sure they match!). Also, keep in mind that the conclusion is a pithy wrap up of everything you have said in your analysis. One or two sentences should be enough in most instances. You should not still be analyzing at this stage. If you find that you are, it may be a clue that you are lacking depth somewhere in the IRA parts of your analysis.

2. When You Can't Remember or Just Don't Know the Law

It happens to the best of us. The mind goes blank. We don't remember the law or any law for that matter. If this happens to you, the key is to not fall apart and drift into some sort of stream of consciousness writing. Remember, you are a law school graduate! You have at your command some law or formulation of law that will get you through this question. So, keep your calm. Don't quit because you can't remember or you can't remember as beautifully as you would like. Pull together what law you can and then IRAC it. Your bar grader must still be able to easily find the rule and its application to the fact pattern. Making it hard for the grader to find the information will only make the situation worse.

Note that if you are following the three-step engagement method as it is set out in Chapter 3 and subsequent chapters and have become a truly "engaged learner" these instances will be few and far between. Nevertheless, this type of forgetfulness can happen. If it does happen, there are methods you can try to ensure you answer as best as possible given the situation.

If you find yourself in this situation, start by using the facts to help figure out what the rule might be. The facts may trigger your memory of the general area of law and the specific topics within that area of law. Also, take your best guess as to what the law might be. It can help to identify the general area of law and then any sub-topics in that general area that might be relevant. For example, you may identify that it is a Torts question. Maybe you can pinpoint Products Liability as the sub-topic. If you can drill deeper, that might help you pinpoint some or a portion of the relevant law.

In addition, use common-sense. When looking at the sub-topic, the law usually follows a common-sense pattern. What parties are the most likely, in a fair and balanced environment, to receive their rights? What parties are most likely to lose those rights? Write your answer from a logical point of view, and you will most likely be on the right track.

Finally, if you can't remember the proper "buzzwords" for that area of law, use the common-sense approach to establish legal language that is relevant to that topic or sub-topic.

BOX NOTE 6-3

How Should I Use the Model Answers?

When you practice essay questions, make sure you also read the model answers. These are super answers provided by your commercial bar course. Do not be intimidated by these super model answers. Instead, use them to improve. If you see a rule statement there that is better than the one you have, copy it into your processing product or lecture notes. If the fact pattern represents an example you did not think of in terms of the applicable rule, summarize it and include it in your processing product or lecture notes. If you see the analysis organized or structured in a way you would not have, outline that structure or organization and include it in your processing product or lecture notes. The key here is not to let your work on the question go to waste. Use what you learn from practicing the questions and reading the super model answers to improve your performance. When you are reading the answers, keep your processing product or lecture notes close so you can incorporate, in the document you will study and memorize from, any valuable information.

---

3. When You Know the Law but Aren't Sure of the Outcome

There may be a situation in a given essay question where you are familiar with the applicable law, but you aren't sure how that law will apply to the question asked. In other words, it could go either way. When a situation like this occurs, the best thing to do is to discuss both eventualities. Keep in mind that MEE essay questions do not always present "either way" situations. Consistent essay practice will reveal to you the specific subject topics that are prone to this type of analysis. Even if you think the outcome could go "either way," always pick a side.

4. Practice, Practice, Practice

Consistent practice is key to success on bar exam essays. Set aside time each day to practice essays. Do not wait until the end of your bar study period. Yes, you want to test your knowledge, but essay work also helps you to advance your knowledge and skills. Thus, practicing essays throughout your bar study will help you to improve by identifying weaknesses in knowledge and skills early enough to remedy them.

In addition, repetitive practice will make you comfortable with the format for essay questions and answers in general and for specific subjects. Because of this, we recommend that you practice as many essays as possible for each bar tested subject. You may be thinking this is impossible given the relatively short study period, but there are many ways to "work" essays besides writing out answers in the traditional way.

Alternative Ways to "Work" Essays

One way to "work" an essay is just by reading it and its answer. When reading, note the facts from the question and whether you are spotting the issues and thinking of the appropriate law. When you read the answer, note whether you matched the facts to the correct issue. If you did match the facts to the correct issue, note whether you recalled the appropriate rule in response to that issue.

If you prefer a more active approach, consider outlining the question and answer. Proceed just as you would if you were only reading, but this time, outline your answer in the margins with abbreviations, mnemonics, and short phrases. Outline the answer as you read. When you are done outlining both, compare the outlines to see if they match.

Lastly, you can reverse outline the question and answer. Read the question call(s) and then the question hypo. Make the question call(s) the heading(s) of your outline. Then read the answer for each question call and outline the answer under each heading. All these methods may take less time than writing out an answer to an essay but will help you to get more essay practice under your belt.

None of these methods should be your primary way of practicing essay problems. That should be done the traditional way—writing each answer in long form. Use these alternative methods for exposure to more essays after already writing a significant number of essays on each subject.

5. Using the Allotted Time to Finish Every Essay

When you receive your bar exam essays during the bar exam, you will be given several of them at one time. For instance, if you are taking the bar exam in a Uniform Bar Exam state, you will be given six essays on the afternoon of

---

BOX NOTE 6-6

On the bar exam, can I take a few extra minutes to finish a question?

The best case scenario is that you time everything correctly and do not mismanage time during any part of the bar exam. But if you do have a timing issue, the best course is to try to isolate it to that question. Do not let it spill over into your other question work. So, in answer to the question above, don't do it! Resist the urge. Every question gets its due time and not one second more. Thus, if you have 30 minutes for each essay, then only use 30 minutes for the essay. Do not rob from the other essays the time needed to produce a well written essay. Instead, maximize your ability to do well on every essay by ensuring that there is full time for each one. If it helps, do not think of the essay questions as islands that stand alone. They are all opportunities for points. So, squeeze as many points as you can out of each one and when time is up for a question, move on to the next question and squeeze as many points out of it. Keep doing that until you come to the end.

If you finish an essay with time left, keep going. DO NOT go back to essays you ran out of time on. But, if you finish ALL essays and still have time at the end , then go back to the ones you ran out of time on. If you feel you answered everything and still have extra time, review your essays for readability.

---

day 1 of the bar exam. You will have three hours to complete the essays. Do the math. If you have three hours to complete all the essays, how much time should you devote to each essay? You should devote 30 minutes to every essay under that scenario. That means that you must remain cognizant of your timing as you practice your essays. Practice under time pressure so that you get used to executing in the given time frame. Keeping as close as you can to the required time period in your practice sessions will ensure that you are on track to write a strong essay during the actual bar exam.

CONCLUSION

By following the three-step engagement process, as set out above, your essay answer should be clearly, concisely, and correctly written. This three-step process will help you understand the template of a successful essay answer. But this cannot happen without significant and consistent practice. Make sure your bar study schedules put you on pace to work as many essay questions as possible for each subject over the course of the bar study period.

CHAPTER 6 RECAP

▶ *CRITICAL PREVIEW*

- Context Building/Critical Reading
  - Read the call of the question
  - Skim the essay
  - Skim/markup the essay

▶ *ORGANIZING ACTIVITY*

- Understanding Material to Build a Knowledge Base
- Outlining your answer
- IRAC style margin notes

▶ *REACHING THE GOAL*

- Producing the Product
- Writing the essay

MEE QUESTIONS

TORTS QUESTIONS

1. Last month, Paul attended a fund-raising lunch at Library, where he purchased and ate a chicken salad sandwich. Later that day, he became severely ill and was diagnosed with food poisoning. As a result of the food poisoning, Paul developed a permanent digestive disorder.

Several other people also became sick after eating at the lunch, and the Health Department determined that the chicken salad was contaminated with salmonella bacteria. According to the Health Department, raw chicken often contains salmonella bacteria. Although the risk of salmonella contamination cannot be eliminated, proper preparation and cooking can ensure that the chicken is safe for eating. The chicken must be thoroughly cooked, and all utensils or surfaces that come in contact with raw chicken must be thoroughly cleaned with hot water and soap before further use.

The Reading Club had initiated and planned the Library's first and only fund-raising lunch. Ann, Bill, and Chuck independently volunteered to make the chicken salad. Each made a separate batch of salad, using their own recipes and working individually at their own homes. Another volunteer combined the three batches of salad at Library, and a Library employee sold sandwiches at the lunch. All lunch profits went to Library.

Ann, Bill, and Chuck each purchased their chicken from Supermarket. The chicken was contained in packages labeled with a prominent warning describing the risk of salmonella contamination and the precautions necessary to avoid those risks.

A Health Department spokesperson has said that "Someone who made the chicken salad did not take proper precautions." Ann, Bill, and Chuck all claim they took the proper precautions.

Paul has consulted an attorney about bringing a tort action against: 1) Library, 2) Supermarket, and 3) Ann, Bill, and Chuck. If Paul can prove only the facts outlined above:

1. Can Library be found liable to Paul under a strict liability theory? Explain.
2. Can Supermarket be found liable to Paul under a strict liability theory? Explain.
3. Can Ann, Bill, and Chuck be found liable to Paul under either a strict liability or negligence theory? Explain.

2. Tenant lives in Landlord's apartment building. The furnace in the building was inoperable during three periods last winter, causing the loss of heat and hot water. On each of those occasions, Landlord made temporary repairs.

On March 25, the furnace again broke down. Landlord was promptly notified of the problem and he ordered the parts needed to fix the furnace on March 26, but they did not arrive until April 6, at which time Landlord fixed the furnace. Between March 25 and April 5, there was no heat or hot water in the building.

In order to bathe from March 25 through April 5, Tenant heated a large pot of water on the stove. After the water boiled, Tenant transferred the water to the bathtub, mixed in cold water, and then used the water to bathe.

On April 3, Nephew, Tenant's eight-year-old nephew, arrived for a visit. On April 4, Tenant was carrying a pot of boiling water down the hall to the bathroom when Nephew, who was chasing a ball out of a bedroom that opened into the hall, collided with Tenant. As a result of the collision, the hot water spilled on Nephew, seriously burning him. Nephew did not look or call out before running into the hall.

A state statute provides that "every apartment building . . . and every part thereof shall be kept in good repair. The owner shall be responsible for compliance . . . . A violation shall be punishable by a fine not exceeding $500."

Nephew, by his guardian, sued Tenant and Landlord for damages. At trial, both Tenant and Landlord argued that Nephew's negligence was the sole cause of the accident.

Based on these facts, may the jury properly award Nephew damages for his personal injury:

1. From Tenant? Explain.
2. From Landlord? Explain.

3. Penny lives in an apartment on Oak Street across from the Fernbury Baseball Park ("the Park"). The Park is owned and maintained by the Fernbury Flies, a professional minor league baseball team. As she left her apartment building one day, Penny was struck in the head by a baseball that had been hit by Dennis, a Flies player, during a game.

The section of Oak Street that adjoins the Park was once lined with single-family homes. Over the past two decades, these homes have been replaced by stores and apartment buildings, causing an increase in both car and pedestrian traffic on Oak Street.

The ball that struck Penny was one of the longest that had been hit at the Park since its construction 40 years ago. During the last 40 years, Flies' records show that only 30 balls had previously been hit over the Park fence adjoining Oak Street. Fifteen of the balls hit out of the Park onto Oak Street were hit during the past decade.

The Park is surrounded by a 10-foot-high fence, which was built during the Park's construction. All other ballparks owned by clubs in the Flies' league are surrounded by fences of similar type and identical height. These fences are typical of those used by other minor league teams in the United States. However, in Japan, where ballparks are often located in congested urban neighborhoods, netting is typically attached to ballpark fences. This netting permits balls to go over a fence but captures balls before they can strike a bystander or car.

After being struck by the ball, Penny was taken by ambulance to a hospital emergency room. After tests, the treating physician told Penny that she had suffered a concussion. The physician prescribed pain medication for Penny. However, because of a preexisting condition, she had an adverse reaction to the medication and suffered neurological damage resulting in the loss of sensation in her extremities.

Penny has sued Dennis, the player who hit the baseball that struck her, for battery and negligence. Penny has also sued the Fernbury Flies. She seeks to recover damages for the concussion and the neurological damage resulting from the medication.

1. Does Penny have a viable tort claim against Dennis? Explain.
2. Does Penny have a viable tort claim against the Fernbury Flies? Explain.

CONTRACTS QUESTIONS

1. Baker is a renowned pastry chef. Café, a sole proprietorship, is a well-known restaurant in need of hiring a pastry chef. Baker and Café's Owner had extensive conversations regarding Baker coming to work at Café. On May 1, a week after those conversations occurred, Baker sent Café a signed letter dated May 1 stating: "I will work for Café as head pastry chef for two years for an annual salary of $100,000."

On the morning of May 7, Café's Owner telephoned Baker and said: "The $100,000 is pretty stiff. Could you possibly consider working for less?" Baker replied: "I am a renowned pastry chef. I will not work for any less!"

Later that morning, Café's Owner sent Baker a signed letter by regular mail stating: "You obviously think you are too good for my restaurant. I am no longer interested in hiring you to work at Café."

Later that afternoon, Café's Owner had a change of heart and sent Baker a registered, express-mail signed letter stating: "Okay, if you really won't work for less, I agree to pay you the $100,000 a year you demand to work as head pastry chef at Café for two years."

On May 10, the registered, express-mail letter was delivered to Baker's office. The regular-mail letter containing the rejection was still on its way. Baker accepted delivery of the registered, express-mail letter from the postal carrier and placed it on his desk without opening it.

On May 11, before Baker read the registered, express-mail letter on his desk, he accepted an offer to work for Restaurant. As a courtesy, Baker called Café's Owner and said, "Sorry, I just took a job at Restaurant. Too bad you couldn't afford me." Café's Owner responded, "You can't work for Restaurant, I already accepted your offer to work at Café for $100,000 a year."

Does Café have an enforceable contract with Baker? Explain.

2. Sam was walking down the sidewalk when he heard shouts coming from a burning house. Sam immediately called 911 on his cell phone and rushed into the house. Inside the house, Sam discovered Resident trying to coax Resident's frightened dog from behind a couch. Sam, at great risk to his safety, crawled behind the couch and pulled the dog from its hiding place. Sam, carrying the dog, and Resident then safely made their way outside.

Once outside, Resident thanked Sam and asked Sam about his work. Sam told Resident, "I was hoping to start training as a paramedic in the fall, but I don't think I'll be able to afford the cost of the program."

Resident responded, "We need all the good paramedics that we can get! If you are going to start paramedic training, I want to help you. Also, my dog means everything to me. I want to compensate you for your heroism. Give me your address, and I will send you a check for a thousand dollars."

Sam said, "Thank you so much! Here is my address. I'll apply to the paramedic program tomorrow."

Sam applied to the paramedic training program but was denied admission. Sam then applied for and was accepted into a cosmetology training program and owes that program $1,000. Sam cannot pay the $1,000 he owes because when Resident learned Sam was not attending the paramedic program, he refused to give Sam the $1,000.

Sam sued Resident to recover the $1,000.

What theories could Sam assert to recover all or some portion of the $1,000, and what is the likelihood of success on each theory? Explain.

AGENCY & PARTNERSHIP QUESTIONS

1. AGENCY & PARTNERSHIP QUESTIONS

1. Principal is an antiques dealer. As is common in the antiques business, Principal acquires inventory by using a group of buyers to purchase antiques on his behalf. Principal pays the buyers a percentage commission on the items they buy for Principal. Principal trains the buyers to be able to evaluate potential purchases and sends them into the field with specific instructions as to the items Principal wants them to buy. The buyers are given credentials identifying them as buyers for Principal, and they use these credentials to introduce themselves to potential sellers. The buyers, using Principal's contract forms, enter into contracts with sellers.

Agent, one of Principal's buyers, was sent out to purchase antiques for Principal. During the next several months, the following three transactions took place:

Using Principal's credentials, Agent bought an antique church bell for $3,500 from Bellseller, who believed that Agent was acting on behalf of Principal. The church bell was on Principal's acquisition list and the price was within the range authorized by Principal. However, Agent did not intend to purchase the bell for Principal. Instead, Agent bought the bell for Greta, a competing antiques dealer, who had agreed to pay Agent $250 to find such a bell. Agent's intention was to use Greta's money to pay for the bell. Greta rejected the bell. Principal, who has received a demand from Bellseller, has decided he does not want the bell and has refused to pay Bellseller.

Agent had a written authorization from Principal to buy several books, including *Looking Backward* by Edward Bellamy. Agent showed this authorization to Tomeseller, who had a first edition of *Looking Backward*. However, Agent did not tell Tomeseller that Principal had given Agent an oral instruction, not to be disclosed to anyone, that Agent should not pay more than $8,000 for the book. Agent bought the book on Principal's behalf for $12,500. Principal now refuses to pay Tomeseller.

When Principal learned of Agent's transactions with Bellseller and Tomeseller, he decided to stop using Agent as his buyer. Principal sent Agent a letter terminating his agency and asking Agent to return the credentials that Principal had provided to Agent.

Several days after Agent received the letter from Principal, Agent purchased for his own account a whale oil lamp for $5,000 from Lampseller. Agent told Lampseller that the purchase was for Principal's account, showed Lampseller his credentials from Principal, and purchased the lamp using the contract forms provided to him by Principal. Agent did not disclose to Lampseller that Principal had terminated Agent as his buyer. Principal now refuses to pay Lampseller because, at the time of the purchase, Principal had terminated Agent and Agent was no longer Principal's buyer.

Is Principal liable to:

1. Bellseller for the purchase of the church bell? Explain.
2. Tomeseller for the purchase of the book? Explain.
3. Lampseller for the purchase of the whale oil lamp? Explain.

2. Sunrise Lodge is a corporation that develops and operates luxury resort hotels. Sunrise recently began constructing a hotel in East Beach, a beach town on the Atlantic coast of the United States. Sunrise hoped to give the East Beach hotel a local flavor by using local sources for materials.

Sunrise hired Adam to be its interior design agent on the East Beach project. The contract between them, which was for a one-year term, included the following language:

Adam has the discretion to make selections for interior floor and wall coverings, works of art, furniture, plumbing fixtures, and lighting fixtures for East Beach hotel, provided that (a) the cost of such purchases does not exceed the budgeted amounts listed in Exhibit A, (b) all purchases will be made from local vendors, and (c) the items selected are within the quantity and style guidelines described in Exhibit B. Adam shall inform vendors that purchases are for Sunrise East Beach and should arrange for Sunrise to be billed on a 30-day net basis.

The style guidelines in Exhibit B include a comprehensive list of themes and styles typical of an Atlantic fishing village like East Beach, including lighthouses, whitewashed wood, lobster traps, wicker furniture, and sailboats.

After hiring Adam, Sunrise sent a letter to prospective local suppliers on Sunrise stationery signed by the Sunrise president, announcing Adam's appointment as follows:

Sunrise Lodge is delighted to announce the appointment of Adam, a well-known local interior designer, to act on its behalf in the selection of interior floor and wall coverings, works of art, furniture, and plumbing and lighting fixtures for the Sunrise East Beach hotel. We are confident that—working only with local suppliers—Adam will exercise a wonderful creative flair in coming up with just the right look for this exciting project. Know that you deal with Sunrise when you deal with Adam on this project.

During the first months of Adam's one-year term, Adam entered into the following transactions with suppliers who had received Sunrise's letter.

First, Adam contracted with Tahini for the main lobby area of the hotel to be decorated entirely in a Tahitian theme. The items for the Tahitian decor are within the budget and are from a local supplier. However, they are not within the Exhibit B style guidelines.

Second, Adam contracted with Moby for the guest rooms to be decorated using authentic themes from the Atlantic seaboard region as required by Exhibit B. The decor selections are within budget and are from local suppliers, but the Sunrise officials do not like the design.

Sunrise has refused to pay either vendor and has terminated Adam's contract.

1. On what agency principles, if any, is Sunrise liable to Tahini and Moby on their respective contracts? Explain.
2. Is Adam liable to Sunrise as a result of the contracts with Tahini and Moby? Explain.
3. May Sunrise terminate Adam's agency before the end of their one-year contract term without incurring liability to Adam? Explain.

3. Lessor owns and manages apartment buildings in the town of Utopia.

Handy is the sole proprietor and only employee of a small business called "Rapid Repairs." Most of the income from this business is generated by making small household repairs for homeowners and apartment dwellers in Utopia. Handy has a good reputation for performing quality work and charging reasonable rates.

One year ago, Lessor contracted for an indefinite period with Handy to perform repair work at several apartment units that Lessor owns in Utopia. The tenants of these units are told to make requests for repairs by calling a telephone number listed as "Lessor's Repair Line."

Under the Lessor/Handy contract, any call to "Lessor's Repair Line" actually rings directly through to Rapid Repairs. Handy is obligated to investigate any tenant's request for repair within 24 hours. Before actually making any repair, however, Handy is required to contact Lessor, describe the nature of the repair, and seek authorization to proceed. Once authorized to make the repair, Handy must make it within 24 hours. Lessor is obligated to pay Handy $50 per hour for any work done pursuant to the contract (including investigating repair requests) and, in addition, to reimburse Handy's out-of-pocket expenses.

The Lessor/Handy contract further provides that Handy:

- may perform similar work on other apartment buildings, but may not perform work "on the side" for Lessor's tenants in Lessor's buildings;
- must provide his own tools;
- may not perform any electrical work, but must subcontract it to a licensed electrician, approved by Lessor, who will work under Handy's supervision.

Last month, Tenant called "Lessor's Repair Line." Handy answered. Tenant said he had a cracked sink drainpipe. Handy immediately investigated. After obtaining permission from Lessor to repair the sink, Handy returned to make the repair. While Handy was making the repair, Tenant asked Handy to install an electrical outlet in the apartment for Tenant's computer. Despite his contract with Lessor, Handy agreed to do so, but told Tenant there would be a charge of $200 as it was an improvement to the apartment, not a repair covered under the lease. Tenant agreed to pay $200 for a new outlet. Tenant assumed that the money would go to Lessor, but Handy intended to keep it for himself.

Handy was negligent in installing the electrical outlet. The outlet caused a fire, which destroyed Tenant's personal property. Tenant never paid for the installation work.

On what alternative theories should Tenant argue that Lessor is liable for Handy's negligence, and what is the likely outcome on each theory? Explain.

4. Best Care Hospital, one of five hospitals in City, operates the largest emergency room in City. Best Care advertises extensively about the quality of care provided in its emergency room. It has billboards strategically placed throughout City urging local citizens to come to Best Care "because Best Care's emergency room doctors are the absolute best and will really care for you." In fact, Best Care employs no doctors; instead it contracts with seven doctors in City to staff the emergency room on a 7-day, 24-hour basis. These contracts provide:

1. Each doctor is an "independent contractor," not an "agent/employee," and may conduct a private practice but may not work in any other emergency room;
2. Each doctor is responsible for the manner in which he or she provides medical care and for the purchase of malpractice insurance;
3. Each doctor is authorized to purchase supplies and equipment for Best Care's emergency room from a list of approved vendors located in City and within Best Care's price guidelines;
4. Each doctor is periodically reviewed by Best Care's governing board to assure that each doctor provides quality care;
5. Each doctor independently bills patients for services provided; and
6. All emergency services are performed in the Best Care emergency room using supplies and equipment provided by Best Care.

Three months ago, Owen, a local orthopedist and one of the doctors with whom Best Care contracts, ordered a portable X-ray machine costing $25,000 from Vision, a company located in a town 450 miles from City. Vision is not on Best Care's approved vendor list and Owen did not consult with anyone at Best Care before he placed the order. When Owen ordered the machine, which was to be custom-designed for Best Care, he truthfully told Vision that he was one of the seven emergency room doctors at Best Care and needed the machine for the emergency room. Owen also stated that he was acting on behalf of Best Care. Vision had had no previous dealings with Owen or Best Care and agreed to make the machine according to the custom specifications provided by Owen. When Vision shipped the X-ray machine, Best Care refused to accept delivery, even though the price for the machine was within its price guidelines. Best Care claimed that Owen had no authority to purchase the machine on its behalf. Vision filed an action for breach of contract against Best Care.

Last month, Anita was hit by a bus. When the ambulance arrived, Anita asked the ambulance driver to take her to Best Care, quoting the billboard claim that "Best Care's emergency room doctors are the absolute best." When Anita arrived at the emergency room, she was treated by Owen. Owen correctly told Anita that she needed immediate surgery. During the operation, Owen negligently severed one of Anita's arteries, and she bled to death. Anita's estate has filed a wrongful death action against Owen and Best Care for damages resulting from Owen's negligence.

1. Is Owen an independent contractor or servant (employee) of Best Care? Explain.
2. Is Best Care liable to Vision for breach of contract? Explain.

Assuming Owen is an independent contractor, is Best Care liable to Anita's estate for Owen's negligence? Explain.

5. For many years, Ruth owned and operated a restaurant as a sole proprietorship doing business as (d/b/a) Ruth's Family Restaurant. In 2001, Ruth sold the assets of the restaurant to Scott. Ruth and Scott agreed that: (1) the restaurant would operate under the name "Ruth's Family Restaurant"; (2) Ruth would manage the restaurant for Scott but would have no ownership interest in the restaurant; (3) all necessary licenses would remain in Ruth's name; and (4) Ruth would hire all employees, but only on an at-will basis (as is customary in the restaurant business). No one other than Ruth and Scott was aware that Scott had bought the restaurant.

Prior to Scott's purchase of the restaurant, Ruth had purchased supplies from Wholesale Restaurant Supply Co. (Wholesale), always signing the contracts as "Ruth, d/b/a Ruth's Family Restaurant." Following Scott's purchase of the restaurant, Scott instructed Ruth in very clear terms not to make any purchases of restaurant supplies from Wholesale in the future. Ruth complied with this instruction for the next several months.

In 2003, Ruth hired Nora, her niece, as assistant manager of the restaurant under a written employment contract for a 20-year term. Ruth signed the contract as "Ruth, d/b/a Ruth's Family Restaurant."

Soon after Nora was hired, she pointed out to Ruth that Wholesale's prices were generally less than those of the other local supply company. Despite Scott's clear prohibition, Ruth resumed buying supplies from Wholesale, again signing all contracts as "Ruth, d/b/a Ruth's Family Restaurant."

When Scott discovered what Ruth had done, Scott took over management of the restaurant, discharged Nora and Ruth, and refused to pay thousands of dollars of invoices from Wholesale for restaurant supplies delivered to the restaurant.

Wholesale has sued Scott to recover on the outstanding invoices. Nora has sued Scott for breach of the employment contract.

Under agency law:

1. Is Scott liable to Wholesale? Explain.
2. Is Scott liable to Nora? Explain.

MBE:[1] The Multiple Choice Portion of the Bar Exam

INTRODUCTION

If we have heard it once, we have heard it 1000 times. "I am really good at essays, but I suck at multiple choice." For the record, and this book shall be the record, if you can read, process, and analyze an essay question, you can do a multiple-choice question. Dare we say, you can even get multiple-choice questions correct!

The MBE section is the multiple-choice section of the bar exam. It consists of 200 multiple-choice questions and is taken over the course of one day — three hours in the morning and three hours in the afternoon for a total of six hours. That amounts to 1.8 minutes per question. The MBE questions are distributed among the following seven subjects: Torts, Contracts, Criminal Law, Criminal Procedure, Evidence, Federal Civil Procedure, and Constitutional Law. Like the other portions of the bar exam, the MEE essay section and MPT section, it pays to fit plenty of practice into your schedule. Chapter 4 shows you how to incorporate daily multiple-choice practice into your weekly schedule.

---

1. All MBE references and materials are printed here pursuant to a licensing agreement with the National Conference of Bar Examiners. (NCBE). Certain publicly disclosed questions and answers from past MBE examinations have been included herein with the permission of the NCBE, the copyright owner. These questions and answers are the only actual MBE questions and answers (as may have been modified with the NCBE's permission) included in this textbook authors' materials. Permission to use NCBE's questions does not constitute an endorsement by NCBE or otherwise signify that NCBE has reviewed or approved any aspect of these materials or the company or individuals who distribute these materials.

The MBE is a 200-question multiple-choice examination that is administered in two three-hour sessions. It is administered by user jurisdictions as part of the bar examination administered twice per year. Areas of law covered on the MBE include the following: Civil Procedure, Constitutional Law, Contracts, Criminal Law and Procedure, Evidence, Real Property, and Torts.

A. CRITICAL PREVIEWING

One of the first things you will need to do is figure out what MBE subject the question is covering. Then you will ascertain the specific subject topic the question is addressing. Discovering which subject matter is being tested is an important first step. Just as you learned in Chapter 6 regarding MEE essays, knowing what subject or subject topic you are being tested on can help you to retrieve the necessary rules and analysis from your memory. Reading the call of the question will typically give you the information you need.

FIGURE 7-2

Multiple Choice Question

A state law provides that a person who has been divorced may not marry again unless he or she is current on all child-support payments. A woman who was refused a marriage license pursuant to this law sued the appropriate state officials.

What standard should the court apply in reviewing the constitutionality of this law?

Multiple-choice questions on the seven MBE subjects will be mixed and will not have labels.

Question call specifically mentions review and constitutionality, which should give a pretty strong clue that this is a constitutional law MC question – subject being tested.

The word "reviewing" also lets you know that judicial scrutiny may be at issue here – specific subject topic.

By reading the question call first, you know all of this before reading the question in full.

B. ORGANIZING ACTIVITY

After you read the call of the question, go back to the beginning and read the entire question. Remember that you may know what subject or subject topic you are being tested on at this point. That means you can easily push out of your mind the other six MBE subjects and think of law and analyses associated with the subject at hand while reading the question.

1. IRAC Processing

The reason you can correctly work a multiple-choice question if you can work an essay question is because it involves the same IRAC processing. The only difference between working an essay and working a multiple-choice question is that you will process faster and you will not have to write your answer out in narrative prose form. As you read the fact pattern, you will pinpoint the issue. You will then think of the precise rule or rules that govern the scenario. After that, you will apply the rule(s) to the facts. Then, you will use this IRAC processing to determine an answer to the question posed in the question call.

Don't be overly concerned if you cannot complete every part of the IRAC processing. This will work for many questions, but for various reasons (question type, subject matter, your knowledge and understanding, etc.), determining the issue, rule, analysis, and answer may not always be possible. Don't abandon this second step in the three-step engagement process, however. If you cannot complete an IRAC outline, consider doing a looser IRAC brainstorm. In a brainstorm, you will just note the things that come to mind as you are reading the question. The brain storm does not have to be long and it doesn't even have to be "correct." But, the brainstorm exercise will help to process your thoughts regardless of what you write down. Whether your produce an outline or brainstorm, what you produce should help you to determine the answer and navigate the answer choices.

BOX NOTE 7-1

Where Do I Record This IRAC Processing?

Depending on your jurisdiction, you may be provided scratch paper for your multiple-choice work. In any event, you can jot down your IRAC processing in the margins of the test booklet as you read the question. You can also circle or underline relevant facts.

BOX NOTE 7-2

I Don't Have Time for IRAC Processing

It is true that you only have 1.8 minutes per question. But, if you practice this strategy, you will become adept at it and it will become intuitive to you such that you will be able to execute it much more quickly.

BOX NOTE 7-3

Clues in the Question Calls

When reading the call of the question, note certain words that may help you discern between answer choices.

For instance, if the question call says, "under the UCC," you likely will have a common law answer in the answer choices. Being cognizant of what you are being asked will help you to resist the answer choices that are meant to capitalize on rushed and hurried reading.

---

2. DO YOU SEE YOUR ANSWER IN THE ANSWER CHOICES?

Once you have completed the IRAC processing, you should have an answer. If you do not have an answer, you still have generated information that should help you navigate the answer choices. If your answer is similar to one of the answer choices, that is the answer choice you should select. But you are not done. You still must read the other answer choices and discount them (i.e., say why they should not be chosen). If you do not see your answer in the choices or do not have an answer before going into the answer choices, read the call of the question again, then go through each answer choice determining whether it is the best answer choice in light of the call of the question.

Perform a true/false analysis on each answer choice even if you see your answer in the answer choices. Try to eliminate some of the answer choices by performing a true/false analysis on them in light of the call of the question. This means you should treat each option as a "true or false" question and, given what the call of the question has asked, try and work out which of the answers would be "false" and eliminate those answers. Then work up from there until you get to the most "true" answer.

A. The state must show that the law is necessary to achieve a compelling government interest.
B. The state must show that the law is intentionally related to an important government interest.
C. The woman must show that the law serves no important public interest.
D. The woman must show that the legislature did not have a rational basis for enacting the law.

FIGURE 7-3

This question requires that you know what level of scrutiny to apply. If you approached the answer choices after IRAC processing with an answer that looked like answer choice A, you were correct. Don't stop. Perform the true/false analysis on the rest.

A is correct because the right to divorce is a fundamental right and claims involving fundamental rights receive strict scrutiny review requiring the state to show that the law is necessary to serve a compelling government interest. — *true*

B is incorrect because even though the facts involve a man and woman, the problem involves a fundamental rights issue and not a gender issue (which requires intermediate scrutiny). Watch out for distractors like this. — *true statement but not applied correctly to the facts*

C is incorrect because this is not a public purpose question and even if it were the state would have the burden. — *false*

D is incorrect because a plaintiff would not typically want a rational basis review (lowest form of scrutiny) and also the burden would be on the state. — *false*

C. REACHING YOUR GOAL — CHOOSING THE CORRECT ANSWER

The final step here is to reach your goal by choosing the correct multiple-choice answer. After you have followed the two steps listed above, you should be ready to take this final step. Don't become preoccupied with trying to learn the "trick" of a question when you are practicing. It is better to use your time memorizing the black letter law and practicing multiple-choice questions so you will be able to easily and accurately retrieve and apply the law most relevant for that question.

D. TIMING

Timing is crucial for the multiple-choice portion of the bar exam. You will answer 200 questions in six hours. That boils down to 1.8 minutes per question. But who can really count eight-tenths of a minute on a time piece? Not many of us can. That's why it is best to think of the time as an average. You want to average 1.8 minutes per question. As you practice multiple-choice questions, pick a standard number to work each day. Let's say you choose to do 25 questions at a time. That should take you 45 minutes to complete. You want to get in the habit of finishing 25 questions in 45 minutes which will average out to 1.8 minutes per question. Practicing questions in a specific time block will help you to set a rhythm for yourself and help you get used to completing questions in the appropriate time frame.

EXERCISE 7-1

Can I Use More Time Than What Is Allotted for a Certain Amount of Questions?

This is not advised.

Let's say you begin your multiple-choice exam at 9:00 am. At 9:00 am, you start on question #1. At 9:44, you see that you are only on question 22. You know you should be working question 25 at this point and readying yourself to move to question 26.

What should you do?

a. Keep working. You're only a few questions behind. You will catch up.
b. Keep working, but skip the questions. You will go back to them, if you have time left after completing the next set of 25 questions.
c. Skip questions 23-25 and start on question 26. You will return to the three skipped questions at the end of the exam.
d. Skip questions 23-25 but fill in a guess answers on the scantron sheet. Circle the skipped questions in the test booklet only. Come back to the skipped questions at the end of the exam if you have time.

The answer is d. If you made a timing error in one set of questions, don't let it bleed into the other sections. Isolate the timing error there. You may have had nervousness about the start of the test or that set may have had questions that were tough for you. Whatever the reason, skip the leftover questions in the set so that your timing error is not compounded. In other words, those extra minutes you used to complete all the questions in the set will grow. This is so because falling behind is likely to create anxiety as you will have that timing hiccup in your mind throughout the test. That is also why it is best not to go back to any missed questions until the very end of the exam.

E. CONCLUSION

Some students love multiple-choice because they feel they have a special knack for this test form. Others don't like it because they feel they can't express themselves in answering these types of questions. Whatever the case may be, try not to distill multiple-choice work to tricks and gimmicks. The best way to conquer bar exam multiple-choice questions is to first, know the law. Then, develop a strategy for working through multiple-choice questions. The strategies described in this chapter should assist you in developing that strategy. Practice multiple-choice questions daily so that you get as many questions under your belt as possible. Wherever you start in terms of your ability, you will see improvement if you work questions consistently over the course of bar study.

CHAPTER 7 RECAP

▶ *CRITICAL PREVIEW*

Context Building/Critical Reading
Read the call of the question

▶ *ORGANIZING ACTIVITY*

Understanding Material to Build a Knowledge Base
IRAC processing
Outlining
Brainstorming

▶ *REACHING THE GOAL*

Choosing the Correct Answer
Perform true/false analysis on each answer choice

SELECTED MBE QUESTIONS

Disclaimer: Certain publicly disclosed questions and answers from past MBE examinations have been included herein with the permission of the NCBE, the copyright owner. These questions and answers are the only actual MBE questions and answers (as may have been modified with the NCBE's permission) included in this textbook authors' materials. Permission to use NCBE's questions does not constitute an endorsement by NCBE or otherwise signify that NCBE has reviewed or approved any aspect of these materials or the company or individuals who distribute these materials.

TORTS MBE QUESTIONS

1. A mother and her six-year-old child were on a walk when the mother stopped to talk with an elderly neighbor. Because the child resented having his mother's attention diverted by the neighbor, the child angrily threw himself against the neighbor and knocked her to the ground. The neighbor suffered a broken wrist as a result of the fall.

   In an action for battery by the neighbor against the child, what is the strongest argument for liability?

   (A) The child intended to throw himself against the neighbor.
   (B) The child was old enough to appreciate that causing a fall could inflict serious injury.
   (C) The child was old enough to appreciate the riskiness of his conduct.
   (D) The child was not justified in his anger.

2. A man tied his dog to a bike rack in front of a store and left the dog there while he went inside to shop. The dog was usually friendly and placid.

   A five-year-old child started to tease the dog by pulling gently on its ears and tail. When the man emerged from the store and saw what the child was doing to the dog, he became extremely upset.

   Does the man have a viable claim against the child for trespass to chattels?

   (A) No, because the child did not injure the dog.
   (B) No, because the child was too young to form the requisite intent.
   (C) Yes, because the child touched the dog without the man's consent.
   (D) Yes, because the child's acts caused the man extreme distress.

3. An assistant to a famous writer surreptitiously observed the writer as the writer typed her private password into her personal computer in order to access her email. On several subsequent occasions in the writer's absence, the assistant read the writer's email messages and printed out selections from them.

   The assistant later quit his job and earned a considerable amount of money by leaking information to the media that he had learned from reading the writer's email messages. All of the information published about the writer as a result of the assistant's conduct was true and concerned matters of public interest.

   The writer's secretary had seen the assistant reading the writer's emails and printing out selections, and she has told the writer what she saw. The writer now wishes to sue the assistant for damages. At trial, the writer can show that the media leaks could have come only from someone reading her email on her personal computer.

Can the writer recover damages from the assistant?

(A) No, because the assistant was an invitee on the premises.

(B) No, because the published information resulting from the assistant's conduct was true and concerned matters of public interest.

(C) Yes, because the assistant invaded the writer's privacy.

(D) Yes, because the published information resulting from the assistant's conduct constituted publication of private facts concerning the writer.

4. Unaware that a lawyer was in the county courthouse library late on a Friday afternoon, when it was unusual for anyone to be using the library, a clerk locked the library door and left. The lawyer found herself locked in when she tried to leave the library at 7 p.m. It was midnight before the lawyer's family could find out where she was and get her out. The lawyer was very annoyed by her detention but was not otherwise harmed by it.

Does the lawyer have a viable claim for false imprisonment against the clerk?

(A) No, because it was unusual for anyone to be using the library late on a Friday afternoon.

(B) No, because the clerk did not intend to confine the lawyer.

(C) Yes, because the clerk should have checked to make sure no one was in the library before the clerk locked the door.

(D) Yes, because the lawyer was aware of being confined.

5. A woman signed up for a bowling class. Before allowing the woman to bowl, the instructor required her to sign a waiver explicitly stating that she assumed all risk of injuries that she might suffer in connection with the class, including injuries due to negligence or any other fault. After she signed the waiver, the woman was injured when the instructor negligently dropped a bowling ball on the woman's foot.

The woman brought a negligence action against the instructor. The instructor has filed a motion for summary judgment based on the waiver.

What is the woman's best argument in opposition to the instructor's motion?

(A) Bowling is an inherently dangerous activity.

(B) In circumstances like these, it is against public policy to enforce agreements that insulate people from the consequences of their own negligence.

(C) It was unreasonable to require the woman to sign the waiver before she was allowed to bowl.

(D) When she signed the form, the woman could not foresee that the instructor would drop a bowling ball on her foot.

6. A boater, caught in a sudden storm and reasonably fearing that her boat would capsize, drove the boat up to a pier, exited the boat, and tied the boat to the pier. The pier was clearly marked with "NO TRESPASSING" signs. The owner of the pier ran up to the boater and told her that the boat could not remain tied to the pier. The boater offered to pay the owner for the use of the pier. Regardless, over the boater's protest, the owner untied the boat and pushed it away from the pier. The boat was lost at sea.

Is the boater likely to prevail in an action against the owner to recover the value of the boat?

(A) No, because the owner told the boater that she could not tie the boat to the pier.

(B) No, because there was a possibility that the boat would not be damaged by the storm.

(C) Yes, because the boater offered to pay the owner for the use of the pier.

(D) Yes, because the boater was privileged to enter the owner's property to save her boat.

CONTRACTS MBE QUESTIONS

1. A seller borrowed $5,000 from a bank. Soon thereafter the seller filed for bankruptcy, having paid nothing on his debt to the bank.

    Five years after the debt had been discharged in bankruptcy, the seller contracted to sell certain goods to a buyer for

    $5,000. The contract provided that the buyer would pay the $5,000 to the bank "as payment of the $5,000 the seller owes the bank." The only debt that the seller ever owed the bank is the $5,000 debt that was discharged in bankruptcy. The seller delivered the goods to the buyer, who accepted them.

    If the bank becomes aware of the contract between the seller and the buyer, and the buyer refuses to pay anything to the bank, is the bank likely to succeed in an action against the buyer for $5,000?

    (A) No, because the buyer's promise to pay the bank was not supported by consideration.
    (B) No, because the seller's debt was discharged in bankruptcy.
    (C) Yes, because the bank was an intended beneficiary of the contract between the buyer and the seller.
    (D) Yes, because no consideration is required to support a promise to pay a debt that has been discharged in bankruptcy.

2. A man sent an email to a friend that stated: "Because you have been a great friend to me, I am going to give you a rare book that I own." The friend replied by an email that said: "Thanks for the rare book. I am going to give you my butterfly collection." The rare book was worth $10,000; the butterfly collection was worth $100. The friend delivered the butterfly collection to the man, but the man refused to deliver the book.

    If the friend sues the man to recover the value of the book, how should the court rule?

    (A) For the man, because there was no bargained-for exchange to support his promise.
    (B) For the man, because the consideration given for his promise was inadequate.
    (C) For the friend, because she gave the butterfly collection to the man in reliance on receiving the book.
    (D) For the friend, because she conferred a benefit on the man by delivering the butterfly collection.

3. A seller sent an email to a potential buyer, offering to sell his house to her for $150,000. The buyer immediately responded via email, asking whether the offer included the house's front porch swing. The seller emailed back: "No, it doesn't." The buyer then ordered a front porch swing and emailed back to the seller: "I accept your offer." The seller refused to sell the house to the buyer, claiming that the offer was no longer open.

    Is there a contract for the sale of the house?

    (A) No, because the buyer's initial email was a counteroffer.
    (B) No, because the offer lapsed before the buyer accepted.
    (C) Yes, because the buyer relied on the offer by ordering the swing.
    (D) Yes, because the buyer's initial email merely asked for information.

4. On June 15, a teacher accepted a contract for a one-year position teaching math at a public high school at a salary of $50,000, starting in September. On June 22, the school informed the teacher that, due to a change in its planned math curriculum, it no longer needed a full-time math teacher. The school offered instead to employ the teacher as a part-time academic counselor at a salary of $20,000, starting in September. The teacher refused the school's offer. On June 29, the teacher was offered a one-year position to teach math at a nearby private academy for $47,000, starting in September. The teacher, however, decided to spend the year completing work on a graduate degree in mathematics and declined the academy's offer.

    If the teacher sues the school for breach of contract, what is her most likely recovery?

    (A) $50,000, the full contract amount.
    (B) $30,000, the full contract amount less the amount the teacher could have earned in the counselor position offered by the school.
    (C) $3,000, the full contract amount less the amount the teacher could have earned in the teaching position at the academy.
    (D) Nothing, because the school notified the teacher of its decision before the teacher had acted in substantial reliance on the contract.

5. A buyer purchased a new car from a dealer under a written contract that provided that the price of the car was $20,000 and that the buyer would receive a "trade-in allowance of $7,000 for the buyer's old car." The old car had recently been damaged in an accident. The contract contained a merger clause stating: "This writing constitutes the entire agreement of the parties, and there are no other understandings or agreements not set forth herein." When the buyer took possession of the new car, she delivered

the old car to the dealer. At that time, the dealer claimed that the trade-in allowance included an assignment of the buyer's claim against her insurance company for damage to the old car. The buyer refused to provide the assignment.

The dealer sued the buyer to recover the insurance payment. The dealer has offered evidence that the parties agreed during their negotiations for the new car that the dealer was entitled to the insurance payment.

Should the court admit this evidence?

(A) No, because the dealer's acceptance of the old car bars any additional claim by the dealer.
(B) No, because the merger clause bars any evidence of the parties' prior discussions concerning the trade-in allowance.
(C) Yes, because a merger clause does not bar evidence of fraud.
(D) Yes, because the merger clause does not bar evidence to explain what the parties meant by "trade-in allowance."

6. An art collector paid a gallery $1,000 to purchase a framed drawing from the gallery's collection. The price included shipping by the gallery to the collector's home. The gallery's owner used inadequate materials to wrap the drawing. The frame broke during shipment and scratched the drawing, reducing the drawing's value to $300. The collector complained to the gallery owner, who told the collector to take the drawing to a specific art restorer to have the drawing repaired. The collector paid the restorer $400 to repair the drawing, but not all of the scratches could be fixed. The drawing, after being repaired, was worth $700. The gallery owner subsequently refused to pay either for the repairs or for the damage to the drawing.

In an action by the collector against the gallery owner for damages, which of the following awards is most likely?

(A) Nothing.
(B) $300.
(C) $400.
(D) $700.

CIVIL PROCEDURE MBE QUESTIONS

1. A retailer brought a federal diversity action against a wholesaler, alleging breach of contract and fraudulent misrepresentation. After the parties presented their evidence at trial, the court instructed the jury on the law. Neither party filed a motion for judgment as a matter of law before the case went to the jury. The jury found for the retailer on both claims. After the court entered judgment on the verdict, the wholesaler moved for a new trial and for judgment as a matter of law, arguing that the evidence was insufficient to support the jury verdict on either claim. The court acknowledged that there had been problems with some of the evidence, but it denied the motions. The wholesaler appealed, challenging the sufficiency of the evidence.

   Should the appellate court consider the wholesaler's challenge?

   (A) No, because a determination of the sufficiency of the evidence is solely within the jury's province.

   (B) No, because the wholesaler did not raise the sufficiency-of-the-evidence issue in a motion for judgment as a matter of law before the case went to the jury.

   (C) Yes, because the challenge was raised and ruled on by the trial court before the wholesaler filed the appeal.

   (D) Yes, because, as the trial court acknowledged, the wholesaler has strong arguments on the challenge.

2. A small commercial airplane crashed in State A. The passengers and pilot, all citizens of State B, were killed in the crash. The airline that owned and operated the airplane is incorporated and has its maintenance facilities and principal place of business in State C. One day before the statute of limitations on their claims would have run, the estates of the pilot and each of the passengers filed a wrongful death action against the airline in federal court in State A. The airline was served one week later and wants to prevent the State A federal court from hearing the action.

   Which of the following motions is most likely to accomplish the airline's goal?

   (A) A motion to dismiss the action for improper venue.

   (B) A motion to dismiss the action for lack of personal jurisdiction.

   (C) A motion to dismiss the action under the doctrine of forum non conveniens.

   (D) A motion to transfer the action to a federal court in State C.

3. A shop owner domiciled in State A sued a distributor in a federal district court in State A for breach of a contract. The shop owner sought $100,000 in damages for allegedly defective goods that the distributor had provided under the contract. The distributor is incorporated in State B, with its principal place of business in State C. The distributor brought in as a third-party defendant the wholesaler that had provided the goods to the distributor, alleging that the wholesaler had a duty to indemnify the distributor for any damages recovered by the shop owner. The wholesaler is incorporated in State B, with its principal place of business in State A. The wholesaler has asserted a $60,000 counterclaim against the distributor for payment for the goods at issue, and the distributor has moved to dismiss the counterclaim for lack of subject-matter jurisdiction.

Should the motion to dismiss be granted?

(A) No, because the wholesaler's and the distributor's principal places of business are diverse.
(B) No, because there is supplemental jurisdiction over the wholesaler's counterclaim.
(C) Yes, because there is no diversity of citizenship between the distributor and the wholesaler.
   Yes, because there is no diversity of citizenship between the shop owner and the wholesaler.
(D) Yes, because there is no diversity of citizenship between the shop owner and the wholesaler.

4. A woman sued her former employer in state court, asserting age and sex discrimination claims under both state and federal law. The woman's attorney had recently been embarrassed in court by the judge to whom the case was assigned. Wishing to avoid difficulties with the judge, the woman's attorney promptly removed the case to federal court on the basis of federal-question jurisdiction. The employer's attorney has timely moved to remand.

How is the federal court likely to proceed?

(A) Remand the entire case.
(B) Remand the state claims but keep the federal claims.
(C) Retain the case to avoid the risk of bias and impropriety in having it proceed before a judge who has shown clear hostility toward the woman's attorney.
(D) Retain the case, because it was timely removed and the woman alleges federal claims.

5. A plaintiff domiciled in State A brought a wrongful death action in a federal court in State A against a State B parent corporation and one of its foreign subsidiaries. The plaintiff alleged that a tire manufactured by the subsidiary in Europe had caused his wife's death in an automobile accident in Europe. The parent corporation does significant business throughout the United States, including in State A. The subsidiary conducts no business and has no employees or bank accounts in State A. The subsidiary manufactures its tires for the European market, but 2% of its tires are distributed in State A by the parent corporation. The subsidiary has moved to dismiss for lack of personal jurisdiction.

    Should the court grant the subsidiary's motion?

    (A) No, because 2% of the subsidiary's tires entered State A through the stream of commerce.
    (B) No, because of the general personal jurisdiction established over the parent corporation.
    (C) Yes, because the accident did not occur in the United States.
    (D) Yes, because the subsidiary lacks continuous, systematic, and substantial contacts with State A.

6. A patient domiciled in State A sued a surgeon domiciled in State B in a federal court in State A, alleging claims for malpractice. The surgeon moved to dismiss the action for lack of personal jurisdiction. The court denied the motion and set discovery cutoff and trial dates. The surgeon has appealed the denial of the motion.

    Should the appellate court hear the merits of the surgeon's appeal?

    (A) No, because the appellate court lacks jurisdiction over the appeal.
    (B) No, because the district court's decision on jurisdiction is final.
    (C) Yes, because a contrary appellate decision could terminate the action.
    (D) Yes, because the surgeon's personal- jurisdiction challenge raises a constitutional question.

Final Study Days: A Macro Organizing Exercise

INTRODUCTION

At some point in your bar study, typically about 10 to 14 days before the bar exam, your commercial bar course lectures and structured guided activities will end. There will be no class to report to or video to watch. You may still have assignments, but the strict structure you will have experienced during your bar study period will be gone. Thus, it is incumbent upon you to build a routine or structure for those final study days – one that will give you the push you need to be successful on the bar exam. So how should you organize your time during this period? What should your focus be in the final days before the bar exam? Let's use the three engagement steps to explore this question.

Up to this point, you have carefully considered the bar exam study process through the three engagement steps—critically previewing, organizing activity, and reaching a goal or producing the product in the context of each bar exam testing format. You began your overall critical review process in Chapter 1 where you learned about the bar exam and the three-step process generally. Chapter 2 continued your critical preview process by guiding you through a review of your life situation and how its different components—personal, professional, and financial—could impact your bar study. You also reviewed your study skills and how those would affect your bar study. Chapter 3 helped you to continue your critical preview process by previewing a specific approach to bar study through the three engagement steps.

Once you critically previewed all aspects of bar study, Chapter 4 introduced you to your first overall organizing activity—scheduling. There, you learned not just

Fewer Topics and Scheduling Travel

Note that the number of days you have left after completing all your commercial bar course lectures will depend on your jurisdiction. Uniform Bar Exam (UBE) jurisdictions will have more time left because UBEs typically test fewer topics than jurisdictions which test state law.

In any event, as you make your final days' study schedule, don't forget to schedule time within those final days for travel to your bar exam test site, particularly if you live a significant distance away.

BOX NOTE 8-1

Reconciling My Commercial Bar Course Schedule

Your commercial bar course will guide your study from start to finish. The commercial course will provide day-to-day instructions as to how you should approach bar study. You have your own schedule and understand the schedule categories so that you may supplement or change that general commercial schedule according to your needs. See Box Note 4-2 for a reminder as to how to use the commercial course schedule. Whichever schedule or combination you use, you will have to adjust it to account for the last days of bar study. To prepare for these final days, check your commercial course schedule so that you are clear when the bar course subject lectures end.

about the different parts of bar study, but also how those parts should be incorporated into a daily scheduled routine that puts you on the path to reaching your goal of passing the bar exam. These organizing activities continued in Chapters 5 through 7 which introduced each bar exam testing form and how the three-step engagement process could be used on a micro basis for each of them—the multistate performance test, essays and multiple-choice questions.

In this chapter, you will learn about your final bar study organizing activity. This last organizing activity is a macro step that encourages you to squarely focus on reviewing each bar exam subject that you may be tested on while taking the bar exam. In reviewing each subject, you will also review your bar exam test taking skills. Don't forget the final step in the three-step engagement process—reaching the goal of producing the product expected by the bar examiners. Consider this last step of determining a final days' schedule a necessary activity in getting you to that point.

A. WHAT SHOULD I DO DURING MY FINAL DAYS OF BAR STUDY?

You should review every bar study subject. You should also continue to work bar exam questions. In many jurisdictions, the final days of bar study will be the last 10 to 14 days before the bar exam. The time seems short and the exercise of reviewing every bar tested subject and continuing to strengthen your test-taking skills daunting.

Just as you may initially have doubted your ability to learn and process 20 or more subjects, work bar questions, and memorize rules during a two-month period, you may have similar feelings again as you plan your final days of study. But remember, at this stage you will not be a bar exam study novice. Just as your coursework throughout law school helped to prime you for bar study, those six or more weeks you will have spent assimilating the substance and sharpening your skills will make you ready for this last bar study organizing activity.

In addition, your assessment of each bar tested subject regarding your strengths and weaknesses will provide you with valuable information as to how much time to spend reviewing each subject during your final study days. You will get through every subject because you will not spend equal time on every subject during this period. This is the final step in readying yourself for the bar exam. The following sections will guide you through the process of assessing your strengths and building a schedule that accurately reflects the right focus for you during your final bar study days.

1. Assessment Categories – There, Almost There, Nowhere

As we end a study period for any type of test, most of us will automatically look at what we've studied and attempt to determine how ready we are to be tested on it. Your thoughts might range anywhere from *I hope I don't get a question on this* to *If I just had two more days to study this subject* to *I wish the whole test could be on this topic because then I would pass for sure*. While these seem like useless meanderings, they can be very helpful to you in building a final days' study schedule. When you are putting together your final days' schedule, assess each bar tested subject in the following terms—*There, Almost There* and *Nowhere*. Assess each subject individually by asking yourself where you are with it. For instance, "For Contracts, am I *There, Almost There* or *Nowhere* with it?"

a. Assess Your Strengths Regarding Each Bar Study Topic

Are you There? If the bar exam was tomorrow, you'd feel confident about the subject and your ability to test well in it. If that accurately describes your feeling regarding a bar subject, then yes, you are *There*! You don't have to be perfect to be *There*. But, the general feeling should be that you understand the subject and feel good about being able to answer a question on it. You will review the material on this topic, but your review can be relatively short as you do not have much to do to be ready to be tested on it. Consider some or all the following as you work to finalize your study on your *There* subjects:

- *Continue to work questions and read the answers.* You want to confirm that your initial assessment is correct. As you work the questions, note whether you are correctly issue spotting and determining the appropriate rule for those issues. In other words, confirm your ability to see facts and determine the appropriate rule and analysis associated with those facts. Make sure you can execute this within the appropriate time allotment.
- *Review your processing product or lecture notes.* Review your processing product or lecture notes and confirm your memorization of the law for each subject and the pattern or structure of analysis related to each topic within the subject.

Are you Almost There? Yes, if you understand the subject, but there are a few aspects of it that you are still having difficulty assimilating. Maybe you keep forgetting a rule, its exception or nuance, or how to apply the rule. Perhaps you frequently mix up scenarios and their applicable rules. Even so, you believe you can remedy these issues. You see the light at the end of the tunnel on this subject and just need to hone in on a few aspects related to it to make you ready for any question on it. You might engage in some or all of the following as you review your *Almost There* subjects.

- *Review as many essay questions as you can.* You should work as many essays as possible. Your study schedule will have already incorporated daily essay work. Thus, you should already have many essays under your belt at this point. But, keep writing. You may not be able to write out every essay. Consider outlining your answer, reverse outlining the question, or reading the essays (and accompanying answers) you cannot write out in long form. See Chapter 6 on *Essays* for a review of the many ways you can "work" essay questions.
- *Continue to work multiple-choice questions.* Even if you have devoted your day of study to a subject that is not tested in the multiple-choice format, schedule multiple-choice work for one of your multiple-choice *Almost There* subjects. Doing multiple-choice questions and reading the answers for those questions will strengthen your grasp of the subject matter as well as provide practice in the skills associated with this test form.
- *Review your processing product or lecture notes.* Review your processing product or lecture notes and confirm your memorization of the law for each subject and the pattern or structure of analysis related to each topic within a subject.

Are you Nowhere? You do not feel confident on the subject at all because there are several aspects you do not understand or are unsure as to how to apply. If you are *Nowhere* on a subject, you may consider some or all of the following:

- *Re-evaluate your processing product.* Perhaps creating flashcards, flowcharts, or tables for the trouble areas may help you to assimilate those topics within your subject that are giving you difficulty. This is especially true if you initially chose a different processing product. Be careful here. You may not need to reprocess the entire subject. Rather, you may just need to "do something different" for the specific subject topics causing you to feel you are *Nowhere* on the subject.
- *Memorize the law.* If you are having trouble remembering the law, re-evaluating your processing product as mentioned above could help. But, also consider whether you know the law well enough. Ask yourself if you know it and have memorized it such that you can correctly spot issues and answer questions regarding that law. In addition, consider active memorization techniques such as mnemonics and acronyms if you are having difficulty remembering the law. Review Chapter 3 on *Active Memorization*.
- *Make sure you are clear on the pattern and structure of analysis associated with each subject topic.* Review as many essay questions as you can. Even if you know the law and have it memorized, you still have to know how to apply it. You still have to know the pattern and structure of analysis for every subject and topic within that subject. If you feel you are *Nowhere* because you cannot marshal

the information to write an answer to a question, get as many looks at the questions as possible. This will give you clear examples of how the law is applied. You will begin to see a pattern amongst the facts, rules, and analysis—one you can note, study, and memorize. While you should continue to work questions by writing them out, you might advance your performance by reviewing as many essay questions on the subject or specific subject topic as possible by outlining the question and answer, reverse outlining the question and answer, or reading the essay and its answer. See Chapter 6 on *Essays* for a review of the many ways you can "work" essay questions.

- *Continue to work multiple-choice questions.* Even if you have devoted your day of study to a subject that is not tested in the multiple-choice format, schedule multiple-choice work for one of your multiple-choice *Nowhere* subjects. Doing multiple-choice questions and reading the answers for those questions will strengthen your grasp of the subject matter as well as provide practice in the skills associated with this test form.

b. Be True in Your Assessment – Honesty Really Is the Best Policy

When performing your assessment, be brutally honest with yourself on both sides. The final days' study period will give you yet another opportunity to review *all* potentially bar tested subjects. But you will not be able to spend equal time on every subject. You must adjust the time depending on the outcome of your assessment. This is why your honest assessment of your position on each subject is crucial.

You must not be afraid to admit that you are *Nowhere* on a topic. It may be very hard to admit, 10 to 14 days before the bar exam, that you are *Nowhere* on a subject. But remember the context. You will have spent roughly six weeks working on numerous topics and honing your skills with respect to those topics. Being *Nowhere* does not mean you do not know the topic or need to start from the beginning on it. It may mean that you are not confident because there are still several topics within that subject you do not feel confident about. That can be remedied. If you use the time correctly, you can move that *Nowhere* assessment to *Almost There* and eventually *There*. Your honest assessment will indicate to you clearly the amount of work you have left in assimilating the topic so you can be ready for any question on it.

Similarly, you must not be afraid to declare yourself *There* on a subject. Being *There* does not mean perfection. Rather, it means you feel confident about all of that subject's topics and their analytic patterns and structures. You may still need to work to bring it all together, but your expectation is that it will come together with relatively little time. This assessment

> **BOX NOTE 8-2**
>
> ### *How Many Topics Should I Expect Under Each Assessment Category?*
>
> For most students, the majority of subjects will fall in the "Almost There" pile with a few subjects falling in the other piles. But, remember that this is about truth — on both ends. Be honest as to what you feel ready for and what you don't. In this way, you'll make the final schedule that is right for you.

category is critical because you do not want to overspend time on a subject you have already assimilated. That time is better spent on *Almost There* and *Nowhere* subjects. We know it's tempting to keep studying your *There* subjects because your knowledge, recall, and ability to nail questions on these subjects, will validate you—especially at the final days stage of your bar study. But, remember that just as no one bar question is an island, no one subject is either. All the potentially tested subjects are opportunities to earn points on the bar exam. Thus, you want to be knowledgeable about them all. Create a final days' schedule that gives you the best chance to achieve that.

2. Now That I Know Where I Stand on Each Topic, How Should I Build My Final Days' Schedule?

Remember that you will go over everything in this period. The *There, Almost There, Nowhere* assessment categories are meant to help you determine how much time to allot to each subject during your final days' study plan—not whether to review the subjects at all. Consider an assessment that looks like the one in Figure 8-2 below.

Once you have made your assessment, determine how you will schedule your final days' study. Think about what you will need to do to be ready for the bar exam on that subject (i.e., how much time do you need to go from *Nowhere* to *There* or from *Almost There* to *There* or even from *There* to "I could answer a question right now, at this very second with complete confidence."). You might also fall somewhere between or slightly askew of the assessment categories. For example, when describing your position regarding Secured Transactions, you might say that you are not quite *Almost There* as you have a lot of work to do to assimilate it. However, you may feel that it is a mischaracterization to say you are *Nowhere* with the subject.

FIGURE 8-2   EXAMPLE OF FINAL DAYS' ASSESSMENT

There	Almost There	Nowhere
Conflicts of Law	Property	Trusts
Torts	Federal Civil Procedure	Corporations
Evidence	Contracts	Family Law
	Criminal Law and Procedure	
	Constitutional Law	
	Secured Transactions	
	Wills	
	Corporations	

How you approach studying when you have a mixture of subjects or subject topics that you are in different stages of assimilating will also determine how you schedule.

a. Scheduling Your Subjects According to Assessment Category

Nowhere Subjects. Depending on how you approach the subject, you may want to work on your *Nowhere* subjects as early as possible in the final days' study period. This may give you comfort that you are making progress on some of your most difficult subjects as the bar exam draws near. Be generous in allotting your time for *Nowhere* subjects. Consider whether your *Nowhere* subjects deserve a portion of the day or the entire day. You may potentially have a number of tasks to complete to move up on the assessment spectrum. You want to make sure you have allotted enough time to make adequate progress.

Almost There Subjects. You might review two of the *Almost There* subjects in one day depending on where you fall on the spectrum. Remember that these subjects are the ones you feel reasonably good about assimilating because you only have a few topics under each subject to work on. Even so, because of the sheer amount of material,
some of these subjects may require an entire day to review. You may have varying tasks to complete to move up on the assessment spectrum depending on the subject or subject topic. Also, don't forget that most subjects will fall under the *Almost There* assessment category.

There Subjects You could do all of the *There* subjects on one day if you feel really secure about them. Consider whether for you, it helps to review them at the beginning or end of the final days' study period. If having a sense of accomplishment helps to motivate you, tackle your *There* subjects at the beginning of the final days' study period or space them out by pairing them with an *Almost There* subject.

See Figure 8-4 for a sample schedule based on the assessment in Figure 8-2.

> **BOX NOTE 8-3**
>
> ***Can I reassess?***
>
> You can and you should reassess as you work through the subjects during your final days' study period. You will definitely improve as you spend concentrated time on each subject. You may also determine that the time you set for the subject was not enough or too much. You want to see your assessment move on the spectrum. If you were *Nowhere*, you want to see yourself moving to *Almost There* and eventually *There* on a subject. Continual assessment will allow you to determine how much time and work you need to continue to invest in the particular topic to see improvement.

FIGURE 8-3

DAY/TIME	NOWHERE			ALMOST THERE					THERE	
	1 Trusts	2 Corps	3 Fam Law	4 Contracts Sec Tran	5 Con Law Fed Civ Pro	6 Wills	7 Prop	8 Crim Law/Pro	9 Conflicts Torts	10 Evidence
Morning 8:00–11:00	Create mnemonics/ Memorize	Flowchart trouble topics	Flash Card different trouble spots	Review Sec Tran trouble spots, Check overall memorization Write/review Sec Tran essay questions	Review Con Law trouble spots, Check overall memorization Write/review Con Law essay questions	Work MPT (use morning to simulate two MPTs if two will be given during bar exam) Review trouble spots if not doing two MPTs	Work MPT Review trouble spots	Review trouble spots, Check overall memorization Write/review Crim Law/ Pro essay questions	Check Conflicts memorization/ do Conflicts questions	Check Evidence memorization/ do Evidence questions
Lunch Break 12:00–1:00										
Afternoon 1:00 – 5:00	Write or review every Trust question in the essay book	Write or review every Corps question in the essay book	Write or review every question Fam Law question in essay book	Review Contracts trouble spots, Check overall memorization Write/review Contracts essay questions	Review Fed Civ Pro trouble spots, Check overall memorization Write/review Fed Civ Pro essay questions	Check overall memorization Write/review Wills essay questions	Check overall memorization Write/review Prop essay questions	Write/review Crim Law/ Pro essay questions	Check Torts memorization and write or review every Torts question is essay book	Write or review Evidence essay questions

NOWHERE				ALMOST THERE					THERE	
DAY/TIME	1 Trusts	2 Corps	3 Fam Law	4 Contracts Sec Tran	5 Con Law Fed Civ Pro	6 Wills	7 Prop	8 Crim Law/Pro	9 Conflicts Torts	10 Evidence
Dinner Break 5:00–7:00										
Evening 7:00–12:00	Finalize memorization Write and review questions Preview Corps Work MC	Finalize memorization Write and review questions Preview Fam Law Work MC	Finalize memorization Write and review questions Review Trusts, Corps and Fam Law Work MC	Finalize memorization Ks and Sec Tran Work MC	Finalize memorization Con Law and Fed Civ Pro Work MC	Finalize Wills memorizatoin Work MC	Finalize memorization Property Work MC	Finalize Crim Law/Pro memorization Work MC Review any previous topics you may still have issues with Reassess your Nowhere and Almost There subjects. Have they moved?	Finalize Conflicts & Torts memorization Work MC Preview Evidence	Finalize Evidence memorization Work MC Review any topics subjects you may still have issues with

b. When Can I Stop Studying for the Bar Exam?

When you bring your bar study to an end depends on a variety of factors related to your sense of readiness. It can also depend on practical matters such as travel. The truth is that bar study never really feels like it's over. There is always something you could use more time on. Ultimately, you should assess your own personal situation and decide when you will stop studying. Below, we offer a bit of advice to help you make that decision.

Perhaps you will begin to wind down on the Sunday afternoon before the last Tuesday and Wednesday in February or July (which is when the bar exam is typically held). If you have to travel and plan to do so on the Sunday before your bar exam, concluding your principal study just before travel begins will leave time for comfortable travel to your bar exam testing site and your hotel. It will also give you a regular week day (Monday) to do a dry run of getting to the testing site on time from your hotel. If you live in the same city as your testing site, you might end late Sunday evening. This would still give you time to do a dry run of getting to the testing site from your home. Even if you are familiar with the area, make sure you know the specific building and what part of it you must access for your exam.

You should determine what day and time are best for you to travel. When doing so, try to pick a day and time that will cause you the least amount of stress. Leave early to avoid traffic or to avoid feeling anxiety if traffic is just part of the drive. If you have to travel a long distance, bring your processing products, a recording, or questions to work while you are traveling. If you drive, you might record a few of your processing products so that you do not feel like you are off task.

It is not uncommon for students to review materials on the eve of the bar exam. If you are traveling a significant distance to the testing site and have to stay in the area overnight, we already know you will lug every commercial bar book and processing product you have with you. This is fine. Even though we do not recommend using every one of these materials on the eve of the bar exam, we know having everything with you will give you calm. We understand the urge to be sure that the information has not somehow left your brain. In any event, a good night's rest will serve you better than last minute studying. So, on the eve of the bar exam, put the study materials away. Do something easy like watching a funny sitcom. Turn in at a decent hour.

CONCLUSION

The end of your final days' schedule will mark the end of your bar study. It will also mark the conclusion of the overall organizing activity step in the three-step engagement process. The only thing left at this point is to demonstrate you have reached your goal by responding to each bar exam question in a way that will maximize your ability to earn points and pass the bar. Use the strategies described in this chapter as you push toward the finish line. The time and effort you put into this stage will get you that much closer to actualizing your ultimate goal of passing the bar.

CHAPTER 8 RECAP

▶ *CREATE A FINAL DAYS' SCHEDULE*

    A. Assess your strengths regarding each subject using the There, Almost There, and Nowhere categories.

    B. Use the results of that assessment to schedule the appropriate time to spend on each subject during the final days' study period.

    C. Determine when you will end your bar exam study.

    D. Don't forget to consider your travel to and from the bar exam testing site.

PART III

REACHING YOUR GOAL

EPILOGUE: Believe You Will Pass the Bar Exam

Believe You Will Pass the Bar

We want the Epilogue of this book to be a strong pep-talk, a loud cheer, and the last piece of sound advice we will offer you about your bar exam preparation. Many have painted bar study as a daunting and difficult exercise that will consume many hours, cause stress in your relationships (familial, platonic and romantic), and cost a heavy sum.[1] And we don't disagree that for some, this will be the case. We hope, however, that after reading the preceding chapters, you are already putting strategies in place to address these matters so you are ready to hit the ground running when your bar study period begins.

Remember that bar study can also be rewarding. *Wait! Don't shut this textbook. Hear us out!* The bar exam is your ticket to law practice; you can't do the latter without the former. Studying for the bar exam is not only about passing the test, it is also about taking the final, and very important step, to becoming a practicing lawyer. **So shift your thinking**. With each lecture you watch, set of lecture notes you process, question you work, or law you memorize, you are passing the bar. One subject at a time, one engagement step at a time, one day at a time, you are passing the bar. And with each step, you are moving closer and closer to becoming a practicing attorney.

YOU CAN DO THIS (PEP-TALK AND LOUD CHEER)

If you made it through three years (or more if you went part time) of law school, you can make it through the last approximately eight to ten weeks of study! Right now, you are reading a book about passing the bar. Right now, you are taking

---

1. Riebe, Denise, A Bar Review for Law Schools: Getting Students on Board to Pass Their Bar Exams 45 Brandeis L.J. 269, fn 2 (2006-2007).

your future into your own hands and doing what you need to do to pass the bar. You have read the chapters and practiced the strategies and techniques. You've reconnected with basic processing and analytical tenets. You've learned new ways of approaching testing. You know what critical previewing and organizing strategies will help you to reach your goal. You have a plan for ordering your study atmosphere and your personal life so you can achieve the hours of studying needed to pass the bar. When we say, you can do this, it is not just a platitude or pie in the sky. We know you can do this because of all you have done to be prepared for this. So, when we say, you can do this, we really mean that *YOU CAN DO THIS!*

YOU HAVE TO BELIEVE TOO (EMBRACE SELF-EFFICACY)

Another concept that students studying for the bar exam should embrace is the concept of self-efficacy. Self-efficacy is an individual's belief about his or her ability to accomplish goals. Students, who embrace self-efficacy, have a high perception of their own competency and control. Studies have shown that, when pursuing a task, students with high self-efficacy are significantly more likely to do the things necessary to succeed at that task.[2] They are also far more likely to persist in the face of adversity than are individuals with low self-efficacy in relation to that specific task.[3]

But how do you engender self-efficacy within yourself? One way is to follow the three-step engagement process set out for you in this text book. Following a method that allows you to create a system for absorbing, processing, and managing the material associated with bar exam study will increase your confidence in your abilities. That increased confidence, based on you executing your system of study, will lead to self-efficacy. Trust that your full engagement in the process and the confidence that comes with it is what will sustain your self-efficacy and push you through the challenging task of studying for a bar exam.

BE RESILIENT (HANDLING TOUGH TIMES)

Resilience is one of the most important skills to have when dealing with the stress associated with bar exam preparation. Resilience is loosely defined as a set of processes that enables good outcomes in spite of serious pressure.[4] Many

---

2. Bandura, A., Self-Efficacy: toward a unifying theory of behavioral change, Psychological review, 84 191-215 (1977).

3. *Id.*

4. Pavlova-Coleman, Tatiana I., "Law Students in Balance: A Proposal for a Well-being Course for Law School Students Founded on the Constructs and Findings of Positive Psychology" (2012). Master of Applied Positive Psychology (MAPP) Capstone Projects. 9:39.

psychologists believe that resilience is a behavior that can be learned.[5] Studies have shown that resilient people, generally, accept the harsh realities facing them, find meaning in terrible times, and have an uncanny ability to improvise, making do with whatever's at hand.[6]

Incorporate these characteristics into the thinking, processing, memorizing and overall studying you will do in your daily bar study life. This will help you handle any adversity that may come your way.

TAKE CARE OF YOUR SELF (YOU ARE THE WHOLE PACKAGE)

Becoming a confident learner imbued with self-efficacy and resilience is a step in the right direction and helps you get your head in the bar study game. But your head is attached to a body. Caring for the whole you is just as important as getting the right mindset.

There is no getting around the fact that the bar preparation period is a stressful time. Many studies have shown that when it's under stress, the body reacts.[7] But stress manifests differently in everyone. For some, it may be stomachaches, headaches, or insomnia. Some over-eat, some under-eat. Still others have a shortened fuse or experience symptoms of depression or anxiety.

Our best advice to you is to know yourself. Understand how stress manifests in you and do what you can to counteract that. Pre-make meals so there is no guesswork or stomachache-inducing ingredients. Create a relaxing haven in your bedroom so that it is quiet and peaceful with no study materials allowed at bedtime. Stick to a pre-set meal schedule so there is little chance of over- or under-eating.

Also engage in general "best practices" to help counteract the stress that is a natural outcropping of bar study. Think about meditation and mindfulness.[8] Both practices lead to a more settled you and can help reduce stress. Making a habit of using these techniques can help you on a daily basis as you go through bar exam preparations.

---

5. Seligman, M. E. P., Learned Optimism: How to Change Your Mind and Your Life. New York, NY: Knopf (1990).

6. Couto, Diane L., How Resilience Works, Harvard Business Review, May 2002.

7. Lin, Nan, et al. "Social Support, Stressful Life Events, and Illness: A Model and an Empirical Test." Journal of Health and Social Behavior, vol. 20, no. 2, 1979, pp. 108–119, JSTOR, www.jstor.org/stable/2136433.

8. Brantley J., Mindfulness-Based Stress Reduction. In: Orsillo S.M., Roemer L. (eds), Acceptance and Mindfulness-Based Approaches to Anxiety. Series in Anxiety and Related Disorders. Springer, Boston, MA. (2005).

Physical exercise is also a great stress reducer.[9] Studies have found that students who participate in some type of exercise report lower emotional distress and lower depression. Finding time to do some type of physical activity—and it doesn't have to be vigorous—provides improvement to health and well-being.[10] So make sure you make time to move during the course of your study day.

CONCLUSION

You have the academic tools and the mental tools to study for and pass the bar exam. Take those tools seriously and use them to fully engage in your bar study. Use the techniques you have learned here. Keep your mind and body in the game. And when you are ready to take the bar on that last Tuesday and Wednesday of February or July, step back, inventory everything you have done to prepare for that moment and believe YOU WILL PASS THE BAR!!

---

9. Ströhle, A., Physical Activity, Exercise, Depression and Anxiety Disorders, J Neural Transm (2009) 116: 777. https://doi.org/10.1007/s00702-008-0092-x.

10. *Id.*

MPT POINT SHEETS

Whitford v. Newberry Middle School District
In re Madert
Acme Resources, Inc. v. Black Hawk et al.
Logan v. Rios
In re Al Merton

POINT SHEET
Whitford v. Newberry Middle School District

Whitford v. Newberry Middle School District
DRAFTERS' POINT SHEET

In this performance test, applicants are asked to write out their closing argument to prepare for their presentation to the court after a hearing on a motion for a preliminary injunction. Under a Newberry Middle School District rule, Annie Whitford, a seventh grader, has been prohibited from trying out for her school's boys-only interscholastic volleyball team. There is no separate girls' or co-ed volleyball team. Annie's federal complaint alleges that the School District rule violates Title IX of the Education Amendments of 1972 and related regulations because the rule deprives her of an equal opportunity to participate in extracurricular athletics. She seeks an order requiring the school district to allow her to try out for the volleyball team.

Applicants are provided a File, which contains a memorandum from the senior partner and the transcript from the hearing on the motion for preliminary injunction conducted by the applicant. The Library contains the relevant portions of Title IX, the regulations, and two decisions of the United States Court of Appeals for the Fifteenth Circuit.

The following discussion covers all the points; the drafters intended to raise in the problem. Applicants need not cover them all to receive passing or even excellent grades. The grading decisions are within the discretion of the graders in the user jurisdictions.

I. Format.

The memorandum directs applicants to write out their closing argument to the court. Applicants must show how the evidence satisfies the requirements for a preliminary injunction enumerated in the law, and how the District's evidence fails to support its case and actually supports Annie's case. Applicants are instructed to tell a persuasive story about why Annie should prevail, to highlight the salient facts, and to otherwise develop a persuasive, organized, well-reasoned, and compelling presentation that concludes with a clear statement .of the relief Annie is seeking. In order to have applicants focus on the likelihood of Annie's success on the merits, they are told not to argue that Annie will suffer irreparable harm; the judge has already determined that Annie would suffer irreparable harm. They are also told not to concern themselves with equal protection considerations that are inherent in the problem. .

II. Content.

- The closing argument should start with introductory fact-based remarks that set a framework sympathetic to Annie. It should contain some or all of the following:
  - Annie Whitford is a seventh-grade student at Newberry Middle School.
  - Annie is a very talented volleyball player who has played for five years

- on various successful co-ed teams; she has received several awards, and aspires to volleyball scholarships and competitive play in college and in the Olympics.
  - The District has a rule that prohibits boys and girls from participating in interscholastic athletic games as mixed teams or against each other as single gender teams. The rule lists volleyball as a contact sport.
  - Annie was prohibited from trying out for her school's volleyball team, which is a boys-only team and the only school volleyball team.
  - The District rule violates Title IX, and Annie seeks an order requiring the District to let her try out for the Newberry Volleyball team.
- Applicants should next provide an overview of the law that reflects their understanding of the statutory, regulatory, and case law. This portion should synthesize and not simply quote the law. It should make the following points:
  - Title IX prohibits gender discrimination in any educational program, of which the interscholastic volleyball program at Newberry Middle School is one.
  - Title IX's regulations allow a school to have single gender teams where selection is based on competitive skill or the activity is a contact sport. However, where a school operates a boys-only team but not a girls-only team in a sport, *and* athletic opportunities for the girls have previously been limited, the girls must be permitted to try out for the team unless the sport is a contact sport.

    NOTE: An applicant who cites the first sentence of 34 § CFR 106.41(b) as applicable to this case would be wrong. It reads, "[A] recipient may operate or sponsor separate teams in a particular sport for members of each gender where selection for such teams is based upon competitive skill or the activity is a contact sport." This section is only applicable where a recipient educational institution operates or sponsors teams for each gender in a particular sport. Here, the record reflects that the school does not have a separate team for each gender.

The next portion of the closing argument should grapple with *whether volleyball is a contact sport*. Discussing this issue first will reflect applicants' recognition that, if volleyball is a contact sport, Annie's claim will fail because 34 CFR § 106.41(b) permits one-gender-only teams when the sport is a contact sport. Applicants should both lay out the law concerning the denomination of a sport as a "contact sport" and argue how the evidence supports Annie's position and diminishes the District's case, as follows:

- The applicable regulation defines a contact sport as one "the purpose or major activity of which involves bodily contact."
- The applicable regulation enumerates examples of contact sports—boxing, wrestling, rugby, ice hockey, football, and basketball—but volleyball is not among the enumerated contact sports.

- The failure of the regulation to enumerate volleyball as a contact sport focuses the inquiry on whether "the purpose or major activity of" volleyball "involved bodily contact."
- The first prong of the inquiry is whether the purpose of volleyball involves bodily contact. This discussion involves league rules and the generally accepted goal of the game. Neither the District nor Annie introduced evidence during the hearing that the purpose of the sport involves bodily contact. Under *Metcalf*, the fact that the rules penalize bodily contact is an important factor in determining whether the purpose of a sport involves bodily contact. The following evidence supports the proposition that the purpose of volleyball does not involve bodily contact:
  - U. S. Volleyball League rules state that volleyball is a non-contact sport and that bodily contact between opposing players will result in a penalty. The purpose of the sport is to try to land the ball in the opponent's court without its being returned successfully. Intentional or threatened physical contact between players can result in a penalty against a player and also against his or her team. (See Wallenstein testimony.)
  - The boy who intentionally injured Annie during an incident at a summer co-ed volleyball camp was penalized. (See Whitford testimony.)
  - The District representative, Grace Huang, gave no testimony as to the purpose of the game of volleyball. She simply testified, without substantiation, that the District had concluded that volleyball is a contact sport.
  - The coach's testimony should be deemed persuasive because of her years of experience coaching middle school and college volleyball and because neither the testimony of the District's witness nor the cross-examination of the coach contradicted the coach's testimony.
- The second prong of the inquiry is whether the *major activity* of volleyball involves bodily contact. The criteria to determine whether the major activity of a sport involves bodily contact are contained in *Metcalf.*
  - A high number of *protective rules* for a sport suggests that bodily contact occur frequently. *Metcalf.*
  - The absence of protective rules in volleyball supports the argument that bodily contact is infrequent and therefore not a major activity of the sport.
  - Even if bodily contact is incidental to the game, an analysis of the *inevitability and frequency* of bodily contact in the actual game determines whether the major activity of a sport involves bodily contact.
    - Although players wear knee pads when they play volleyball and common sense would dictate that players not wear jewelry, league rules do not require players to wear any protective equipment, including knee pads, elbow pads, mouth protectors, or shin guards, nor do they prohibit the wearing of jewelry during a game. (See Wallenstein testimony.) No District evidence contradicted the coach's testimony.

- Annie has suffered only two injuries in all the years she has played volleyball. (See Whitford testimony.)
- Collisions between teammates when they are scrambling for the ball are infrequent. (See Whitford and Wallenstein testimony.)
- In the course of trying to spike a ball over the net, a player may physically strike a player on the other team, but such an incident is rare. (See Wallenstein testimony.)
- Even though Wallenstein testified that a good volleyball player should use all her power, speed, and strength to get the volleyball over the net, the District did not introduce any evidence that such effort makes bodily contact inevitable or frequent.

- After concluding that volleyball is not a contact sport, the applicant must argue that under the applicable regulation, Annie should be allowed to join the boys-only team because *there is no girls-only or co-ed team and the athletic opportunities for girls at Newberry Middle School have previously been limited.*
  - It is undisputed that there is neither a girls-only nor a co-ed volleyball team.
  - In arguing that athletic opportunities for girls at Newberry have previously been limited, applicant should point out that, under *Milley*, such an inquiry is not sports-specific: "[T]he obligation of an educational institution in complying with the requirements of Title IX in [interscholastic athletics] cannot be measured only by comparing types of teams available to each gender, but instead must turn on whether disparities of a substantial and unjustified nature exist in the benefits, treatment, services, or opportunities afforded male and female athletes in the institution's sports program as a whole."
  NOTE: An applicant who argues that the absence of a girls-only volleyball team proves that athletic opportunities for girls at Newberry were previously limited demonstrates a misunderstanding of the law as expressed in *Milley*.
  - *Milley* is consistent with the applicable regulation, 34 CFR § 106.4l(c),
  - "Equal Opportunity," which enumerates a set of factors to consider in determining whether equal athletic opportunities are available.
  - Applicants should then apply the relevant factors under 34 CFR § J06.4l (c) to the facts of Annie's case to prove that athletic opportunities for female students at Newberry were previously limited.
  - The factors that are relevant to Annie's case are:
    Factor l: Whether the selection of sports and levels of competition effectively accommodate the interests and abilities of members of both genders.
    Factor 2: Provision of equipment and supplies.
    Factor 4: Travel and per diem allowance.
    Factor 5: Opportunity to receive coaching and academic tutoring.

Factor 6:   Assignment and compensation of coaches and tutors.
Factor 10:   Publicity.

- Application of these factors to the following evidence supports the conclusion that female Newberry students were denied equal athletic opportunities:
  - Girls and their parents had previously tried to get Newberry to start a girls' interscholastic volleyball team, but the District denied the requests for monetary and logistical reasons (e.g., difficulty in scheduling practice and games times, need to spend more money on coaching and expanded facilities). (See Wallenstein and Huang testimony.)
- In looking at Newberry's athletic program as a whole, there is disproportionate support for male athletics.
  - Of 1,000 student in the seventh and eighth grades at Newberry, approximately 600 are female and 400 are male.
  - There are 10 interscholastic sports teams, none of which is co-ed.
  - Approximately 100 girls play on the four all-girls teams (cross-country, basketball, swimming, and tennis) and approximately 200 boys play on the six all-boys teams (football, basketball, baseball, ice hockey, volleyball, and wrestling). (See Huang and Wallenstein testimony.)
  - The athletic budget pays for coaches' salaries, facilities upkeep, equipment and uniform purchases, athlete transportation, and publicity. Seventy percent of the athletic budget is spent on the boys' teams. (See Wallenstein testimony.)
- Applicants should end the argument by summarizing briefly:
  - The evidence supports the conclusion that the District's refusal to let Annie try out for the school volleyball team violates Title IX:
    - Volleyball is not a contact sport because it is not enumerated in the regulation and neither the purpose nor major activity of volleyball involves bodily contact.
    - Newberry does not have a co-ed or girls-only volleyball team, and athletic opportunities for female students have previously been limited.
      - The court should therefore issue an order requiring the District to allow Annie to try out for Newberry's inter-scholastic volleyball team.
      - Applicants who argue that Annie should actually be placed on the team have missed the point.

POINT SHEET
In re Madert

In re Madert
DRAFTERS'POINT SHEET

Allie and Bruce Madert have met with the supervising partner at the firm to complain about their neighbors, Adrian and Evelyn Doyle. The Doyles, who moved next door about a year ago, are part-time musicians trying to start a rock band; he plays the bass guitar, and she plays the drums. They practice their extremely loud rock music at all hours of the night and on weekends, sometimes just the two of them and at other times with an ever-changing group of other musicians. They practiced in the house for a time until they finished remodeling a shed behind their house, which they made into a studio.

The side yard between the Maderts' home and the Doyles' is only 12 feet wide. When the Doyles and their musician friends are practicing, the music is so loud that the Maderts and their children have trouble sleeping. The children are distracted while trying to do their homework and their sleep time is reduced to the point where their lack of sleep adversely affects their extracurricular activities.

The Maderts have repeatedly complained to the Doyles to no avail. They even went so far as to give the Doyles a letter threatening litigation if the Doyles didn't do something to reduce the noise. The Doyles responded by blithely referring the Maderts to their lawyer. The problem continues. The Maderts prefer to try to settle the matter short of litigation but are prepared to sue if they need to. The supervising partner suggests writing a letter to the Doyles' lawyer to see if that will help solve the problem.

The task for the applicants is to draft a letter to the Doyles' lawyer to see if, through him, the Doyles can be persuaded to abate the nuisance.

The following discussion covers all the points the drafters intended to raise in the problem. Applicants need not cover them all to receive passing or even excellent grades. The grading decisions are within the discretion of the graders in the user jurisdictions.

I. **Overview.** The work product of the applicants should be in the form of a letter and should be written in language that one would expect to be in a letter from one lawyer to another. Quotations from and citations to the cases and other authorities would be in order. Better applicants will recognize that the letter is an initial effort to conciliate the dispute and will avoid a belligerent approach.

The supervising partner's instructions tell the applicants that the letter should:

- be persuasive (as opposed to objective);
- emphasize the key facts;
- use the legal authorities (i.e., cases);
- point out that, if the Maderts sue, a court will likely issue an injunction and award damages;
- state what relief the Maderts expect; and

- include constructive suggestions for steps that the Doyles could take to abate the noise and avoid litigation.

Thus, graders should be looking for all of those points to be covered in the letter. The File materials—a transcript of an interview with the Maderts, the letter from the Maderts to the Doyles, and a report on noise pollution and control—provide the factual support. The three Franklin court cases in the Library furnish the legal authority.

II. **Factual Recitation.** Some applicants may choose to include all the facts at the beginning of the letter in a sort of "statement of the facts" and others may opt instead to weave them into the argument later on in the letter. Either approach is acceptable. The important thing is that the introductory part of the letter should sufficiently inform the reader of the essence of the dispute.

The Background. The letter should recite the nature of the dispute and how it got started, including the following facts:

- Adrian and Evelyn Doyle moved next door to the Maderts about a year ago;
- The Doyles are aspiring musicians who are trying to start a rock band; Adrian plays the bass guitar, and Evelyn plays the drums;
- They practice their music either alone or with other band members on weeknights and weekends;
- At first, they practiced in their house and more recently in a shed they converted into a studio at the rear of the house;
- The music is loud and raucous and is very disturbing to the Madert family; and
- The noise has gotten louder and more frequent since the Doyles began practicing in the shed, which appears to have been renovated without insulating materials.

The Effect on the Maderts. The applicants' letters should describe how the noise affects the Maderts:

- It is not uncommon on weeknights for the Doyles to practice with their instruments late into the night-frequently as late as midnight;
- The repetitive beat of the bass guitar and drums permeates the Maderts' home and keeps the Maderts from sleeping;
- The problem is exacerbated when the Doyles' musician friends join them on weekends and the loud music of the entire band goes on until 2 or 3 o'clock in the morning;
- The Madert children, 9 and 13 years old, are unable to focus on their homework because the noise is so loud;
- The entire Madert family is unable to get to sleep until very late;
- The Maderts' 13-year-old daughter plays the violin and, on at least one occasion, was unable to get enough sleep on the night before an 8:30 a.m. recital because of a loud Friday night session at the Doyles';

- On the same occasion, the Maderts' 9-year-old son wasn't able to get to sleep until after midnight and had to get up at 7 a.m. for a Saturday morning basketball game;
- On that same occasion, Bruce and Allie Madert weren't able to get to sleep until 3 a.m.;
- Thus, the noise is interfering significantly with the regular activities of the Maderts' lives.

<u>Notice to the Doyles that the Noise Was Intolerable</u>. The letters should also include a history of the Maderts' complaints and the Doyles' responses:

- Early on, Allie Madert told Evelyn Doyle that the noise that emanated from the Doyle house when they were practicing disturbed her;
  - Evelyn Doyle's response was that the Doyles were looking for ways to dampen the sound in the renovation of the shed at the rear of their house;
- The design of the renovation added a lot of glass to the shed, which Allie Madert observed would exacerbate the problem when the Doyles began practicing in the shed;
  - Evelyn Doyle simply said they were "dealing with it";
- Once, Allie Madert complained to Adrian Doyle that the noise was distracting the children when they were doing their homework;
  - His response was that it would be better once the shed was done and that they (the Doyles) would try to keep the noise down;
- After a particularly loud and late Friday night, the Maderts put a letter of complaint in the Doyles' mailbox, suggesting that they might be forced to bring legal action;
  - The response from Adrian Doyle was "see my lawyer."
- All efforts to conciliate the dispute have failed. The Doyles, while they say the right things, are unrepentant and appear intent on continuing, as they have.

<u>The Windsor Neighborhood</u>. The applicants' letters should describe the character of the neighborhood.

- The Windsor neighborhood is residential and the homes have large backyards;
- But the homes are fairly close together-the side yards are only 12 feet wide;
- The residents include all sorts of artistic and ecologically minded types;
- The neighbors sponsor a wide variety of musical and theatrical productions;
- The productions are usually held in the commercial district or at the artists' cooperatives and community centers that are available for the purpose of accommodating such affairs; and
- The neighbors have installed speed bumps in the streets to discourage motorcycles and noisy trucks from using them.

III. Application of the Facts (Argument). In this part of the letter the applicants should apply the facts to the authorities and argue persuasively that

- the activities of the Doyles constitute a private nuisance; and
- if the Maderts sue, the court would likely issue an injunction granting them the relief they seek and award them significant damages.

The Doyles' Activities Constitute a Nuisance. The *Meadowbrook and Gorman* cases supply the foundation of the argument that noise can be a private nuisance:

- In Meadowbrook, the court held that any activity ("trade or business"), even though it might be lawful and carried on in a reasonable method, can be a nuisance if it "interferes with the reasonable and comfortable enjoyment by another of his property."
- The *Meadowbrook* court also said that "noise alone may be a nuisance."
- *Gorman* says that noise constitutes a private nuisance if it "causes physical discomfort and annoyance to those of ordinary sensibilities, tastes and habits and seriously interferes with the ordinary comfort and enjoyment of their homes."
- And the *Arundel Fish & Game Club* case adopts the Restatement rule and defines "intentional" broadly enough to encompass the Doyles' conduct.
  - The court rejected the notion that, to be considered intentional, the conduct would have to be inspired by ill will or malice. Conduct is "intentional" if it continues after the actor has been put on notice of the harm.
- There can be no doubt in this case that the loud music played by the Doyles at night interferes substantially with the Maderts' use and enjoyment of their property and is therefore a private nuisance.
  - The music is loud and persistent.
  - The Maderts can't sleep at night when the Doyles and their fellow musicians are playing.
  - The Madert children are having trouble focusing on their homework.
  - The noise is interfering with the ability of the Madert children to engage in ordinary extracurricular activities (soccer, violin recitals, and basketball) because they aren't able to get enough sleep on nights before they engage in those activities.
  - Implicit in the facts is the underlying tension and aggravation accompanying the circumstances.
    - As stated in a report by the University of Franklin's Department of Ecological Studies, "Home should be a place for rest and quiet after the labor and cares of each day."
      - The apprehension of anticipating the next raucous jam session renders rest and quiet impossible.
- The character of the neighborhood is also a consideration in determining whether the activity constitutes a nuisance.

- In *Meadowbrook*, the court stated, "Any habitual noise, [even if] produced by . . . skilled musicians, which is so loud, continuous, insistent, not inherent to the character of the neighborhood and unusual therein, that normal people are so seriously incommoded that they cannot sleep, study, read, converse, or concentrate until it stops, is unreasonable."
- This describes perfectly the situation in this case—the Doyles' activity is not suited to the neighborhood.
  - It is a residential area where people are entitled to peace and quiet in their homes.
  - The houses are close together (12-foot side yards).
  - Although many of the residents are artistic, musical types, they carry out those pursuits either in the commercial areas of town or in the cooperatives and community centers that are available for those purposes.
  - The neighbors go to lengths to preserve the quiet, even going so far as to install speed bumps in the streets to discourage motorcycle and truck traffic.

<u>If the Maderts Were to Sue, the Court Would Likely Issue an Injunction Granting Them the Relief They Seek and Award Damages</u>. At this point, the applicants should describe the relief the Maderts want and argue that a court would likely grant it and award damages:

<u>Injunction</u>.

- It is not absolutely clear from the facts exactly what the Maderts want by way of relief.
  - Allie Madert says, "I'd be happy enough if they kept the noise from reaching our house-the whole year. So I guess they'd have to change the times they play and practice. And I bet there are alterations they could make to the studio to muffle the noise a lot."
- This suggests a number of things:
  - That the Maderts want a complete abatement so that the noise does not enter their home;
  - That they want the Doyles to play and practice only at certain hours when it would not interfere with the Maderts; and
  - That they want sound-muffling alterations made to the studio.
  - The case law supports a combination of all three things, so it would not be inappropriate for the Maderts to demand initially a complete abatement and, in the final analysis, to suggest something short of that as a means of resolving the dispute without litigation.
- According to *Meadowbrook*, the court could simply issue a broad injunction preventing the Doyles from "the playing of loud music . . . in such [a] manner that the noise is transmitted onto the propert[y] of the plaintiffs, so as to deprive them . . . of the reasonable use and comfortable enjoyment of their . . . home[]."

- The burden would then be on the Doyles to "adopt any effective method of so reducing the volume of sound transmitted to the [Madert home] that [the Maderts] will no longer be disturbed."
- Likewise, the court in Arundel Fish & Game affirmed a very broadly worded injunction giving the Club six months to "design and implement a noise abatement system . . . so as to reduce the noise [to acceptable levels]" and, further, limiting their activities during those six months "to certain hours calculated to reduce the likelihood of interference with the use and enjoyment of the residents' properties."
  - The court also found that injunctive relief could be granted even though the Club was specifically exempt from the Franklin environmental regulations.
- The relevance of these holdings to the Madert/Doyle situation is this:
  - The absence of any laws or regulations specifically preventing the Doyles from playing loud music would not deter the court from issuing an injunction (See *Arundel Fish & Game*, where the fact that the Club was exempted from regulations that apply only in commercial areas did not deter the court.);
  - The likely injunction would be very broad, simply ordering the Doyles to implement an effective abatement, putting on them the entire burden of figuring out how to do it;
  - The Doyles would be given a time limit within which to implement the abatement and, in the meantime, they could be enjoined from creating any noise that disturbs the Maderts; and
  - Thus, the very real risk to the Doyles is that the court could enjoin them completely and permanently unless they come up with a failsafe method of abatement.

Damages.

- The Doyles are also exposed to the risk of significant compensatory damages and perhaps even punitive damages.
  - *Meadowbrook and Gorman* both support a claim for damages.
    - Meadowbrook holds that, under the circumstances, "an action lies at law or equity."
    - Under *Gorman*, damages may be recovered for "the diminution in the value of the use of the property as a home . . . for any actual inconvenience and physical discomfort . . . [and] for illness, pain and discomfort, and annoyance caused by a nuisance."
      - There is no question that the Maderts have suffered such injuries and that they could produce "sufficient evidence of the ill effects suffered by them to entitle them to substantial damages." *Gorman*.
- There is even a possibility that the court would award punitive damages.

- In *Gorman*, the court agreed that the evidence that the defendants had acted willfully and maliciously was sufficient to justify punitive damages.
  - In the present case, there is similar evidence:
  - The Doyles simply ignored repeated complaints by the Maderts that the noise was having serious effects on their lives;
  - Adrian Doyle's response when the Maderts finally put it in writing was, "See my lawyer."
  - Notwithstanding the frequent complaints, the Doyles persisted in their disruptive activities.
- Although it may be problematic under the facts, applicants should argue that a finder of fact could conclude that the Doyles acted willfully and maliciously.

Constructive Suggestions for Abatement. This part of the letter should carry a conciliatory tone. It should suggest that, although the Maderts will file suit if they have to, they would prefer to resolve the matter short of litigation. There are any number of combinations the applicants could come up with for means of abatement. Below are some things suggested in the materials, including the University of Franklin article on noise pollution and control.

- The Doyles could practice and play at one of the artists' cooperatives or community centers in town. This option would not be expensive and is what all the other musical groups do.
- Although it might not completely abate the noise, the Doyles could agree to install insulation materials and acoustical glass in the studio at the back of their house that would vastly reduce the amount of noise that escapes.
- Until such modifications are made, they could agree either to stop practicing and playing altogether or to do so only at one of the community locations.
- After the modifications are made, they could agree that they will practice and play only in the studio (not in the house) and that they will limit their hours of play and practice to times when the noise will not disturb the Maderts.
- They could agree to build some sort of protective buffer around the studio which, in combination with the insulation and acoustical glass, would further dampen the noise.
- They could agree to outer noise limits that practicing and playing would produce. They could install noise measuring devices on their property and on the Maderts' property. The devices would be monitored and, if the noise exceeded the agreed upon levels, further abatement steps would be taken.
- Applicants might also suggest that the Maderts are open to ideas from the Doyles. Finally, the applicants should probably set a reasonable deadline for a response from the Doyles.

POINT SHEET
Acme Resources, Inc. v. Black Hawk et al.

Acme Resources, Inc. v. Robert Black Hawk et al.
DRAFTERS' POINT SHEET

This performance test requires applicants, as associates in a law firm, to draft a persuasive brief in a federal court action contesting whether an Indian tribal court may exercise civil jurisdiction over a nonmember of the tribe.

Applicants' law firm represents Robert Black Hawk and seven other members of the Black Eagle Indian Tribe (collectively, "tribe members" or "Black Hawk et al."). The tribe members have filed a lawsuit in tribal court against a mining company, Acme Resources, Inc. (Acme), for damages caused by Acme's extraction of coal bed methane from under reservation land. The process used to develop the coal bed methane has depleted the water table, causing many of the tribe members' wells to begin to run dry, leaving them without water for their livestock or crops. A geologist predicts that all wells on the Reservation will go dry in five years if Acme's methane extraction continues.

In response to the Tribal Court complaint, Acme filed an answer denying liability and jurisdiction. At the same time, Acme commenced an action in federal court requesting a declaratory judgment that the Tribal Court has no jurisdiction over Acme and seeking an injunction against prosecution of the Tribal Court action. Applicants' task is to analyze the law relating to Tribal Court jurisdiction and draft the argument section of a brief in support of a motion for summary judgment in the federal action or to dismiss or stay the federal action to allow the Tribal Court to consider its jurisdiction first.

The File contains: (1) a memorandum from the supervising attorney describing the assignment; (2) a transcript of an interview with the client, Robert Black Hawk; (3) a copy of Acme's complaint filed in U.S. District Court; (4) a draft motion for summary judgment or, in the alternative, to dismiss or stay; (5) an affidavit signed by Robert Black Hawk; and (6) an affidavit by a geologist who has studied the cause of the Reservation water table depletion.

The Library contains excerpts from the Black Eagle Tribal Constitution and Tribal Code, and a Fifteenth Circuit opinion relating to tribal court jurisdiction.

The following discussion covers all the points the drafters intended to raise in the problem. Applicants need not cover them all to receive passing or even excellent grades. Grading is entirely within the discretion of the user jurisdictions.

I. Format and Overview

The supervising attorney's memo requests that applicants draft two arguments: that the court should grant summary judgment to the defendant Tribe members because there is no genuine issue of material fact that the Tribal Court has jurisdiction over Acme; and that, as an alternative basis for relief, the district court should stay or dismiss (without prejudice) Acme's action in federal court to allow the Tribal Court to consider the question of its jurisdiction.

The memorandum provides the template for applicants' argument section of the brief in support of the draft motion. Jurisdictions will have to decide how to weigh the subjective component of "persuasiveness." One guide is that an applicant's work product is not considered responsive to the instructions if it is in the form of an objective memo that takes the on-the-one-hand/on-the-other-hand approach. The argument section of the brief should be broken into its major components with well-crafted headings that summarize applicants' arguments. The arguments should weave the law and facts together into a persuasive statement of the argument, citing to the appropriate authorities and including contrary authorities that are to be addressed, explained, or distinguished. Applicants are instructed that a statement of facts is not necessary.

Applicants should argue that under the two *Montana* exceptions to the general rule against tribal court jurisdiction over nonmembers, the Black Eagle Tribal Court has jurisdiction over Acme. Acme entered into a "consensual relationship" with the Tribe through the lease agreement giving Acme the right to mine the methane gas under the Reservation. Acme's methane operations also threaten the Tribe's economic security by depleting its water supply. Thus, the district court should grant defendants' summary judgment motion. Further, applicants should argue that the Tribal Court has not yet had an opportunity to rule on the jurisdictional issue, and under the exhaustion rule of *National Farmers Union*, the district court should stay or dismiss the federal action to allow the Tribal Court to address the jurisdiction issue first.

II. The Facts

Applicants are to incorporate the relevant facts into the argument sections of their briefs, emphasizing those facts favorable to tribe members' position.

- The eight defendants, Black Hawk et al., are all members of the Black Eagle Tribe (the Tribe) and operate farms and ranches within the Black Eagle Reservation.
- Black Hawk et al. are neighbors of Patrick Mulroney, a nonmember of the Tribe who owns fee land within the Reservation.
- Acme, a mining company, is not a member of the Black Eagle Tribe.
- Mulroney granted a permit to Acme to use his land for the infrastructure necessary to explore for coal bed methane under his land. Acme pays Mulroney a royalty in exchange for access to his land.
- The Tribe owns the mineral rights to the methane under Mulroney's land. It leased to Acme the right to extract the methane in exchange for a 20 percent royalty for the Tribe.
- Acme's methane development requires pumping out huge quantities of groundwater. Within six months of the development of the coal bed methane field, the wells of Mulroney's neighbors, Black Hawk et al., began to run dry.

- Black Hawk and his co-defendants cannot survive economically without water to run their farms and ranches, and there is no other water reasonably available.
- Geologist Jesse Bellingham, Ph.D., defendants' expert, states that all Reservation wells will run dry within five years if the coal bed methane development continues.
- The Black Eagle Constitution recognizes the importance of preserving the Reservation's environment, and the Black Eagle Tribal Code authorizes a civil action by a party aggrieved by another's degradation of the environment.
- Black Hawk et al. brought an action in Black Eagle Tribal Court against Acme for damages and injunctive relief. Acme denied both liability and the Tribal Court's jurisdiction. No further proceedings have been held in tribal court.
- Acme filed an action in federal court seeking declaratory relief and an injunction against prosecution of the tribal court action.
- No federal statute or treaty addresses the Black Eagle Tribal Court's civil jurisdiction.

III. Legal Issues

Applicants must address two issues:

- Whether there is any genuine issue of material fact as to whether the Tribal Court has jurisdiction over the action pending before it and whether summary judgment should be entered in favor of Robert Black Hawk et al., and
- Whether the district court action should be dismissed or stayed because Acme failed to exhaust tribal court remedies before seeking relief in federal court.

Applicants might appropriately frame the questions in any number of ways, but should recognize the jurisdiction and exhaustion of tribal remedies issues.

IV. Argument

To formulate a good argument, applicants must digest the legal authority contained in *AO Architects v. Red Fox et al.*, the Fifteenth Circuit decision, and the cases cited therein as well as the File materials. *AO Architects* summarizes the governing United States Supreme Court precedent regarding tribal court jurisdiction. The following argument headings are suggestions only and should not be taken by the graders as the only acceptable ones.

A. Because Acme Entered Into a Consensual Relationship With the Black Eagle Tribe, and Because Its Mining Poses a Threat to the Tribe's Economic Security, There Is No Genuine Issue of Material Fact as to Whether the Tribal Court Has Jurisdiction Over Acme and, Therefore, Black Hawk Et Al. Are Entitled to Summary Judgment.

- Absent express authorization by Congress or a treaty provision authorizing jurisdiction over nonmembers, a tribal court may not exercise civil jurisdiction over a nonmember. *Montana v. United States*, 450 U.S. 544 (1981).
- There are two exceptions to this general rule: (1) the consensual relationship exception; and (2) the security of the tribe exception. If the controversy arises out of a consensual relationship between the nonmember and the tribe or its members, or if the nonmember's conduct directly threatens the political integrity, economic security, or health and welfare of the tribe, the tribal court may exercise jurisdiction over the nonmember. *Id.*

Applicants should argue that, although Acme is not a member of the Tribe and is engaged in activities on the surface of land held in fee simple by another nonmember (Mulroney), the controversy arises out of a consensual relationship (the lease agreement) and also threatens the economic security of the tribe (no water to raise crops or livestock). Applicants should use the facts in the File to argue that both *Montana* exceptions apply, and should distinguish *Strate* and *Funmaker*, cases cited in *AO Architects* in which the court declined to find a consensual relationship or tribal security exception, and thus found that the tribal court had no jurisdiction over nonmembers.

The Acme/Tribe Lease Constitutes a Consensual Relationship and Therefore the Tribal Court Has Jurisdiction Under the First *Montana* Exception.

- The first *Montana* exception confers civil jurisdiction over a nonmember where the nonmember has a consensual relationship with the tribe through commercial dealings. *AO Architects,* citing *Montana.*
- The Tribe/Acme lease satisfies this commercial dealing requirement: it is a direct business relationship between the Tribe and Acme. It gives Acme a sustained (as opposed to fleeting) presence within the Reservation, and it has significant (as opposed to minimal) financial and environmental implications for Tribe members and the Tribe as a whole.
- The Acme/Tribe relationship is thus distinguishable from a "commonplace" reservation highway accident between two nonmembers that the *Strate* court rejected as an insufficient basis for conferring tribal jurisdiction.
- In *Franklin Motor Credit Co. v. Funmaker* (cited in *AO Architects*), the 15th Circuit Court of Appeals noted that tribal court jurisdiction will not be conferred under the consensual relationship exception unless there is a "direct nexus" between the underlying business relationship and the subject of the lawsuit against the nonmember.
  - Thus, in *Funmaker*, the court rejected tribal court jurisdiction over a car dealership's financing company in a products liability suit brought by a tribe member who was injured while driving a vehicle leased by the tribe and financed by the finance company.

- Here, by contrast, there is a "direct nexus" between Acme and the Tribe.
  - The Tribe and Acme entered into a lease agreement giving Acme the right to extract methane from mineral reserves belonging to the Tribe and located within the Reservation in exchange for a 20 percent royalty payment to the Tribe on all methane produced.
  - The subject of the Tribe members' lawsuit is the harm allegedly caused by Acme's methane mining.
- Applicants might anticipate that Acme will attempt to argue that the consensual relationship at issue, Acme's lease of the mineral rights, is a consensual relationship with the Tribe, and not with one Black Hawk et al., the parties suing Acme.
- However, the applicable case law does not suggest that there must be a direct match between the parties involved in the consensual relationship and the parties to the suit in tribal court. The key is that there be a consensual relationship with the tribe or its members and that there be a connection between the facts giving rise to the litigation in tribal court and that relationship. *See Funmaker.*

Acme's Mining Activities Threaten the Tribe's Economic Security by Depleting the Reservation Water Supply, Thereby Satisfying the Second *Montana* Exception.

The second *Montana* exception permits a tribal court to exercise civil jurisdiction over a nonmember of the tribe where the nonmember's conduct "on fee lands within [the tribe's] reservation . . . threatens or has some direct effect on the political integrity, the economic security, or the health and welfare of the tribe." *AO Architects* (quoting *Montana*). It is important that applicants recognize that a conclusory reference to the negative effect of Acme's activities on the Tribe is not sufficient. Rather, applicants are expected to identify the particular interest(s) of the Tribe (e.g., its economic security) that are at risk from Acme's extraction of coal bed methane.

- Black Hawk et al. have identified a real and substantial risk to the Tribe's economic security: if Acme's mining activities continue, it is likely that within five years all the wells on the Reservation will run dry. (*See* Bellingham Aff.)
- The fact that the wells of eight Tribe members with ranches and farms abutting Patrick Mulroney's land (the site of Acme's methane extraction) began running dry within six months of the start of Acme's mining operations shows the immediate impact that the mining has had and the potential magnitude of the risk. (*See* Black Hawk Aff.)
- The Black Eagle Tribal Constitution, article IV, § 1, stresses the importance of the environment to the Tribe: "The land of the Black Eagle Tribal Reservation shall be preserved in a clean and healthful environment for the benefit of the Tribe and future generations."

- The Tribal Code reiterates this concern for the environment and creates a cause of action in Tribal Court for any person harmed by those who "pollute or otherwise degrade the environment of the Black Eagle Reservation." Tribal Code § 23-5.
- Obviously, depleting the water table in order to extract coal bed methane degrades the environment of the Reservation.
- Moreover, without a stable and plentiful water supply, Tribe members will be unable to raise crops or livestock, in the absence of securing an alternate water supply that is economical and practical. Thus, the lack of water will directly threaten the Tribe's economic security.
- The specific risk here (which threatens the entire Tribe and is directly related to Acme's conduct) stands in sharp contrast to the interest in preventing careless driving on a reservation's public highways at issue in *Strate*, where the Supreme Court refused to find jurisdiction, reasoning that such a broad public safety interest, such as preventing auto accidents, would swallow the rule of *Montana*.
- Applicants may also argue that the Tribe's health and safety and welfare are threatened by Acme's depletion of the water table through its methane mining.
  - While Black Hawk's affidavit and interview focus on the threat to the Tribe's economic security (inability to support crops and livestock), applicants could reasonably argue that tribal health and safety may also eventually be at risk, especially given Bellingham's prediction that *all* wells will run dry in five years. In short, the Tribe could end up without adequate water for basic health and sanitation as a result of Acme's mining.
- Astute applicants might note that Acme could argue that even if the Tribe eventually has to find another source of water, for the term of Acme's lease, the Tribe will receive a royalty of 20 percent of all methane production. Presumably, that is a significant amount (in his interview notes, Black Hawk states that ". . . the promises of easy money carried the day").
- Applicants should contend that the royalty income from Acme cannot offset the permanent damage to the Reservation and the Tribe's long-term economic security if there is no water available on the Reservation.
- The fact that Acme's mining operation is based on land owned in fee simple by Patrick Mulroney, a nonmember of the Tribe, does not deprive the Tribal Court of jurisdiction.
- Acme is extracting coal bed methane that belongs to the Tribe and the aquifer being depleted by Acme's activities serves all the wells on the Reservation.
- The probability, as stated in the Bellingham Affidavit, that *all* the wells on the Reservation will run dry within five years, counters the argument that the economic security of the entire Black Eagle Tribe (as opposed to only the eight tribe members involved in the current litigation) is not at stake.

- Applicants could argue that the fact that the Tribal Council granted Acme a mining concession does not affect defendants' rights, as the Tribal Constitution and Tribal Code addresses threats to the Reservation's environment and provides an independent basis for Tribe members' standing to bring suit.
- In sum, contrary to what Acme alleges in its complaint, it is clear that the Tribal Court has jurisdiction because both exceptions to *Montana*'s main rule apply. Therefore, the court should grant summary judgment to Black Hawk et al.

B. The Tribal Exhaustion Doctrine of *National Farmers Union* Requires the District Court to Dismiss or Stay Acme's Federal Action on the Grounds That the Tribal Court Has Not Been Afforded an Opportunity to Consider Its Own Jurisdiction.

Applicants' argument discussing the exhaustion rule should mention the following points:

- *National Farmers Union Ins. Cos.* v. *Crow Tribe*, 471 U.S. 845 (1985), announced a tribal exhaustion requirement: a tribal court should ordinarily first be given an opportunity to consider its jurisdiction before a party may seek relief in federal court. *See AO Architects.*
- The exhaustion rule is a prudential rule and is to be applied as a matter of comity (deference) unless it is clear that the tribal court lacks jurisdiction over the action involving the nonmember.
- Here, the Black Eagle Tribal Court has not had an opportunity to consider and rule on whether it has jurisdiction over Acme.
- Acme has answered the complaint in Tribal Court, but no further proceedings have been held there.
- Applicants should argue that the Black Eagle Tribal Court has jurisdiction over the action before it because both *Montana* exceptions apply, and therefore Black Hawk et al. are entitled to summary judgment on that issue. In addition, applicants should state that if the court determines that it is unclear whether the Tribal Court has jurisdiction, the court should, consistent with the principle of comity discussed in *AO Architects* and *National Farmers Union*, dismiss or at least stay the action to give the Tribal Court an opportunity to consider the question.

POINT SHEET
Logan v. Rios

Logan v. Rios
DRAFTERS' POINT SHEET

The task for the applicants in this performance test item is to prepare the initial draft of one part of the Early Dispute Resolution (EDR) statement that the supervising attorney will submit to the EDR judge, on behalf of the firm's client, Trina Rios, the defendant in a slip-and-fall case. Plaintiff Karen Logan was shopping at Trina's Toys, the toy store owned by Trina Rios, when she slipped on a small puddle of water and fell in one of the aisles, injuring her ankle in the process. As a result, Logan sued Rios, claiming that Rios violated her duty as a premises owner. Rios pled an affirmative defense of contributory negligence, which, if proven, would be a complete bar to Logan's recovery under Franklin law.

The File contains the instructional memo from the supervising attorney, Local Rule 12 concerning EDR conferences, Form 12 (the form to be completed for the EDR statement), the plaintiff's complaint, the defendant's investigator's report, and excerpts of the depositions of the plaintiff, Karen Logan, and Nick Patel, an employee of the defendant.

The Library includes a Franklin Supreme Court Approved Jury Instruction concerning the premises liability of property owners. The Jury Instruction contains commentary on the duty of property owners and the affirmative defense of contributory negligence.

The following discussion covers all the points the drafters of the item intended to incorporate, but applicants may receive passing and even excellent grades without covering them all. Grading is left entirely to the discretion of user jurisdictions.

I. Overview

Applicants are expected to draft one component of the EDR statement in accord with the description set forth in Form 12, item 6:

A candid discussion of the strengths and weaknesses of the party's claims, counterclaims, and/or defenses and affirmative defenses. For each element that must be proven, parties should discuss the specific strengths and weaknesses of the evidence gathered to date relating to that element in light of the jury instruction and any commentary thereto.

Applicants are told to carefully review the evidence gathered to date and identify and evaluate the proof available for each legal element of the claim and the affirmative defense. They are told to organize the facts relating to each legal element as defined in the jury instruction, to address both strengths and weaknesses of the case, and to analyze the case in light of the evidence available to Logan and Rios. Note that applicants have been told not to discuss Logan's damages (e.g., pain and suffering and the costs of medical care, etc.). Except as described below, applicants who do discuss damages may receive less than full credit as a result of their failure to follow directions. Applicants have been told to limit themselves to the evidence gathered to date. Speculation regarding evidence that may come to light as discovery proceeds is beyond the scope of the call memo.

Applicants are expected to extract from the jury instruction the elements of proof of liability that the plaintiff must establish and each element of the defendant's affirmative defense. From the depositions and other evidence provided, applicants should identify the evidence that supports the elements. Using the law and facts, they should assess the strengths and weaknesses of the evidence in relation to their client's case. Applicants are told that the EDR statement is confidential and will not be shared with the other party. Thus, they should be candid. Applicants who ignore the weaknesses of Rios's case—both in terms of their assessment of Logan's case and in terms of Rios's affirmative defense of contributory negligence—should be penalized.

Although applicants are not given a specific organizational format, they are directed in the call memo to organize the facts relating to each element as set forth in the jury instruction and to assess the strengths and weaknesses of their case. The outline provided below is an example of an organizational structure that complies with that instruction. Applicants should include citations to the cases cited in the Commentary to Jury Instruction 35 where appropriate. They need not cite to the factual record; record references are provided for graders' convenience.

II. Arguments concerning the strengths and weaknesses of defendant Rios's case including any affirmative defenses

A. <u>There was a condition which presented an unreasonable risk of harm to people on the defendant's property: namely, the presence of water on the floor (Jury Instruction 35; Complaint ¶ 4)</u>

Strengths of Rios's case:

- Applicants might point out that an indisputably small and thin puddle of water on the middle of a floor in a well-lit store hardly constitutes an unreasonable risk of harm.

Weaknesses of Rios's case:

- Applicants should note that it is undisputed that there was water on the floor where there was customer traffic. (Patel Dep. Tr., Logan Dep. Tr.)
  - It is possible that a jury would find that *any* amount of water on a slippery tile floor constituted an unreasonable risk.
- It is also undisputed that there was no warning about the water on the floor—no employee saw it, and no signs or cones were posted. (Patel Dep. Tr.) Had there been some notice to customers that there was water on the floor, the condition would not have presented an unreasonable risk of harm.

B. <u>The defendant knew or in the exercise of reasonable care should have known of both the condition and the risk. (Jury Instruction 35; Complaint ¶ 4)</u>

Strengths of Rios's case:

- Patel, one of Rios's employees, was in the store at the time of the fall. Neither he nor Rios knew about the water and thus could not have prevented it or warned customers about it. (Patel Dep. Tr.)
- Further, it was not unreasonable that Rios and her employees were unaware of the water.
  - There are no sources of water in the area of the fall that would have caused water to accumulate there: no leaking ceiling, no squirt gun displays. In fact, aisle 3 was an area of puzzles and games. (Patel Dep. Tr.)
  - It was not raining or snowing on the day of the incident. (Logan Dep. Tr.)
  - Trina's Toys is not a store that sells refreshments or toys containing water, so it is arguably unexpected for there to be a spill on the floor.
  - Patel mops the floors at night, after the store closes, so the floors would presumably dry by the next morning.
  - No one reported to store employees that there was water in the aisle, even though the store had had a steady stream of customers that day. (Patel Dep. Tr.)
  - If a customer spilled the water, neither Rios nor Patel had knowledge of the spill. (Patel Dep. Tr.)
  - A key factor in determining whether a premises owner acted with reasonable care is the length of time an unsafe condition existed. (JI 35 Commentary) Here, even if Logan relies on Patel's admission that no store employee had checked on the aisle for two hours (Patel was in the aisle just before the store opened at 10 a.m..; Logan fell before noon), there was no reason to anticipate spills in the toy store and thus no duty to periodically check for them. (Patel Dep. Tr.) (*Chad v. Bill's Camera Shop* (Fr. Ct. App. 2006))
    - By contrast, the owner of a coffee shop was liable for a fall that occurred when coffee had "just spilled" because it was reasonably foreseeable that customers would spill coffee. *Owens v. Coffee Corner* (Fr. Ct. App. 2007).
    - Unlike the mini-golf operator found liable for a fall caused by a liquid spill in *Rollins v. Maryville Mini-Golf Park* (Fr. Ct. App. 2002), Rios does not serve food in her establishment.

Weaknesses of Rios's case:

- There is no evidence to narrow the possible time period that the water was on the floor.
- It is undisputed that Patel failed to patrol the aisles each hour. (Patel Dep. Tr.)
  - Had he done so, he almost certainly would have found the water, as it was in plain view.

- There were two other employees there—Rios herself and Naomi Feldman—who presumably were capable of checking the aisles themselves, but did not.
- Trina's Toys is a store frequented by children, who, like the little boy in the store at the time of Logan's fall, could be expected to have various containers like baby bottles and sippy cups containing beverages that could spill.
- Thus, a jury could conclude that two hours is too long for a puddle of water to be in a busy area of a toy store.

C. <u>The defendant could reasonably expect that people on the property would not discover the danger, and the defendant failed to warn that water had accumulated on the floor. (Jury Instruction 35) However, the defendant could not be liable for harm caused by a condition which was open and obvious, nor must the defendant warn of conditions on the premises that are open and obvious. (Townsend v. Upwater)</u>

Strengths of Rios's case:

- Water on the floor is usually an open and obvious condition.
  - Logan admitted that nothing blocked her view of the water. (Logan Dep. Tr.)
  - Logan admitted that she was not looking at the floor. (Logan Dep. Tr.)
- Logan also conceded that the store was brightly lit, so there is no evidence of a problem with the lighting that would have prevented a reasonable person from noticing the water. (Logan Dep. Tr., Patel Dep. Tr.)
- Logan had been on her cell phone just prior to the fall and may have been distracted by the call. (Logan Dep. Tr.)

Weaknesses of Rios's case:

- Rios failed to warn of the water. (Patel Dep. Tr.) In fact, the toy store is not equipped to warn of spills—it does not have warning signs or cones to put out on the floor. (*Id.*)
- The water, being odorless and colorless, may not have been readily apparent to customers. (*Id.*) Also, this was not a large spill but a thin "trail of water." (Logan Dep. Tr.)
- Rios's customers could not necessarily be expected to scour the store's floor searching for hazards. Many of Rios's customers are children who would be focusing on the toys displayed. Adults, too, would reasonably be expected to be looking at the toys on display, as Logan said she was doing just before the fall (e.g., Wii bowling game).

D. <u>If the defendant created a distraction in the area such that the defendant had reason to suspect that the plaintiff might not appreciate the obvious nature of the unsafe condition, the defendant had a duty to warn the plaintiff. (*Ward v. ShopMart*)</u>

Strengths of Rios's case:

- Had Logan been looking where she was walking, she would have seen the water, which was an open and obvious condition. (Logan Dep. Tr.)
- The store was well lit. (Logan Dep. Tr., Patel Dep. Tr.)
- The distraction exception should stay just that—an exception. If it is construed as applying to all stores that make an effort to attractively display merchandise, all retail stores will become insurers of their customers' safety.

Weaknesses of Rios's case:

- Although Rios has no duty to warn of open and obvious conditions, she does have a duty to warn if a customer is likely to be distracted and therefore fail to notice the dangerous condition. (*Ward v. ShopMart*)
  - Holiday decorations may constitute a distraction. If so, the "distraction exception" to the open and obvious rule applies and the defendant is not relieved of liability for the plaintiff's injury. (*Gardner v. Wendt*)
  - But *Gardner* is distinguishable—holiday decorations qualify as a distraction because they are not usually present.
  - In this case, the aisle where Logan fell—indeed, the entire store—is filled with merchandise that is meant to attract customers. (Patel Dep. Tr.)
    - The end of the aisle had a computer-animated display of games. (*Id.*) This display may have distracted Logan from noticing where she was walking.
    - She claims to have been looking at the merchandise ahead of her, further down the aisle. (Logan Dep. Tr.)
  - The store also had a Wii game available for play, which Logan had been playing just before her fall. (*Id.*) She may have been distracted by it.
  - If it was reasonable to expect that the store displays would distract Logan from watching for open and obvious conditions, Rios had a duty to warn of the puddle.
    - It is undisputed that there were no warnings about the water puddle that could have alerted Logan to it.
  - However, the distraction exception does not apply when those claiming injury created the distraction. In *Brown v. City of De Forest* (Fr. Ct. App. 2005), the plaintiff could not recover where she had tripped on an uneven sidewalk while chasing after a runaway child. She admitted that her attention was diverted from the sidewalk by her concern for the child. The court held that the distraction exception did not apply because the distraction was the result of the plaintiff's concern for the child and inattentiveness to where she was going, and the city could not be held responsible.
    - In light of Logan's questionable credibility as a witness (see below), a jury might find it more likely than not that she was still using her cell

phone when she slipped and so, under *Brown*, the "distraction" was of her own making, and the exception would not apply.

E. <u>Defendant's Affirmative Defense: Contributory Negligence. The plaintiff was negligent in spilling the water on which she slipped, and that negligence was the proximate cause of her injury. (Jury Instruction 35)</u>

Strengths of Rios's affirmative defense:

- Franklin is a contributory negligence jurisdiction. Thus, any negligence by Logan that contributed to her fall is a complete bar to recovery.
- While Logan has denied that she spilled water on the floor, there is circumstantial evidence that she did so.
  - She admits that she had a water bottle with her in the store. (Logan Dep. Tr.)
  - The water bottle was on the floor next to her after she fell. (Patel Dep. Tr.)
  - According to Patel, the water bottle was empty when he put it in Logan's backpack after she fell. (*Id.*)
  - Logan claims the bottle was full when she left for the store. (Logan Dep. Tr.)
  - She is equivocal regarding how much water was in the bottle when she was in the store and whether she had consumed any of it. (*Id.*)
  - The fact that there was no reason for water to be in aisle 3 and that no other customer saw the water creates a strong circumstantial case that Logan herself spilled the water, fell, and then lied about it.
- Given the false and inconsistent statements that Logan has made about the impact her ankle injury had on her employment and her scholarship, the jury may well believe that Logan herself spilled the water that caused her fall.

Weaknesses of Rios's affirmative defense:

- No witness actually *saw* Logan spill the water.
  - Patel testified that he is unaware of any witnesses to Logan's fall who might be able to apportion some blame to her. (Patel Dep. Tr.)
  - Logan herself testified that she did not see anyone else spill any water, including the toddler using the sippy cup. (Logan Dep. Tr.)
- Nevertheless, while there were no witnesses, it cannot be ruled out that the toddler with the sippy cup or another customer with water caused the spill.

F. <u>Defendant's Affirmative Defense: Contributory Negligence: The plaintiff was negligent in failing to exercise due care for her safety by wearing shoes that were unsafe, especially while carrying a heavy backpack, and that negligence was the proximate cause of her injury. (Jury Instruction 35)</u>

Strengths of Rios's affirmative defense:

- Logan was wearing shoes with approximately three-inch heels and leather soles, which she was wearing for only the fourth time. The shoes were backless, high-heeled sandals. (Logan Dep. Tr.)
- The shoes looked like they were "not too steady." (Patel Dep. Tr.)
- It is likely that the leather soles were slippery and that the shoes, along with the weight of the backpack, caused Logan to fall. She could have expected that her relative inexperience in those particular shoes coupled with the heavy backpack could potentially lead to slipping and falling under any conditions.

Weaknesses of Rios's affirmative defense:

- No one saw how or why Logan fell.
- It is undisputed that she fell where the water puddle was.
- Stores like Trina's Toys can reasonably anticipate that customers will be wearing a variety of footwear.

G. Additional Strengths of Rios's Case

- Logan has the burden of proving by a preponderance of the *credible* evidence, including testimony, that she was injured as a result of Rios's negligence. (Jury Instruction 35)
  - Logan is vulnerable to impeachment as a witness.
  - Rios will present evidence that Logan has lied about some of her damages, and therefore Logan's account of how she fell is suspect.
    - Logan lied about her injury causing the loss of her job.
    - According to Joe Nyugen, Logan's supervisor at Fresh Grocers, Logan lost her job because she failed to report to work for three days and failed to call in. Nyugen may testify that Logan was absent for three days without notice to her employer and that the employer had no knowledge of her injury when it fired her. (Ling's report)
  - Logan lied about her injury causing the loss of her basketball scholarship.
    - Logan claimed that she lost the basketball scholarship after the fall because she could not practice with her injured ankle. Rios may call university officials to show that Logan lost the scholarship prior to the injury and that the reason was "academic difficulties." (Ling's report)

Being able to show that Logan has lied about these facts will undermine the credibility of her testimony about the fall itself.

POINT SHEET
In re Al Merton

In re Al Merton
DRAFTERS' POINT SHEET

On the day before he is scheduled to undergo open heart surgery, the client, Al Merton, meets with the supervising partner in the firm about getting his will updated. He is concerned that he might not survive the surgery and wants to set his affairs in order.

The task for the applicants is to draft the introductory and dispositive clauses of a will in accordance with the wishes expressed by Mr. Merton in his interview with the partner. In addition, applicants must deal with Stuart Merton (the adopted son whom Mr. Merton wants to disinherit) and the disposition of the corporate stock and explain why they have dealt with these issues as they have. The applicants are also told to follow the instructions in the firm's Will Drafting Guidelines, which are included in the File.

The File contains the will of Henry Merton, from whom Al Merton inherited the Merton Office Supply Corporation ("MOSC") and associated property, and the latest will of Al Merton himself. These documents are in the File to give the applicants some idea of what a will looks like and the sort of language that might be used to express a disposition of property. The two wills are sufficiently different from the one the applicants are assigned to write so that the exercise does not become one of simply copying from the wills of Henry and Al Merton.

The File also contains an excerpt from a treatise, Walker's Treatise on Wills, explaining the classifications of bequests, to aid the applicants in placing Mr. Merton's bequests in the proper order in the new will. It also contains an appraisal of MOSC. The appraisal furnishes some background information regarding the corporation's assets, the number of shares owned by Mr. Merton, and the history and future prospects for carrying on the business, but is otherwise irrelevant to the task. Finally, the File contains a family tree to assist the applicants in keeping the parties straight.

The Library contains some relevant, definitional statutes on descent of property and basic corporations law, including a provision regarding voting trusts, which is relevant to Mr. Merton's desire to vest control of MOSC in Sara, one of his adopted children.

The Library also contains two cases, including Barry v. Allen, a Franklin case that stands for the proposition that a voting trust cannot last longer than 10 years unless certain conditions exist. The applicants should use that case in molding the will language regarding the establishment of a voting trust.

The following discussion covers all of the points the drafters intended to raise in the problem. Applicants need not cover them all to receive passing or even excellent grades. Grading decisions are within the discretion of the graders in the user jurisdictions.

Overview: There are two things the applicants are required to do:

(1) Draft the introductory and dispositive provisions of a new will for Mr. Merton. In doing so, applicants must follow the instructions in the firm's guidelines and adhere to Mr. Merton's wishes as expressed in the transcript of the interview.

The will should include numbered paragraphs setting forth the provisions in the order prescribed in the guidelines. That organization will require the applicants to determine the character of each bequest as defined in the excerpt from Walker's Treatise on Wills and to order them according to the guidelines.

The provisions should be stated concisely and written in the structure and format of a will.

(2) Follow the dispositive provisions regarding the disposition of the MOSC stock with a short explanation of why the dispositive language says what it does. This part of the exercise offers the applicants the opportunity to state in narrative, expository form what the language they have drafted means and why. They must also explain how they have dealt with Stuart Merton, and why, irrespective of whether they included language about Stuart in the will (see infra).

Graders can decide for themselves how much weight, if any, to ascribe to artful exposition and facial format.

PART ONE - The Introductory Clauses: This should be a fairly easy task. The Will Drafting Guidelines are clear. These clauses should recite that:

- The document is Mr. Merton's will;
- He is a resident of Griffin County, Franklin; this comes from his prior will and information contained in the interview.
- His immediate family consists of the two adopted children, Sara and Stuart, and his two nephews, Daniel and Louis.
- He revokes all prior wills and codicils.

PART TWO - The Dispositive Clauses: The order of bequests should follow the directions set forth in the guidelines. First the specific bequests: real property (of which the only one is the land and the building comprising the Lincoln Street Property); tangible personal property (none); and other specific bequests (the stock in MOSC).

The guidelines also tell applicants that they are to set forth "any other clauses stating conditions that might affect the disposition of specific bequests." It is unclear whether such clauses should be part of the dispositive clauses themselves or whether they should be separate clauses referring back to the dispositive clauses. Either way will work, but it will be more efficient if the applicants state the conditions in the dispositive clauses themselves.

Then, in sequence, applicants should set forth the general bequests (gifts of money to Sara, Daniel, and Louis, and to Franklin College for the Henry Merton Small Business Assistance Program); next, the demonstrative bequest to Sara to be paid from the savings account; and, finally, the residuary bequest.

At some point in the exercise, they must also deal with Mr. Merton's desire to disinherit Stuart.

SPECIFIC BEQUESTS

- **Real Property—Disposition of the Lincoln Street Property:** The interview and the business appraisal make it clear that the Lincoln Street Property consists of the land and the building and that it is not among the assets of MOSC. In order to "link" the Lincoln Street Property with the business, Mr. Merton has decided simply to will the Lincoln Street Property to MOSC. Thus, the applicants should simply draft a clause giving the land and buildings to MOSC.
  - NOTE: It would be erroneous to mention Mr. Merton's residence in this section because it falls into the residuary bequest.
- **Other Specific Bequests—Disposition of the Corporate Stock:** Under the facts, Mr. Merton wants to leave "an equal share of the business" to Sara, Daniel, and Louis and have them all share in the profits but wants to ensure that Sara retains the power to "make the decisions" for at least 15 years. This will require, as the supervising attorney put it, laying the groundwork in the will for the later creation of a voting trust. Drawing upon the wishes Mr. Merton expressed in the interview, § 102 of the Franklin Corporations Code, and the holdings in *Barry v. Allen* and In re *Estate of Tourneau*, the applicants should draft language reflecting that:
  - Sara, Daniel, and Louis are each to receive one-third (or 50 shares) of the MOSC stock;
  - Sara is to have the right to vote all shares, a goal that is to be accomplished by the later creation of a voting trust;
  - Accordingly, Sara, Daniel, and Louis must agree that their respective shares will be placed in a voting trust for up to 15 years and that Sara is to have the sole right to vote the shares.
  - They will also have to agree that, if MOSC's articles of incorporation do not provide that a voting trust can last for more than 10 years (which they appear not to), the articles will be amended so to provide. (See Barry v. Allen, In re Estate of Tourneau, and Franklin Corporations Code § 102(b).)
  - If either Daniel or Louis should refuse to agree to these conditions, the shares of the corporate stock that each would receive under the will would go to Sara.
  - This would be the "gift over" that appears as a requirement in Tourneau.
- The applicants might also draft language specifying that Mr. Merton wants all three to share in the profits. However, omission of such language is not fatal because the statute (§102(c)) provides that dividends paid on account of stock in a voting trust shall be paid to the beneficial owners (Sara, Daniel, and Louis). If applicants omit such language they should cover it in their explanations.

Explanation: Applicants should explain that the language used in the dispositive provisions is intended to make sure that Sara retains the right to run the business for up to 15 years even though all three of them will share in the profits (and, unless applicants have explicitly included "share-the-profits" language, they must explain that sharing results automatically by operation of § 102(c)); that, although each beneficiary is getting one-third of the stock, it is on the condition that they all agree to put it into a 15-year voting trust giving Sara the sole power to vote the stock; that the beneficiaries must agree that the articles of incorporation may be amended to carry out that intent; and that if either Daniel or Louis refuses to agree to these conditions, that beneficiary will lose his shares to Sara.

- It should be implicit in applicants' treatment of this subject that they understand that a bequest of the corporate stock conveys ownership of the assets of the corporation, i.e., the inventory, the lease, and the corporate name (see the appraisal of the corporation). Applicants who attempt to bequeath these assets separately have missed the point and should receive reduced credit.
  - It should also be implicit that applicants recognize that this bequest falls into the category of "other specific bequests" as opposed to a bequest of "tangible personal property," i.e., stock in a corporation is not tangible personal property in the ordinary sense of the word. See *Barry v. Allen*.

GENERAL BEQUESTS

- **The general gifts of money or estate assets:** There are two categories of such gifts: the bequest of $100,000 each to Sara, Daniel, and Louis; and the gift of $1,000,000 to Franklin College to endow a specific entity.
  - The gifts of $100,000 each to Sara, Daniel, and Louis can be stated in a single dispositive paragraph (e.g., "I give Sara, Daniel, and Louis $100,000 each.") or in separate paragraphs reciting the gift for each of them.
  - The gift of $1,000,000 out of general estate assets to Franklin College should recite that it is to endow the small business program and is conditioned on the program's being named after Mr. Merton's father: The Henry Merton Small Business Assistance Program.

DEMONSTRATIVE BEQUEST

- **The gift to Sara to be paid from the savings account:** This is a demonstrative bequest because its payment is to be made from a designated fund— the savings account.
  - The language of the bequest should state that the gift is to be paid first out of the savings account and that it is a separate bequest to furnish money to enable Sara to finish college.

RESIDUARY BEQUEST

- **The gift of the remainder of the estate:** The language of this clause should recite clearly that the remainder of the estate goes to the Franklin College Faculty Development Fund (e.g., "the rest, residue, and remainder" or "all my property not otherwise disposed of by this will.")
  - Note that the residue also contains Al Merton's home, which is realty. It is not disposed of as a specific bequest because Mr. Merton did not direct that it be given to the Faculty Development Fund separately and distinctly from the residue.

DISINHERITING STUART

- **The intent to disinherit Stuart:** At some point in the exercise, applicants will have to deal with Mr. Merton's desire to disinherit Stuart. It can be done either at the beginning or at the end of the document.
  - It can be accomplished by an express statement in the will that Mr. Merton wants to disinherit Stuart. (e.g., "It is my intention that my adopted child, Stuart Merton, take nothing under my will.") It can also be accomplished by saying nothing in the will, inasmuch as Stuart had been adopted several years before Mr. Merton's visit with the partner and therefore he is the legal equivalent of a child in being before the will was written. Better applicants will definitely opt to make the express statement rather than leave it open to interpretation.
  - Explanation: This is the only point in the exercise, other than a reference in the introductory clause, where the fact that Mr. Merton adopted Sara and Stuart is called into play. As to Sara, it makes no difference because she is a named beneficiary and takes under the terms of the will, irrespective of the adoption.
  - With regard to Stuart, applicants should discuss whether he would be a pretermitted heir if he is not provided for in the will. Under Franklin Probate Code § 101(e), Stuart is deemed for all purposes to be Mr. Merton's lineal descendant. Section 206 raises the issue of pretermission, and it is abundantly clear that Stuart would not be pretermitted because he was not adopted after the will was made. Applicants should make it clear that they understand this. An applicant who includes language expressly disinheriting Stuart so to pre-vent Stuart from claiming as a pretermitted heir shows a lack of understanding. If, on the other hand, an applicant chooses to leave the will silent as to Stuart, it is essential that he or she explain why, i.e., that there is no need to mention him because the will was made after Stuart became a child of Mr. Merton and, therefore, Stuart is not pretermitted.

MEE ANSWERS

Contracts Question Analyses
Torts Question Analyses
Agency & Partnership Question Analyses

TORTS QUESTION ANALYSES

1. **Legal Problems:**
   (1)   Is Library, an occasional, noncommercial product seller, strictly liable to Paul?
   (2)(a) Is Supermarket, a commercial product seller, strictly liable for injuries to Paul when it did not produce or alter the defective product and did not sell the product to Paul?
   (2)(b) Is a product defective when the risk cannot be eliminated and the product comes with adequate warnings?
   (3)   May Paul recover damages from any of Ann, Bill, or Chuck when he cannot show who was negligent and caused his injury?

DISCUSSION

Summary

If Paul proves only the facts given in the problem, he will not be able to recover damages from any of the parties. Paul cannot recover damages from Library because, as an occasional, noncommercial seller of food, Library is not strictly liable for injuries caused by its food. Paul cannot recover damages from Supermarket either. Although Supermarket, as a commercial seller, is strictly liable for defective products, here the product was not defective as it was prominently labeled as possibly having salmonella bacteria, and the risk of salmonella contamination cannot be eliminated. There is evidence that at least one of Ann, Bill, or Chuck was negligent in the preparation of the chicken salad that caused Paul's injury. If Paul could establish which party was negligent, he could recover damages from that individual. However, Paul cannot establish which party was negligent, and the doctrines of res ipsa loquitur, alternative liability, and joint enterprise liability are all unavailable to assist Paul in his claim.

Point One: (15–25%)

Strict products liability is only available against commercial product sellers. Thus Library cannot be liable because it is not a commercial product seller.

"One who sells any product in a defective condition unreasonably dangerous to the user or consumer . . . is subject to liability for physical harm thereby caused. . . ." RESTATEMENT (SECOND) OF TORTS § 402A (1966). The chicken salad sandwich that Paul consumed was unreasonably dangerous to the consumer because it contained salmonella bacteria. Thus, if Library had been a restaurant or other commercial entity, Paul would have a viable products liability action. In that action, he would not need to establish negligence on the part of Library.

However, a strict products liability action is only available against a "person engaged in the business of selling products for use or consumption." *Id.* § 402A cmt. f; RESTATEMENT (THIRD) OF THE LAW OF PRODUCTS LIABILITY § 1 (1998). Because the facts do not establish that Library is a commercial seller, Paul's action against Library will fail on that ground.

Point Two(a): (10–20%)

A commercial seller may be found strictly liable for a defective product it sells even if the seller did not produce the product and the injured party did not purchase the product from the seller.

Strict products liability applies to all commercial sellers. Even a retailer who has no control over the design and manufacture of a product may be found strictly liable if that retailer sells a defective product. Because Supermarket is a commercial seller, it may be found liable if the chicken it sold was defective. *See* RESTATEMENT (SECOND) OF TORTS § 402A.

The fact that Paul did not purchase the chicken himself does not alter the result. Modern products liability law applies to bystanders as well as purchasers. The "privity of contract" approach has everywhere been abandoned. *See id.* (establishing strict liability for injuries to "ultimate user or consumer"); *see also* 2 DAN DOBBS, THE LAW OF TORTS § 353 (2001).

Point Two(b): (15–25%)

A product seller is liable only for a defective product. Because the risk of salmonella contamination cannot be eliminated from raw chicken and the product was accompanied by detailed warnings, the chicken sold by Supermarket was not defective.

A product is defective when it is unreasonably dangerous. A product may be defective because it has a manufacturing defect, because it is defective in design, or because it provides inadequate instructions or warnings. The chicken sold by Supermarket carried adequate warnings of the risk of salmonella contamination and instructions on how to cook the chicken to ensure that it was safe for eating. The chicken sold by Supermarket did not contain a manufacturing or design defect as the risk of salmonella contamination is inherent in raw chicken and cannot be eliminated. Thus, the chicken conformed to the producer's specifications, and those specifications could not be altered. Because the chicken was not defective, Paul cannot recover damages from Supermarket. *See generally* DOBBS, *supra*, § 354.

Point Three: (25–35%)

Paul could recover on a negligence theory against Ann, Bill, or Chuck *if, and only if,* he could show which of them was negligent in preparing the chicken salad. Furthermore, merely the fact that these batches of chicken salad were mixed together doesn't make Ann, Bill, and Chuck joint tortfeasors because there is no evidence they were engaged in a joint venture or joint enterprise. In fact they acted independently of one another. Paul cannot recover on a strict liability theory because Ann, Bill, and Chuck are not product sellers.

The Health Department said that someone who made the chicken salad that Paul ate used improper precautions. The evidence thus shows that one of Ann, Bill, or Chuck was negligent, that is, failed to exercise reasonable care under the circumstances.

Even though Paul cannot show how the negligence occurred, he could still recover if only one individual had made the salad. In such a situation, Paul could use the doctrine of res ipsa loquitur, which permits the jury to infer negligence when "the event is of a kind which ordinarily does not occur in the absence of negligence; . . . other responsible causes . . . are sufficiently eliminated by the evidence; . . . and the indicated negligence is within the scope of the defendant's duty to the plaintiff." RESTATEMENT (SECOND) OF TORTS § 328D(1)(a)-(c). Paul can meet the first and third of these requirements: the Health Department has said that salmonella contamination does not occur when chicken is cooked and prepared properly. The salad preparers owed a duty to Paul as he was a lunch patron who would foreseeably have been expected to consume the chicken salad. However, Paul cannot establish that any *one* defendant had control of the chicken salad, as there were two other individuals who made salad independently. *See Samson v. Riesing,* 215 N.W.2d 662, 667-68 (Wis. 1974). Nor can Paul show that Ann, Bill, and Chuck have better information about who was negligent or are engaged in a conspiracy of silence. *See Ybarra v. Spangard,* 154 P.2d 687 (Cal. 1944).

There are other doctrines that permit the jury to find a defendant liable even when there is more than one defendant and the plaintiff cannot show which defendant's conduct caused his injury. However, none of these doctrines would help Paul to establish the liability of Ann, Bill, or Chuck. The "alternative liability" doctrine, which permits the jury to find two defendants liable when each was negligent and either individual could have caused the plaintiff's injuries, is unavailable because Paul cannot show that all defendants were negligent. *See Summers v. Tice,* 199 P.2d 1 (Cal. 1948); RESTATEMENT (SECOND) OF TORTS

§ 433B(3). The "joint venture" or "joint enterprise" doctrine allows the jury to impute one defendant's negligence to other defendants who are engaged in a common project or enterprise and who have an explicit or implied understanding about how the project is to be carried out. *See* DOBBS, THE LAW OF TORTS § 340. However, Paul cannot show that Ann, Bill, and Chuck had any common understanding. The facts state that Ann, Bill, and Chuck acted independently in making their respective batches of chicken salad.

Thus, because Paul cannot show which defendant was negligent, he cannot recover damages from Ann, Bill, or Chuck.

A strict products liability action would not be available against Ann, Bill, or Chuck because none is a product seller. Moreover, even if a products liability action were available, it would still be necessary to identify the source of the defective product, here the contaminated chicken salad.

2. **Legal Problems:**
   (1) Does Nephew have a cause of action against Tenant for negligence?
   (2) What is the standard of care applicable to Nephew?
   (3) Will Nephew's negligence prevent Nephew from recovering damages from Tenant or Landlord?
   (4) Did Landlord's violation of a state statute requiring that every part of a building be kept "in good repair" represent negligence *per se*?
   (5) Was Landlord's failure to repair the furnace a proximate cause of Nephew's injuries?

DISCUSSION

Summary

The jury could award Nephew damages in his action against Tenant. In a negligence action, an adult defendant's conduct is measured against that of a reasonable, prudent person engaged in a similar activity; a minor's conduct is measured against that of a minor of like age, intelligence, and experience. The determination of whether a party's conduct conforms to the applicable standard of care is a question of fact that is normally left to the jury. Here the jury could conclude that Tenant was negligent and that his negligence was the cause in fact and proximate cause of Nephew's injuries. Even if the jury also concluded that Nephew was negligent, under modern comparative negligence rules Nephew could still recover from Tenant.

It is less clear that the jury could award Nephew damages in his action against Landlord. Although violation of a state statute is normally considered negligence *per se*, it is unclear that the injuries Nephew suffered were within the category of harms the legislature aimed to prevent when enacting the statute. It is equally unclear whether Landlord's failure to repair the furnace was a proximate cause of the injuries.

Point One: (15–25%)

A reasonable jury could conclude that Tenant was negligent and that his negligence caused Nephew's injuries.

In any negligence action, a plaintiff must show that the defendant owed the plaintiff a duty to conform his conduct to a standard necessary to avoid an unreasonable risk of harm to others, that the defendant's conduct fell below the applicable standard of care, and that the defendant's conduct was both the cause in fact and the proximate cause of his injuries.

Nephew would have no difficulty in establishing that Tenant owed him a duty of care. Nephew was Tenant's household guest whose presence was known to Tenant. Thus, Tenant owed Nephew an obligation to exercise reasonable care to avoid foreseeable risks. *See* RICHARD A. EPSTEIN, CASES AND MATERIALS ON TORTS 154–55 (7th ed. 2000).

In determining whether Tenant's conduct fell below the standard of care, the jury would measure that conduct against the conduct of a reasonable, prudent person engaged in a like activity. A reasonable, prudent person takes precautions to avoid foreseeable risks. *See id.* at 162–63. A large pot of boiling water, if it spills, clearly poses a foreseeable risk of serious burns. A jury might also conclude that it was foreseeable that someone would come out of the bedroom quickly and collide with the boiling water. The burden of taking precautions to avert this possibility was small; Tenant could have yelled, "I'm coming with a pot of boiling water," or closed the bedroom door. Given the foreseeability of serious harm and the small burden of taking precautions, a jury might conclude that Tenant was negligent.

Tenant's conduct also was the cause in fact and proximate cause of the injuries. Tenant's failure to take precautions appears to have been a substantial factor in producing the accident. Burns were a foreseeable result of collision with a pot containing boiling water. Thus, based on the facts, a jury could properly award damages to Nephew.

Point Two: (15–25%)

Although Nephew's age makes it unlikely, a jury could find that Nephew was negligent and that Nephew's negligence was a contributing factor in causing his injuries.

Nephew, like Tenant, had a duty to prevent foreseeable risks to himself and others. In judging whether Nephew exercised reasonable care under the circumstances, the jury would measure Nephew's conduct against that of a minor of like age, intelligence, and experience. *See* RESTATEMENT (SECOND) OF TORTS §§ 283, 283A (1965); *Roberts v. Ring*, 173 N.W. 437 (Minn. 1919). A few jurisdictions apply the so-called "tender years doctrine," under which a minor of less than seven years of age cannot be found negligent, but Nephew was age eight when the accident occurred.

Nephew chased a ball into the hall without looking or calling out. To an adult, this conduct would create a foreseeable risk of collision with someone walking in the hall. Age is the key factor here. A normal toddler does not foresee risks, particularly when engaged in an activity like chasing a ball; a normal adolescent does foresee such risks. Nephew, age eight, falls between a toddler and an adolescent. Therefore, it is possible, but not likely, that a jury would find that Nephew's conduct was negligent.

Point Three: (10–20%)

Even if the jury found that Nephew was negligent in running into the hall, under modern comparative negligence rules, Nephew's negligence would reduce his recovery from Tenant but would not eliminate Tenant's liability.

At common law, if the jury found the plaintiff's negligence to be a cause in fact and proximate cause of his injuries, the plaintiff could not recover from the defendant. This all-or-nothing approach was frequently criticized; it has now been abandoned by virtually all states. *See* EPSTEIN, *supra*, at 369.

Under the modern "comparative negligence" approach, if the jury finds that two or more parties are negligent, it apportions fault between them. The plaintiff's fault share is subtracted from the total damages awarded by the jury. Thus, even if the jury found Nephew to be negligent, that finding would reduce his recovery from Tenant but not eliminate Tenant's liability, except in a state that has preserved the all-or-nothing approach to contributory negligence or in a comparative negligence state where recovery is barred if the victim was more than 50 percent negligent.

Point Four: (15–25%)

The unexcused violation of a statutory standard is negligence *per se* if the statute was designed to protect against the type of accident the actor's conduct caused and the injured party is within the class of persons the statute was designed to protect. Under this standard, it is unclear whether Landlord's conduct constituted negligence *per se.*

The governing state statute requires that "every apartment building . . . and every part thereof shall be kept in good repair." Arguably, Landlord violated the statute, as the furnace was "part" of the "apartment building" owned by Landlord, and it malfunctioned on three different occasions before Landlord took steps to correct the problem permanently. "An actor is negligent if, without excuse, the actor violates a statute that is designed to protect against the type of accident the actor's conduct causes, and if the accident victim is within the class of persons the statute is designed to protect." RESTATEMENT (THIRD) OF TORTS § 14 (P.F.D. No. 1 2005). In such a case, the jury is *required* to find that the actor is negligent.

Landlord's failure to permanently fix the furnace was unexcused. On three earlier occasions, he was given notice of problems with the furnace but made only temporary repairs. Nephew, as the guest of a tenant, is within the class of persons the statute is designed to protect. Loss of heat and hot water is certainly among the types of harms the statute was designed to protect against. However, it is not clear that the accident which occurred—burns due to a collision—was within the category of harms the statute was designed to protect against. *See* EPSTEIN, *supra*, at 259-60 (describing conflicting authority on whether statutes criminalizing the act of leaving a key in a car ignition are designed to protect against injuries caused by a car thief).

Point Five: (20–30%)

In a negligence action, a defendant is liable only if his conduct was the proximate cause of the plaintiff's injury. A reasonable jury could find that the type of harm Nephew suffered was too remote from Landlord's negligence in failing to provide adequate heat and hot water.

It is unclear whether Landlord's failure to repair the furnace was a proximate cause of Nephew's injuries. (Indeed, the "right type of harm" requirement for use of a statutory standard to establish negligence is probably just another way of stating the proximate cause requirement.) Even when the defendant is negligent, his conduct must have "such an effect in producing the harm as to lead reasonable men to regard it as a cause, using that word in the popular sense, in which there always lurks the idea of responsibility, rather than in the so-called 'philosophic sense,' which includes every one of the great number of events without which any happening would not have occurred." RESTATEMENT (SECOND) OF TORTS § 431, cmt. a.

Intervening actors or events that produce harm different in kind from that which one would normally anticipate from the defendant's negligence may break the chain of causation and lead a fact-finder to conclude that the defendant's acts are not the proximate cause of the plaintiff's injury. Thus, a defendant who negligently exceeds a speed limit and therefore happens to be on the spot where a tree falls during a violent windstorm is not liable for injuries caused by the tree (*see Berry v. Sugar Notch Borough*, 43 A. 240 (Pa. 1899)), and a defendant who negligently fails to stop a train at a station is not liable for the passenger's injuries when she elects to walk the mile back to the station along a dangerous route and is assaulted. *See Hines v. Garrett*, 108 S.E. 690 (Va. 1921). These harms are simply too remote from the defendant's negligent conduct.

On similar facts, courts have not agreed on whether a landlord's conduct was the proximate cause of a plaintiff's injury. Some courts have found that the landlord's negligence in failing to timely repair a furnace is too remote from burn injuries like Nephew's based on the intervening and arguably unforeseeable conduct of actors like Nephew and Tenant as well as the nature of the injuries, which are different in kind from those that would typically be produced by an inoperable heating system. Other courts have held that a jury might reasonably find heating hot water to be a foreseeable result of not having hot water and collisions from carrying hot water a foreseeable result of heating it. *Compare Martinez v. Lazaroff*, 399 N.E.2d 1148 (N.Y. 1979), *with Enis v. Ba-Call Bldg. Corp.*, 639 F.2d 359 (7th Cir. 1980). *See generally* Annotation, *Landlord and Tenant: Violation of Statute or Ordinance Requiring Landlord to Furnish Specified Facilities or Services as Ground of Liability for Injury Resulting from Tenant's Attempt to Deal with Deficiency*, 63 A.L.R.4th 883 (1988).

[NOTE: The applicant's conclusion on the proximate cause issue is less important than his or her analysis. The applicant should receive full credit if he or she recognizes and discusses the applicable legal principles.]

3. **Legal Problems:**
    (1) What must Penny establish in a battery action against Dennis?
    (2) What must Penny establish in a negligence action against Dennis?
    (3) What must Penny establish in an action against the Flies based on the team's employment relationship with Dennis?
    (4) What must Penny establish in a negligence action against the Flies?
    (5) If Penny succeeds in her action against either Dennis or the Flies, can she recover for damages for the neurological harm that resulted from a preexisting condition?

DISCUSSION

Summary

Penny does not have a viable battery action against Dennis because Dennis neither intended, nor knew with substantial certainty, that the ball he hit out of the Park would strike anyone. Penny does not have a viable negligence action against Dennis because there is no reasonable means by which Dennis could have avoided hitting Penny. Because Penny does not have a viable claim against Dennis, she has no viable claim against the Flies based on the team's employment of Dennis even though Dennis was acting within the scope of his employment. However, Penny might have a viable negligence action against the Flies based on the team's failure to attach netting to the fence adjoining Oak Street. The fact that the Flies have conformed to customary standards for minor league baseball fence construction is relevant but not determinative. If the jury finds that the Flies' failure to install netting along the Oak Street fence was negligent, Penny could recover for harm suffered as a result of her adverse reaction to medication even though this harm resulted from a preexisting condition.

Point One (25%)

Dennis did not commit a battery when the ball he hit struck Penny. Therefore Penny does not have a viable battery action against Dennis.

In a battery action, the plaintiff must show that the defendant *intentionally* caused a harmful or offensive bodily contact. A defendant intentionally causes such a contact if he "acts with the desire to bring about that harm" or engages "in action knowing that harm is substantially certain to occur." RESTATEMENT (THIRD) OF TORTS § 1, cmt. d. In this case, Dennis neither desired to bring about a harmful contact between the baseball and Penny nor, in light of his location inside the Park, could he have known that such a contact would or was substantially certain to occur. As a result, Penny does not have a viable battery claim against Dennis.

Point Two (25%)

Dennis was not negligent in hitting the ball that struck Penny over the Oak Street fence. Therefore Penny does not have a viable negligence claim against Dennis.

In a negligence action, the plaintiff must show that the defendant owed the plaintiff a duty to conform his conduct to a standard necessary to avoid an unreasonable risk of harm to others, that the defendant's conduct fell below the applicable standard of care, and that the defendant's conduct was both the cause in fact and the proximate cause of the plaintiff's injuries.

In determining whether Dennis's conduct fell below the standard of care, the jury would measure that conduct against the actions of a reasonable, prudent person engaged in a like activity. A reasonable, prudent person takes appropriate precautions to avoid foreseeable risks; in measuring whether a particular precaution was warranted, the jury weighs the burden of taking such precautions against the gravity of the risk and the likelihood that it will eventuate. *See* RICHARD A. EPSTEIN, CASES AND MATERIALS ON TORTS 150–51 (7th ed. 2004); *United States v. Carroll Towing Co.*, 159 F.2d 169 (2d Cir. 1947).

Here the burden of taking the precaution against the risk is high. The only meaningful precautions that Dennis might have taken were not hitting the ball at all or trying to hit it with less than maximum force. Either precaution would generally be inconsistent with Dennis's job as a professional baseball player, which includes the obligation to hit the ball and to hit a home run if possible. For Dennis, the cost of taking precautions could mean the loss of his career.

The gravity of the risk created by his hitting the ball cannot be determined easily. Being hit with an errant baseball could cause harm ranging from minimal bruising to far more serious injury. The likelihood of the harm occurring is low—in 40 years only 30 balls had previously been hit into Oak Street.

Thus Dennis was not negligent in hitting the ball that caused Penny's injury.

Point Three (10%)

<u>Penny does not have a viable claim against the Flies based on the team's employ-
ment of Dennis.</u>

An employer is vicariously liable for the tortious actions of his employee that are
within the scope of the tortfeasor's employment. *See* RESTATEMENT (SECOND)
OF AGENCY §§ 219, 229; RESTATEMENT (THIRD) OF AGENCY § 2.04. In this case,
there is no question that Dennis was acting within the scope of his employment;
he was a baseball player engaged in hitting a baseball. But Penny does not have
a viable tort action against Dennis because Dennis's conduct was not tortious.
Therefore, the Flies are not vicariously liable for his conduct.

Point Four (25%)

<u>Penny may have a viable negligence action against the Flies based on the team's
failure to attach netting to the Oak Street fence despite the fact that the fence
conforms to customary standards within professional baseball.</u>

Just as a jury would measure Dennis's conduct against the actions of a reasonable,
prudent person engaged in a like activity, it would measure the Flies' conduct in
constructing and maintaining the Oak Street fence against that of a reasonably
prudent ballpark owner. And while Dennis had no means of avoiding the injury
to Penny other than not hitting the ball, the Flies could have added netting to the
Oak Street fence, and that netting would have prevented Penny's injury.

Custom is relevant in a negligence action, but it is not determinative. *See
The T.J. Hooper*, 53 F.2d 107 (S.D.N.Y. 1931). Thus, even though the Flies' conduct conformed to the industry standard, Penny may succeed in her negligence
action if she can establish that the cost of adding netting to the fence was relatively modest in relation to the risk of injuries from balls exiting the Park onto
Oak Street. Given the changed character of the street, the increasing number
of balls hit onto the street in recent years, and the widespread adoption of netting in another country, it is possible that Penny may succeed in making such a
showing.

Point Five (15%)

<u>Because a tort defendant "takes his victim as he finds him," Penny could recover
for harm suffered due to her adverse reaction to medication.</u>

A tort defendant takes his victim as he finds him. The plaintiff with an "eggshell
skull" who suffers damage greatly in excess of those that a normal victim would
suffer thus is entitled to recover fully for his injuries. *See* Epstein, *supra,* at 476–
77. Because Penny's sensitivity to the prescribed medication was a preexisting
condition, if Penny succeeds in her lawsuit against the Flies, she could recover
for all injuries suffered as a result of that sensitivity.

CONTRACTS QUESTION ANALYSES

1. **Legal Problems:**
   (1)(a) Did Baker's letter of May 1 constitute an offer?
   (1)(b) Did Café Owner's oral response on the morning of May 7 constitute a counteroffer?
   (2)   Did Café accept Baker's offer?
   (3)   Did the contract between Baker and Café satisfy the Statute of Frauds?

DISCUSSION

Summary

A valid contract requires an offer, an acceptance and, when as here, the contract cannot be performed within one year, a writing that satisfies the Statute of Frauds. Here, Baker made an offer to work for Café that was accepted when Café's Owner sent an acceptance by express mail to Baker. It is irrelevant that Baker did not read the acceptance. The fact that an earlier rejection was mailed is also irrelevant because a rejection, unlike an acceptance, is effective only upon receipt, and Baker did not receive the rejection before receiving the acceptance. When both a rejection and an acceptance are sent, whichever is received first is effective. Lastly, the writings, being signed, satisfy the requirements of the Statute of Frauds. Therefore, Café has an enforceable contract.

Point One(a): (20-30%)

<u>Baker's signed letter of May 1 to Café agreeing to work as a pastry chef for Café is a valid offer.</u>

A person makes an offer when the person communicates to another a statement of "willingness to enter into a bargain, so made as to justify" the other person who hears the statement "in understanding that his assent to that bargain is invited and will conclude it." Restatement (Second) of Contracts § 24 (1981). Here, Baker's letter of May 1 to Café was an offer because an objective recipient of the letter, such as Café, would reasonably conclude that assent would create a contract.

An offer cannot ripen into a contract by acceptance unless its terms are reasonably certain. Id. § 33(1). Here, the terms were clear and certain and identified the parties, the subject matter, and the price.

Point One(b): (20-30%)

<u>Café Owner's phone call to Baker on the morning of May 7 asking if he would possibly work for less was not a counteroffer but merely a request for changed terms.</u>

A counteroffer is a statement from the offeree to the offeror, relating to the same subject matter as the original offer but suggesting a substituted bargain from the original terms. Id. § 39(1). Generally, if an offeree makes a counteroffer, the offeree can no longer accept the original offer. Id. § 39(2). Here, Café's Owner said to Baker "The $100,000 is pretty stiff. Could you possibly consider working for less?" This utterance is not a counteroffer because it did not offer substitute terms to Baker and did not indicate any unwillingness to conclude the bargain on Baker's terms if Baker would not accept an alternative salary. All Café's Owner did was ask Baker if he could possibly work for less. Café's Owner proposed no alternative salary. Because Café's Owner's call to Baker was not a counteroffer, but merely a request for unspecified changed terms, it did not preclude Café's later acceptance of Baker's offer.

Point Two: (25-35%)

<u>Although Café's Owner initially rejected Baker's offer in writing, he later accepted the offer. Because Baker received the acceptance before he received the rejection, Baker's offer is deemed accepted.</u>

A rejection is a manifestation of intent not to accept an offer. Id. § 38(2). A rejection terminates the offeree's power to accept an offer. Id. § 38(1). However, a rejection does not extinguish the offeree's right to accept an offer until the rejection is received by the offeror. Id. § 40. Here, Café's Owner's letter stating "I am no longer interested in hiring you" clearly manifests an intent not to go forward with the bargain and constitutes a rejection of Baker's offer.

However, Café's Owner's second letter, in which Café agreed to Baker's terms, was an acceptance because it was a manifestation of assent to the terms of an offer made in a manner invited by the offer. Id. § 50(1). The question then becomes which of the two letters sent by Café's Owner is effective, the rejection or the acceptance.

An acceptance is effective upon dispatch under the so-called "mailbox rule." Id. § 63. A rejection is effective only upon receipt. But when an acceptance is sent after a rejection (that is, both the acceptance and the rejection are sent), whichever gets to the recipient first is effective. Id. § 40. Here, Café's letter of acceptance was received by Baker first, while the letter containing the rejection was still on the way to Baker. See id. § 68 (a communication is received when it comes into the possession of the person to whom it is addressed). The fact that Baker did not read the letter does not alter this result. Because the acceptance was the first communication received, it is effective. Therefore, Café accepted Baker's offer to work for Café, and a contract was created.

Point Three: (25-35%)

If a contract cannot be performed within a year, it must meet the requirements of the Statute of Frauds. Here the contract satisfies that statute and, therefore, is enforceable.

A contract must satisfy the Statute of Frauds if it cannot be fully performed within one year. Id. § 130. Here, the two-year employment requirement cannot be completed in one year, and therefore the contract is within the purview of the Statute of Frauds and must satisfy the requirements of the Statute of Frauds to be enforceable.

A contract within the Statute of Frauds satisfies that statute and is enforceable if it is evidenced by a writing signed by "the party to be charged," which (a) reasonably identifies the subject matter of the contract; (b) is sufficient to indicate that a contract has been made; and (c) "states with reasonable certainty the essential terms" of the contract. Id. § 131.

Here, each party signed a writing that is sufficient under these criteria as it identifies the position, person, term, and salary. Therefore, the Statute of Frauds is satisfied and the employment contract is enforceable. Because this is a personal services contract, if Baker refuses to work for Café, Café can sue Baker for damages, but cannot get specific performance.

2. **Legal Problems:**
   (1) Was Resident's promise to pay Sam $1,000 supported by consideration?
   (2) In the absence of bargained-for consideration, can Sam enforce Resident's promise under the material benefit (moral consideration) rule?
   (3) In the absence of bargained-for consideration, can Sam enforce Resident's promise under the theory of promissory estoppel?

DISCUSSION

Summary

Sam cannot recover the $1,000 under the theory that Resident's promise was supported by consideration as there is no evidence of a bargained-for exchange.

Sam may be able to recover if the material benefit (or moral consideration) rule applies because Resident made the promise to pay $1,000 in recognition of a benefit received. Sam may also be able to recover under the theory of promissory estoppel if he acted in reasonable reliance on Resident's promise. However,

Sam may recover less than the full $1,000 under both the material benefit rule and the theory of promissory estoppel.

Point One: (25–35%)

<u>Sam cannot recover under the theory that Resident's promise was supported by consideration because that promise was not part of a bargained-for exchange.</u>

To be legally enforceable, a promise generally must be supported by consideration, which is shown through bargained-for exchange. This means that the promisor must have sought and received something of legal value in exchange for the promise. *See* RESTATEMENT (SECOND) OF CONTRACTS § 71. Here, there was no bargained-for exchange.

Sam might argue that his action in rescuing the dog and/or Sam's promise to apply for paramedic training constitutes consideration for Resident's promise to pay $1,000. However, neither of those arguments will prevail. Resident's promise to pay the $1,000 was not made in exchange for Sam's rescue of the dog, but instead was made in recognition of that prior action. With regard to Sam's promise to apply for paramedic training, Resident did not seek that promise in exchange for the promise to pay the $1,000. Resident's promise was not part of an exchange and therefore the consideration necessary to make Resident's promise legally enforceable is absent.

Point Two: (15–25%)

<u>Sam may be able to recover if the material benefit (moral consideration) rule applies, but possibly may not receive the full $1,000 Resident promised him.</u>

Some states recognize an exception to the past consideration limitation in cases in which the promise is made after receipt of a significant benefit. This exception is set out in the Restatement (Second) of Contracts § 86 (the material benefit rule) and encapsulates cases in which moral consideration was found to provide a basis for recovery. The material benefit rule states that a promise not supported by consideration may be enforceable if it is "made in recognition of a benefit previously received by the promisor from the promisee . . . ." RESTATEMENT (SECOND) OF CONTRACTS § 86(1); *see Webb v. McGowin*, 168 So. 196 (Ala. 1935). Here, Resident promised to give Sam $1,000 in recognition of Sam's act of saving Resident's dog. Thus, it could be argued that the material benefit rule applies because Resident received a benefit from Sam and made the promise to give Sam $1,000 in recognition of that benefit.

However, the material benefit rule does not apply (and the promise is not enforceable) if the promisee conferred the benefit as a gift, or to the extent that the value of the promise is disproportionate to the benefit conferred. RESTATEMENT (SECOND) OF CONTRACTS § 86(2). Here, it is unclear whether Sam intended to confer a gift upon Resident. He may have been acting out of pure selflessness when he rescued the dog, or he may have believed that his heroic action would result in a financial reward.

Even if it is determined that Sam did not intend to confer a gift (and that Resident's promise is therefore enforceable), a court might limit recovery to something less than the full $1,000 if it finds that $1,000 is disproportionate to the value of the rescue of the dog.

Point Three: (35–45%)

Sam may be able to recover some or all of the $1,000 if the doctrine of promissory estoppel applies. Promissory estoppel requires that the promisee show that a promise existed, that a detrimental change in position was made in reasonable reliance on the promise, and that enforcement of the promise is the only way to avoid injustice.

The doctrine of promissory estoppel allows the enforcement of gratuitous promises to avoid harm to individuals who have relied on those promises. *See* RESTATEMENT (SECOND) OF CONTRACTS § 90. In order to establish a promissory estoppel claim, all of the following must be shown: (1) the promisor, when making the promise, should have reasonably expected that the promisee would change his position in reliance on the promise; (2) the promisee did in fact change position in reliance on the promise; (3) the change in position was to the promisee's detriment and injustice can be avoided only by enforcing the promise. *Id.*

Here, the facts state that Resident promised to pay $1,000. Sam did change his position in reliance on that promise by incurring a $1,000 debt. Resident might argue that Sam's applying to the cosmetology program was not reasonable reliance because the promise was specific to a different program—Resident said, "If you are going to start paramedic training, I want to help you." However, Resident also said, "I want to compensate you for your heroism," and Sam could reasonably interpret that remark as indicating that Resident's promise to give him $1,000 was a promise to compensate him for rescuing Resident's dog and was not conditioned on his career choice. Thus, it is possible that Sam could recover that portion of the $1,000 promised by Resident that is determined to be the amount required to avoid injustice.

AGENCY & PARTNERSHIP
QUESTION ANALYSES

1. **Legal Problems:**
    (1) Is a principal bound when an agent who has actual authority enters into an obligation apparently for the benefit of the principal but in fact for the benefit of a third party?
    (2) Is a principal bound when an agent who has actual authority enters into an obligation in violation of an undisclosed limitation placed on the agent's authority by the principal?
    (3) Is a principal bound when an agent whose actual authority has been terminated but who continues to have apparent authority enters into an obligation on behalf of the principal?

DISCUSSION

Point One (25-35%)

<u>Principal is liable to Bellseller for the church bell. Principal is bound by Agent's purchase of the church bell apparently on Principal's behalf, even though Agent was in fact operating on Greta's behalf, since Bellseller was unaware of that fact.</u>

There is no doubt that Principal is liable. However, different jurisdictions are likely to reach this result based on different theories.

First, some jurisdictions would conclude that Agent had actual authority to bind Principal to the contract with Bellseller because Agent was expressly authorized by Principal to purchase the bell and the price that Agent agreed to pay was within the range authorized by Principal. Moreover, because the contract entered into by Agent disclosed that Principal was Agent's principal, Bellseller knew that Agent was acting as agent for a third party. This makes Principal a disclosed principal who is "subject to liability upon a contract purported to be made on his account by an agent authorized to make it for the principal's benefit, *although the agent acts for his own or another's improper purposes,* unless the [third] party has notice that the agent is not acting for the principal's benefit." RESTATEMENT (SECOND) OF AGENCY § 165. *See also U.S. Fidelity & Guaranty Co. v. Anderson Constr. Co.,* 260 F.2d 172 (9th Cir. 1958). Here, Bellseller had no knowledge that Agent was not acting for Principal's benefit, and as a result, Principal is liable to Bellseller for the price of the church bell. (In some jurisdictions, this same reasoning would be used to hold Principal liable on an "inherent authority" rationale. *See* Comment a to RESTATEMENT (SECOND) OF AGENCY § 165.) Agent, on the other hand, could be liable to Principal for breach of fiduciary duty.

Other jurisdictions would conclude that Agent did not have actual authority. Agent did not make the purchase for Principal, he made the purchase for Greta and his act of *purchasing the bell for Greta* was NOT within the actual authority given by Principal: Principal only authorized agent to make the purchase *for the benefit of Principal. See* Draft, RESTATEMENT (THIRD) OF AGENCY § 2.01, comment e (an "act that would be within the agent's actual authority had the agent acted to serve the interests of the principal . . . falls outside actual authority [if] the agent acted to serve the agent's own purposes or other improper purposes.") Thus, although he purported to be acting for Principal, Agent probably lacked actual authority *to make this purchase for Greta,* though he would have had authority to purchase for Principal. Consequently, Principal would probably not be bound simply on the basis of actual authority.

Nevertheless, jurisdictions that conclude that Agent lacked actual authority would probably also conclude that Agent had *apparent* authority to make this purchase. Apparent authority is created "by written or spoken words or any other conduct of the principal which, reasonably interpreted, causes the third person to believe that the principal consents to have the act done on his behalf by the person purporting to act for him." *See* RESTATEMENT (SECOND) OF AGENCY § 27. *See also Mohr v. State Bank of Stanley*, 241 Kan. 42, 734 P.2d 1071, 1076 (1987); *Lewis v. Washington Metro. Area Transit Auth.,* 463 A.2d 666 (D.C. 1983). The principal must "be responsible for the information which comes to the mind of the third person," but this can occur if the principal provides "documents or other indicia of authority" to the agent that are subsequently shown to the third party. RESTATEMENT (SECOND) OF AGENCY § 27, comment a.

In this case, Principal provided Agent with written credentials which, when they were shown to Bellseller, caused Bellseller to believe that Agent was authorized to purchase the bell on behalf of Principal. Agent then purported to act within the scope of this apparent authority, and Bellseller believed him to be so acting. Consequently, Principal is liable for the contract made by Agent within the scope of his apparent authority. *See* RESTATEMENT (SECOND) OF AGENCY § 159.

In any event, the basic justification for imposing liability on Principal is simply that Principal created a situation where Bellseller reasonably relied on Agent's claims to be acting for Principal. Agency law typically protects third parties who act in reliance on appearances created by a purported principal, and a court is likely to protect Bellseller for this reason, whether the result is explained on grounds of apparent authority, inherent authority, or estoppel. *See* RESTATEMENT (SECOND) OF AGENCY § 8, comments d, e & f; § 8A.

Point Two (25-35%)

Agent acted with actual authority to purchase the book, and with apparent authority because Tomeseller was unaware of Principal's price limitation. Therefore, Principal is liable even though Agent exceeded the terms of his authorization.

Principal specifically authorized Agent to buy the book, so Agent had actual authority to purchase the book on Principal's behalf. RESTATEMENT (SECOND) OF AGENCY § 26. However, Agent exceeded the limitation on price imposed by Principal, and therefore exceeded the scope of his actual authority. Although Agent is liable to Principal for breach of duty to obey instructions, Principal will nevertheless be liable to Tomeseller.

Agent showed the written authorization to Tomeseller, and the purchase contract identified Principal as the principal, so Principal was a disclosed principal, and Agent had apparent authority. Apparent authority is created "by written or spoken words or any other conduct of the principal which, reasonably interpreted, causes the third person to believe that the principal consents to have the act done on his behalf by the person purporting to act for him." RESTATEMENT (SECOND) OF AGENCY § 27. *See also Mohr v. State Bank of Stanley,* 241 Kan. 42, 734 P.2d 1071, 1076 (1987); *Lewis v. Washington Metro. Area Transit Auth.,* 463 A.2d 666 (D.C. 1983). When Agent presented Tomeseller with the written authorization, which did not include the limitation, Tomeseller reasonably understood that Agent was authorized to purchase the book on Principal's behalf, creating apparent authority on behalf of Agent.

Because the price limitation was not included on the written authorization shown to Tomeseller, she was unaware of the limitation. "A disclosed or partially disclosed principal authorizing an agent to make a contract, but imposing upon him limitations as to incidental terms intended not to be revealed is subject to liability upon a contract made in violation of such limitations with a third person who has no notice of them." RESTATEMENT (SECOND) OF AGENCY § 160. *See also Hunt v. Davis,* 387 So. 2d 209 (Ala. Civ. App. 1980)(holding that secret limitations on an agent's authority do not bind third parties); *Wittlin v. Giacalone,* 171 F.2d 147 (D.C. Cir. 1948). Therefore, Principal remains liable to Tomeseller for payment of the book.

Point Three (25-30%)

Because Agent was acting with apparent authority, even though Principal had terminated all actual authority, Principal is liable to Lampseller for the purchase of the lamp.

Principal had terminated the agency relationship by delivery of the letter to Agent, so Agent did not have actual authority to buy the lamp. RESTATEMENT (SECOND) OF AGENCY § 119. Agent did, however, continue to have apparent authority. Once apparent authority is created, it can be terminated only when the third party has notice of termination or when the authority is terminated due to impossibility or lack of capacity. Reuschlein & Gregory, THE LAW OF AGENCY AND PARTNERSHIP § 46 at 95, (2d ed. 1990); RESTATEMENT (SECOND) OF AGENCY § 125.

When Principal engaged Agent, Principal gave Agent credentials and form contracts used to buy antiques on Principal's behalf. Agent showed Lampseller the credentials and used Principal's form to purchase the lamp, so Lampseller could reasonably have understood that Agent had authority from Principal to buy antiques, including the lamp. When Principal entrusted Agent with "indicia of authority," Principal became obliged to give notice of any termination of that authority to third persons who relied upon Agent's possession of the credentials. Since Lampseller had no notice that Agent's credentials were no longer valid, the apparent authority continued as to Lampseller and, as a result, Principal is liable for payment to Lampseller for the $5,000 purchase price.

2. **Legal Problems:**
   (1)(a) Did Adam act with either actual or apparent authority in contracting for the Tahitian lobby decorations?
   (1)(b) Did Adam act with either actual or apparent authority in contracting with Moby for the guest room furnishings?
   (2) Does Sunrise have a claim for indemnification from Adam for either of the contracts for which Sunrise is liable?
   (3) Can Sunrise terminate Adam's agency prior to the expiration of the one- year term, and if so, is Sunrise liable to Adam for damages based on the early termination?

DISCUSSION

Summary

Adam acted with apparent but not actual authority with respect to the contract with Tahini. Adam acted with apparent authority because Sunrise advised Tahini of the agency agreement but not of the limitations on Adam's authority. On the other hand, Adam acted with actual authority with respect to the Moby contract which was consistent with all of the terms of the agency contract between Sunrise and Adam. Thus, Sunrise is liable to both Tahini and Moby, albeit on diffcrent theories. Sunrise can seek indemnification from Adam for its liability under the Tahini contract but not under the Moby contract. Because Adam materially breached the agency contract, Sunrise can terminate that contract prior to the end of the fixed term in the contract without any liability to Adam.

Point One(a): (20-30%)

Sunrise is liable on the contract for the purchase of the Tahitian decorations because Adam acted with apparent authority.

Adam had no actual authority to purchase the Tahitian lobby items on Sunrise's behalf. Under the Restatement (Second) of Agency, actual "authority to do an act can be created by written or spoken words or other conduct of the principal which, reasonably interpreted, causes the agent to believe that the principal desires him so to act on the principal's account." Restatement (Second) of Agency § 26. Sunrise made it clear to Adam that the items had to be within the style guidelines described in Exhibit B. The Tahitian items were inconsistent with the guidelines, and thus Adam had no actual authority to purchase them.

On the other hand, Adam did have apparent authority to purchase the Tahitian lobby items on Sunrise's behalf. Under the Restatement, "apparent authority to do an act is created as to a third person by written or spoken words or any other conduct of the principal which, reasonably interpreted, causes the third person to believe that the principal consents to have the act done on his behalf by the person purporting to act for him." Restatement (Second) of Agency § 27. Sunrise had sent a letter to Tahini appointing Adam "to act on its behalf in the selection of interior floor and wall coverings, works of art, furniture, and plumbing and lighting fixtures for the Sunrise East Beach hotel." The Sunrise letter emphasized Adam's authority by stating: "Know that you deal with Sunrise when you deal with Adam on this project." Sunrise did not indicate to Tahini that there were any restrictions on Adam's scope of discretion or authority, and the facts do not suggest that Tahini had knowledge of any limitations through other means. As a result, it was reasonable for Tahini to conclude that Adam acted with authority when he ordered the decorations. Since Adam acted with apparent authority, Sunrise is liable to Tahini. Restatement (Second) of Agency § 140(b).

Point One(b): (10-20%)

Adam acted with actual authority in contracting with Moby for the guest room furnishings and therefore Sunrise is liable on the contract.

When Adam contracted with Moby for the guest room furnishings, he was within the budget and style limitations required by Sunrise and Moby was a local supplier. Therefore, he acted within the scope of the actual authority granted by Sunrise. Restatement (Second) of Agency § 26. Because Adam acted within the scope of the grant of actual authority, Sunrise is liable on the contract to Moby for the guest room furnishings. In addition, Adam also acted with apparent authority because Moby received the letter from Sunrise. See Point One(a) above.

Point Two: (10-20%)

Sunrise has a claim against Adam for the amount of Sunrise's liability to Tahini but does not have a claim against Adam for its liability to Moby for the guest room furnishings.

Sunrise has a claim against Adam for the amount of its liability to Tahini because Adam did not act within the scope of his actual authority and, therefore, breached his duty to follow directions. Restatement (Second) of Agency §§ 399, 401.

Sunrise has no claim against Adam for reimbursement of its liability to Moby for guest room furnishings because Adam acted within the scope of his grant of authority. Restatement (Second) of Agency § 399. He followed directions and fulfilled his fiduciary obligations.

Point Three: (20-30%)

Sunrise can terminate Adam's agency at any time and end Adam's authority to bind Sunrise. Early termination of Adam's agency may expose Sunrise to liability for damages to Adam, but in this case Sunrise has a defense to such a claim.

Although the general rule is that authority conferred for a specific time terminates at the expiration of the period, Restatement (Second) of Agency §§ 105 and 118 provide that: "[a]uthority terminates if the principal . . . manifests to the [agent] dissent to its continuance." Therefore, Sunrise may terminate Adam as its agent at any time, including before the end of the one-year term.

The principal has the power to terminate the agency even in violation of the agency contract: "The principal has power to revoke . . . although doing so is in violation of a contract between the parties . . ." Restatement (Second) of Agency § 118 cmt. b. However, the principal "has a duty not to repudiate or terminate the employment in violation of the contract of employment." Restatement (Second) of Agency § 450. In such a situation, the principal may be liable to the agent for damages. Restatement (Second) of Agency § 455.

Given Adam's deviation from the terms of his contract with Sunrise, Adam is not likely to recover from Sunrise for early termination. First, if a termination is based upon the agent's breach of contract, then the principal has an offset against the agent's damages. Restatement (Second) of Agency § 456. Second, "[a] principal is privileged to discharge before the time fixed by the contract of employment an agent who has committed such a violation of duty that his conduct constitutes a material breach of contract." Restatement (Second) of Agency § 409(1). That appears to be the case in this situation.

3. **Legal Problems:**
   (1)(a) Does Lessor exercise sufficient control over Handy to establish Handy as Lessor's "servant" so that Lessor is liable for Handy's torts?
   (1)(b) If Handy is Lessor's servant, is Handy's conduct within the scope of employment?
   (2) If Handy is not a servant, did Tenant reasonably rely upon Handy's apparent authority to install an electrical outlet so that Lessor is nonetheless liable for Handy's tort?

DISCUSSION

Summary

Lessor may be held liable for Handy's tortious conduct under either of two theories. First, if the Lessor-Handy relationship is one of master and servant, Lessor is liable for Handy's torts if Handy was acting within the scope of his employment when he committed them. See Restatement (Second) of Agency § 219. Second, even if the relationship between Lessor and Handy does not rise to the level of a master-servant relationship, Lessor will be liable for Handy's tort if Tenant relied on statements or conduct by Handy that were within Handy's apparent authority. Restatement (Second) of Agency § 265.

Point One(a) (30-40%):

The relationship between Handy and Lessor may be a master-servant relationship such that Lessor is liable for torts committed by Handy while acting within the scope of his employment.

A master is liable for the torts of the master's servants committed while acting in the scope of their employment. Restatement (Second) of Agency § 219(1). Handy is clearly an agent as he agreed to work for, and subject to the control of, Lessor. The more difficult question is whether Handy would be considered to be Lessor's servant.

Note: The Restatement (Third) of Agency has adopted "Employer-Employee" language in place of the traditional "Master-Servant" terminology and applicants may of course use this newer terminology.

Whether Handy performed the work for Tenant as Lessor's "servant" or as an independent contractor agent depends on the degree of control exercised by Lessor over Handy's activities. The Restatement (Second) of Agency § 2(2) provides that a "servant is an agent employed by a master to perform service in his affairs whose physical conduct in the performance of the service is controlled or is subject to the right to control by the master." Conversely, the Restatement (Second) of Agency § 2(3) provides that "an independent contractor is a person who contracts with another to do something for him but who is not controlled by the other nor subject to the other's right to control with respect to his physical conduct in the performance of the undertaking." The Restatement (Second) of Agency § 220(2) lists factors used to determine whether an agent is a servant. These factors are:

(a) the extent of control which, by the agreement, the master may exercise over the details of the work;
(b) whether or not the one employed is engaged in a distinct occupation or business;

(c) the kind of occupation, with reference to whether, in the locality, the work is usually done under the direction of the employer or by a specialist without supervision;

(d) the skill required in the particular occupation;

(e) whether the employer or the workman supplies the instrumentalities, tools, and the place of work for the person doing the work;

(f) the length of time for which the person is employed;

(g) the method of payment, whether by the time or by the job;

(h) whether or not the work is a part of the regular business of the employer;

(i) whether or not the parties believe they are creating the relation of master and servant; and

(j) whether the principal is or is not in business.

In Handy's case, the facts permit a persuasive argument on either side. Several factors suggest that Handy should be considered a servant of Lessor. First, Lessor exercises significant control over Handy, in insisting that any repair be approved by Lessor. Second, the relationship appears to be long term, not a temporary arrangement for a small number of repair jobs; it has already lasted for a year. Third, payment is by time worked, not by the particular job. Finally, the work performed is a necessary part of Lessor's business of owning and operating apartment buildings.

On the other hand, several factors support an argument for classifying Handy as an independent contractor. First, Handy, as a repairman, is engaged in a distinct occupation and business that requires some degree of special skill. Second, Handy provides his own tools. Third, Handy has his own separate repair business and appears to have taken on Lessor's work in the course of operating that separate business. Fourth, Lessor approves repairs to his properties but does not specify the methods that Handy must use.

Note: Either analysis of the servant issue is plausible. The point is that Lessor is only liable under the theory of *respondeat superior* if Handy is a servant.

Point One (b): (15-25%)

If Handy is a servant, his actions were within the scope of employment because, although not authorized, adding an electrical outlet was incidental to authorized conduct.

Conduct is within the scope of employment if the conduct is of the "same general nature authorized or incidental to the conduct authorized." Restatement (Second) of Agency § 229(1).

Factors examined in determining whether conduct is within the scope of employment include whether the conduct is the kind the servant is employed to perform; whether it occurs substantially within the authorized time and space;

and whether it was performed, at least in part, to serve the master. *See* Restatement (Second) of Agency § 228.

In this case, Handy was not authorized to add the electrical outlet as Handy's contract with Lessor expressly prohibited him from doing electrical work. It also prohibited him from doing work "on the side" for a tenant. However, even forbidden activity can be within the scope of employment. Restatement (Second) of Agency § 230.

The Restatement (Second) of Agency § 229(2) sets forth factors to consider in determining whether an action is incidental to the authorized conduct so that it comes within the scope of employment. These factors include:

(a) whether or not the act is one commonly done by such servants;
(b) the time, place and purpose of the act;
(c) the previous relations between the master and the servant;
(d) the extent to which the business of the master is apportioned between different servants;
(e) whether or not the act is outside the enterprise of the master or, if within the enterprise, has not been entrusted to any servant;
(f) whether or not the master has reason to expect that such an act will be done;
(g) the similarity in quality of the act done to the act authorized;
(h) whether or not the instrumentality by which the harm is done has been furnished by the master to the servant;
(i) the extent of departure from the normal method of accomplishing an authorized result; and
(j) whether or not the act is seriously criminal.

A key fact that points to the conclusion that adding the electrical outlet was incidental to the scope of employment is the fact that Handy did the electrical work while providing Tenant with authorized services.

Point Two (50-60%)

<u>Even if Handy is not a servant, or is a servant not acting within the scope of employment, Lessor is liable if Tenant reasonably believes Handy was Lessor's agent and relied on what appeared to be authority for Handy to perform the work.</u>

Restatement (Second) of Agency § 265 sets out the general rule: "(1) A master or other principal is subject to liability for torts which result from reliance upon, or belief in, statements or other conduct within an agent's apparent authority." Section 265(2) conditions this liability upon reliance.

An agent is clothed with apparent authority when a principal "by written or spoken words or any other conduct of the principal which, reasonably interpreted, causes the third party to believe that the principal consents to have the act done on his behalf by the person purporting to act for him." Restatement (Second) of Agency § 27. The facts indicate that Lessor clothed Handy with apparent authority by advising tenants to call the "Lessor's Repair Line" when they needed repairs, and then using Handy's business phone number as the "Lessor's Repair Line." The act of using Handy's number reasonably caused Tenant to believe that Handy was authorized by Lessor to act on Lessor's behalf. There are no facts to suggest that Tenant knew or could expect to know that a person authorized to make general repairs was prohibited by contract from adding an electrical outlet.

With respect to reliance, the facts permit a persuasive argument on either side. Arguably, Tenant did not reasonably rely on Handy's apparent authority because Tenant was told that adding an electrical outlet was an improvement, not a repair, and Handy made repairs. Further, Handy indicated that there was a charge for the electrical work.

However, the alternative argument could also be made. Lessor arranged to have "Lessor's Repair Line" ring directly to Handy's office. Tenant knew that Handy was working for Lessor; in fact Handy was present doing work on behalf of Lessor. It is not unreasonable to believe that the same person designated to make repairs would also make improvements. Further, the facts indicate that Tenant believed the payment for the work ($200) was to go to Lessor.

4. **Legal Problems:**
   (1) Is Owen an independent contractor or a servant (employee) of Best Care?
   (2) Did Owen have actual or apparent authority to bind Best Care to the contract to purchase the X-ray machine?
   (3) Is Best Care liable to Anita's estate for Owen's negligence on an apparent (ostensible) agency theory?

DISCUSSION

Summary

Whether Owen is an independent contractor or a servant (employee) is a question of fact. The degree of control is generally the distinguishing factor between an independent contractor and a servant (employee). Traditionally, Owen would have been an independent contractor because Best Care did not retain substantial control over how Owen was to practice medicine; however, recent opinions have moderated this position and look to the right to control rather than actual exercise of control.

Best Care is not liable on the Vision-Owen contract. Owen lacked actual authority to enter into the contract with Vision on behalf of Best Care because Vision was not a vendor in City. Further, Best Care had made no manifestations to provide Vision with a reasonable basis to believe that Owen was acting as an agent of Best Care.

Even if Owen is an independent contractor, he appears to the outside world—and to Anita in particular—to be an employee of Best Care as a result of Best Care's representations made on the billboards. Because of this apparent (ostensible) agency, Best Care would be estopped from denying liability for Owen's negligence and Anita's resulting death.

Point One (35-45%)

Owen was probably an independent contractor and not an employee of Best Care, but the facts could be argued differently.

Owen is either an independent contractor or a servant (employee). "An independent contractor is a person who contracts with another to do something for him but who is not controlled by the other nor subject to the other's right to control with respect to his physical conduct in the performance of the undertaking. He may or may not be an agent." Restatement (Second) of

Agency § 2(3). "A servant [employee] is an agent employed by a master [employer] to perform service in his affairs whose physical conduct in the performance of the service is controlled or is subject to the right to control by the master." Id. at § 2(2). A number of factors are relevant in distinguishing an independent contractor from a servant. The crucial factor is the extent of control that the employer may exercise over the details of the work. See Restatement (Second) of Agency § 220. Traditionally, doctors were considered independent contractors because of their high level of skill and the use of their independent judgment. See McMurdo v. Getter, 10 N.E.2d 139 (Mass. 1937). However, in recent years, courts have placed greater emphasis on the employer's "right to interfere or control rather than [the employer's] actual interference or exercise of control." See Knorp v. Albert, 28 P.3d. 1024 (Kan. Ct. App. 2001); Kelly v. Rossi, 481 N.E.2d 1340 (Mass. 1985). Other factors used to distinguish between a servant and an independent contractor are: (1) whether the one employed is engaged in a distinct occupation or business, (2) the skill required in the particular occupation, (3) who supplies the materials to perform and the place to perform the service, (4) method of payment, and (5) how the parties characterize the transaction. Restatement (Second) of Agency § 220 (2); Chapman v. Black, 741 P.2d 998 (Wash. App. 1987).

These facts could be argued either way. Here, most of the factors suggest that Owen is an independent contractor and not an employee or servant of Best Care. In particular items 1, 2, and 5 of the contract favor characterizing Owen as an independent contractor, while items 4 and 6 of the contract indicate some level of oversight and control on the part of Best Care. The self-labeling in item 1 is evidence, but is not decisive.

Point Two (30-40%)

<u>Owen had neither actual nor apparent authority to bind Best Care to the contract to purchase the X-ray machine. Thus, Best Care is not liable to Vision for breach of contract.</u>

Agency arises where one person consents that another shall act on his behalf and, at least as respects matters within the agency, subject to his control. See generally Restatement (Second) of Agency § 1(1).

Actual authority arises where the principal communicates the authority to act to the agent. See generally Restatement (Second) of Agency § 7; William A. Gregory, The Law of Agency and Partnership, 3d ed. § 14. A principal is bound by contracts entered into between an agent with actual authority and a third party. See generally Restatement (second) of agency § 144.

Item 3 of the contract provides that "[e]ach doctor is authorized to purchase supplies and equipment for Best Care's emergency room from a list of approved vendors located in City and within Best Care's price guidelines." This contract provision gave Owen actual authority to buy equipment for Best Care so long as it was within specified price guidelines from suppliers located in City for Best Care's account. If Owen had acted within this authority, Best Care would be bound even if Vision was unaware of the authorization. However, Owen exceeded his authority by purchasing equipment from Vision, which was not an approved vendor and was located 450 miles away from City. Therefore, Best Care is not liable under the contract because Owen did not have actual authority.

Further, Best Care is not liable under the theory of apparent authority. Apparent authority is created as to a "third person by written or spoken words or any other conduct of the principal which, reasonably interpreted, causes the third person to believe that the principal consents to have the act done on his behalf by the person purporting to act for him." Restatement (Second) of Agency § 27. There are no facts to suggest that Best Care made any representations that would create a reasonable basis for Vision to believe that Owen was authorized to purchase the X-ray machine.

Point Three (25-35%)

Even if Owen is an independent contractor, Best Care is liable for Owen's negligence if Anita reasonably believed that Owen was acting as an agent of Best Care.

While a master is liable for the torts of its servant (employee) conducted within the scope of employment, a principal is not necessarily liable for the torts of its independent contractor agent. See Restatement (Second) of Agency §§ 219, 250. A principal, however, may be estopped from denying liability for the torts of its independent contractor if the principal has created indicia of apparent authority. See Restatement (Second) of Agency § 8B. This is sometimes referred to as the "holding out" theory or ostensible agency. See Adamski v. Tacoma General Hospital, 579 P.2d 970 (Wash. Ct. App. 1978) (The hospital may be liable under the "holding out" theory so long as the hospital acted in some way that leads the patient to a reasonable belief that he is being treated by a hospital employee).

Restatement (Second) of Agency § 267 provides that "one who represents that another is his servant or other agent and thereby causes a third person justifiably to rely upon the care or skill of such apparent agent is subject to liability to the third person for harm caused by the lack of care or skill of the one appearing to be a servant or other agent as if he were such." Here, Best Care publicly advertised, on billboards strategically placed throughout City, that people should come to its emergency room because "Best Care's emergency room doctors are the absolute best and will really care for you." Anita apparently saw and believed the slogan on the billboards because she expressly requested the ambulance driver to take her to Best Care because "Best Care's emergency room doctors are the absolute best." It would be reasonable for a prospective patient to conclude, based on the billboards, that all doctors in Best Care's emergency room are employees of Best Care. As it was reasonable for Anita to believe that Owen was an agent of Best Care, under the general principle that a principal is liable for the torts committed by its agents Best Care would be liable to Anita's estate for Owen's actions (negligently severing an artery so that she bled to death).

NOTE: Most jurisdictions provide that a principal who hires an independent contractor to perform an "ultrahazardous" or "inherently dangerous" activity has a nondelegable duty to exercise due care to provide for the safety of persons who may be harmed by that activity. However, the usual tort and agency law definitions of ultrahazardous activity would not cover surgery, and there is no line of authority holding that a doctor's performance of surgery falls within this rule.

5. **Legal Problems:**
   (1) What is the nature of the legal relationship between Scott and Ruth?
   (2) Does an agent have actual authority to bind an undisclosed principal to contracts that are made in violation of the principal's instructions to the agent?
   (3) Does an agent have apparent authority to bind an undisclosed principal to contracts that are made in violation of the principal's instructions to the agent?
   (4) Does an agent have inherent agency power to bind an undisclosed principal to contracts that are made in violation of the principal's instructions to the agent?

DISCUSSION

Summary

Ruth was Scott's agent for purposes of operating the restaurant. However, Ruth did not have actual authority to purchase supplies from Wholesale or to employ Nora for a 20-year term because these actions violated Scott's express instructions to Ruth. Ruth also lacked apparent authority to bind Scott because Scott was an undisclosed principal, and neither Wholesale nor Nora was aware that Ruth was acting in an agency capacity. Scott did nothing to manifest to Wholesale or Nora that Ruth had authority to act on his behalf.

Nevertheless, Ruth probably had inherent agency power to bind Scott to pay for the supplies purchased from Wholesale. The purchase of restaurant supplies is the kind of transaction usually performed by a restaurant manager, and the principal is appropriately held responsible for that transaction, even if Ruth violated Scott's orders in the way in which she carried it out. By contrast, hiring an assistant manager for a 20-year term is not the type of transaction one would ordinarily expect to be performed by a restaurant manager, and Ruth's inherent agency power probably did not extend to binding Scott to such a contract.

Point One (10-20%)

Ruth was Scott's general agent for the operation of the restaurant. Because the agency was not disclosed to persons dealing with Ruth's Family Restaurant, Scott was an "undisclosed principal."

Ruth and Scott agreed that Ruth would act as Scott's agent. Moreover, Ruth was a "general agent" for Scott, having been authorized, as manager of the restaurant, to conduct a series of transactions to ensure continuity of service for Scott, as owner of Ruth's Family Restaurant. *See* RESTATEMENT (SECOND) OF AGENCY § 3(1) (1958). However, neither party disclosed the agency relationship to outsiders. As a result, Scott was Ruth's "undisclosed principal." *See* RESTATEMENT (SECOND) OF AGENCY § 4(3) (1958) (defining undisclosed principal).

As Scott's agent, Ruth could bind Scott to contracts with Wholesale or Nora if Ruth had actual authority, apparent authority, or inherent agency power to enter such contracts. The issue in this problem is whether an agent has the power to bind an undisclosed principal to contracts that the agent enters in violation of instructions from the principal.

Point Two (20-30%)

Because her actions violated Scott's express instructions, Ruth had no actual authority to purchase restaurant supplies from Wholesale or to hire Nora for a 20-year term.

Actual authority "to affect the legal relations of the principal" exists only if the agent's acts are "done in accordance with the principal's manifestations of consent." RESTATEMENT (SECOND) OF AGENCY § 7 (1958). Thus, Ruth had actual authority to bind Scott only insofar as Ruth acted consistently with Scott's "manifestations of consent" to her.

Here, Ruth's acts were completely contrary to Scott's instructions. Ruth was told not to contract with Wholesale, yet she did so. Ruth was instructed to hire employees only on an at-will basis, yet she hired Nora for a 20-year term. Because these acts were done contrary to Scott's "manifestations of consent" to Ruth, they were not done with actual authority.

Point Three (20-30%)

<u>Ruth had no apparent authority to bind Scott because Scott was an undisclosed principal, and neither Nora nor Wholesale was aware that Ruth was Scott's agent.</u>

Apparent authority is created when a purported principal causes third persons to believe that the purported agent has the power to act on behalf of the principal. In other words, apparent authority depends on a person's manifestations to a third person "that another is his agent." *See* RESTATEMENT (SECOND) OF AGENCY § 8 & comment a (1958).

Ruth could not have apparent authority to bind Scott because Scott made no manifestations to anyone that Ruth was his agent. In fact, no one other than Ruth or Scott was aware of their agency relationship. Furthermore, Scott and Ruth took pains to avoid disclosing the agency, even to the extent of Ruth's signing all contracts as "Ruth, d/b/a Ruth's Family Restaurant." "Apparent authority exists only with regard to those who believe and have reason to believe that there is authority; there can be no apparent authority created by an undisclosed principal." *Id.* Neither Nora nor Wholesale was aware that Scott was Ruth's principal.

Point Four (25-35%)

<u>Scott might be liable to Wholesale on the theory that Ruth had inherent agency power to bind Scott to contracts for the purchase of restaurant supplies, but a court is unlikely to conclude that Ruth had inherent agency power to bind Scott to an extraordinary employment contract.</u>

Even if Ruth lacked actual or apparent authority to bind Scott, as Scott's agent, Ruth might have had "inherent agency power" to bind Scott to transactions undertaken to benefit Scott that were similar to the types of activities authorized, even if those transactions were in violation of orders. *See* RESTATEMENT (SECOND) OF AGENCY § 8A and comment a (1958). The concept of "inherent agency power" provides a means for courts to protect persons dealing with agents even when the agent violates orders. The theory is that an agent is generally acting "in the principal's interests" and is "trusted and controlled" by the principal. When such an agent's disobedience causes a loss, it is "fairer" that the loss fall upon the principal than on a third party, at least if the agent is engaged in acts generally of a kind that would fall within his or her actual authority, but for the violation of instructions.

Inherent agency power has generally been found in precisely the kind of situation presented on these factsCan agent has been given general power to manage a business and has done acts for the principal's account, albeit in violation of instructions. *See* RESTATEMENT (SECOND) OF AGENCY §§ 161, 194-195 (1958).

Under the facts of this problem, Ruth probably did have inherent agency power to contract with Wholesale for the delivery of restaurant supplies. Ruth was a general agent and was authorized to purchase restaurant supplies. Purchasing restaurant supplies from the local supply company that offered the best prices would be a "usual" or ordinary transaction for an agent managing a restaurant. If Ruth somehow violated Scott's special instructions, Scott should nonetheless be liable to Wholesale, especially since Scott's business certainly benefitted by purchasing cheaper supplies from Wholesale. *See* RESTATEMENT (SECOND) OF AGENCY § 194 (1958).

On the other hand, Scott is not likely to be held liable to Nora. Ruth's entry into a contract to employ Nora as an assistant manager for a 20-year term was not a transaction that would be "usual" in the restaurant business. Although restaurant managers regularly hire and fire employees, at-will employment contracts are the norm. An employment contract specifying a 20-year term would be extraordinary and unusual in any business; certainly a 20-year term of employment is neither usual nor necessary in employing an assistant restaurant manager. A restaurant's business manager would not ordinarily have the power to enter such a contract. Therefore, Ruth had no inherent agency power to bind Scott to a 20-year employment contract with Nora.

Another fact to consider is that Nora was Ruth's niece, which suggests that the fairness concern that undergirds inherent agency analysis may, in fact, cut in Scott's favor here. It would seem unfair to hold Scott responsible for Ruth's violation of instructions when the violation was done to benefit a member of Ruth's family.

NOTE: The draft Third Restatement of Agency eliminates the concept of inherent agency power, but would reach the same results in the case of an undisclosed agency relationship under a theory that it calls "estoppel of undisclosed principal." *See* RESTATEMENT (THIRD) OF AGENCY, TENTATIVE DRAFT NO. 2, §2.06.

MBE ANSWERS

Torts MBE Questions Analyses
Contracts MBE Questions Analyses
Civil Procedure MBE Questions Answers

Disclaimer: Certain publicly disclosed questions and answers from past MBE examinations have been included herein with the permission of the NCBE, the copyright owner. These questions and answers are the only actual MBE questions and answers (as may have been modified with the NCBE's permission) included in this textbook authors' materials. Permission to use NCBE's questions does not constitute an endorsement by NCBE or otherwise signify that NCBE has reviewed or approved any aspect of these materials or the company or individuals who distribute these materials.

TORTS MBE QUESTIONS ANALYSES

1. A mother and her six-year-old child were **on** a walk when the mother stopped to talk with an elderly neighbor. Because the child resented having his mother's attention diverted by the neighbor, the child angrily threw himself against the neighbor and knocked her to the ground. The neighbor suffered a broken wrist as a result of the fall.

In an action for battery by the neighbor against the child, what is the strongest argument for liability?

(A) The child intended to throw himself against the neighbor.

Correct. To recover on a claim for battery, it is sufficient for the neighbor to show that the child intended to touch the neighbor in a way that would be considered harmful or offensive, even though the child may have been too young to understand that what he was doing was wrong or to appreciate that the neighbor might be unusually vulnerable to injury.

(B) The child was old enough to appreciate that causing a fall could inflict serious injury.

Incorrect. Proof of intent to cause injury or knowledge that injury may result is not necessary to recover on a claim of battery. Instead, it is sufficient that the child intended to touch the neighbor in a way that would be considered harmful or offensive, even though the child may have been too young to understand that what he was doing was wrong or to appreciate that the neighbor might be unusually vulnerable to injury.

(C) The child was old enough to appreciate the riskiness of his conduct.

Incorrect. Whether the child was old enough to appreciate the riskiness of his conduct is irrelevant to the neighbor's battery claim. It is sufficient that the child intended to touch the neighbor in a way that would be considered harmful or offensive, even though the child may have been too young to understand that what he was doing was wrong. Whether a child is old enough to appreciate a given risk would be relevant in a negligence action, but not in an action for battery.

(D) The child was not justified in his anger.

Incorrect. It is sufficient that the child intended to touch the neighbor in a way that would be considered harmful or offensive, whether or not the child was justifiably angry. The motive for a defendant's actions may be relevant to an affirmative defense in some situations, but even justified anger is not a defense to an intentional tort.

2. A man tied his dog to a bike rack in front of a store and left the dog there while he went inside to shop. The dog was usually friendly and placid.

A five-year-old child started to tease the dog by pulling gently on its ears and tail. When the man emerged from the store and saw what the child was doing to the dog, he became extremely upset.

Does the man have a viable claim against the child for trespass to chattels?

(A) No, because the child did not injure the dog.

Correct. Trespass to chattels requires that the plaintiff show actual harm to or deprivation of the use of the chattel for a substantial time. Here the child's acts caused emotional distress to the man, but the acts did not result in harm to the man's material interest in the dog.

(B) No, because the child was too young to form the requisite intent.

Incorrect. Even a small child can commit an intentional tort, such as trespass to chattels, so long as the child is old enough to form an intent to touch. But trespass to chattels requires that the plaintiff show actual harm to or deprivation of the use of the chattel for a substantial time. Here the child's acts caused emotional distress to the man, but the acts did not result in harm to the man's material interest in the dog.

(C) Yes, because the child touched the dog without the man's consent.

Incorrect. Trespass to chattels requires that the plaintiff show actual harm to or deprivation of the use of the chattel for a substantial time. Here the child's acts caused emotional distress to the man (because they were without his consent), but the acts did not result in harm to the man's material interest in the dog.

(D) Yes, because the child's acts caused the man extreme distress.

Incorrect. Trespass to chattels requires that the plaintiff show actual harm to or deprivation of the use of the chattel for a substantial time. Here the child's acts caused emotional distress to the man, but the acts did not result in harm to the man's material interest in the dog.

3. An assistant to a famous writer surreptitiously observed the writer as the writer typed her private password into her personal computer in order to access her email. On several subsequent occasions in the writer's absence, the assistant read the writer's email messages and printed out selections from them.

The assistant later quit his job and earned a considerable amount of money by leaking information to the media that he had learned from reading the writer's email messages. All of the information published about the writer as a result of the assistant's conduct was true and concerned matters of public interest.

The writer's secretary had seen the assistant reading the writer's emails and printing out selections, and she has told the writer what she saw. The writer now wishes to sue the assistant for damages. At trial, the writer can show that the media leaks could have come only from someone reading her email.

Can the writer recover damages from the assistant?

(A) No, because the assistant was an invitee on the premises.

Incorrect. The assistant exceeded the scope of any invitation, whether through his employment as an assistant or through the invitation to work on the premises. The writer did not leave the emails exposed so that others might see them. An invitation to enter premises does not normally include permission to access personal email, especially when the email account is password-protected.

(B) No, because the published information resulting from the assistant's conduct was true and concerned matters of public interest.

Incorrect. Truth is a common law defense to defamation but not to invasion of privacy. In some circumstances, the First Amendment or a common law defense based on the public interest in the material disclosed can provide a defense to an action for disclosure of private matters. However, even if these defenses were applicable to the disclosure aspect of this case, they would not provide a defense to a privacy action based on intrusion. A news-gathering purpose does not provide general immunity from tort law.

(C) **Yes, because the assistant invaded the writer's privacy.**

Correct. By accessing the writer's email, the assistant was intruding upon her privacy. "Intrusion upon seclusion" is one category of the tort of invasion of privacy that is recognized in many states. The assistant did not have permission to access the emails, and the writer did not leave the emails exposed so that others might see them.

(D) Yes, because the published information resulting from the assistant's conduct constituted publication of private facts concerning the writer.

Incorrect. The most appropriate privacy action here would be for "intrusion" rather than for "public disclosure of embarrassing private facts," in part because there is no indication that the facts published were embarrassing to the writer. Publication is irrelevant to whether a cause of action for intrusion has been established. By accessing the writer's email, the assistant was intruding upon her privacy. "Intrusion upon seclusion" is one category of the tort of invasion of privacy that is recognized in many states. The assistant did not have permission to access the emails, and the writer did not leave the emails exposed so that others might see them.

4. Unaware that a lawyer was in the county courthouse library late on a Friday afternoon, when it was unusual for anyone to be using the library, a clerk locked the library door and left. The lawyer found herself locked in when she tried to leave the library at 7 p.m. It was midnight before the lawyer's family could find out where she was and get her out. The lawyer was very annoyed by her detention but was not otherwise harmed by it.

Does the lawyer have a viable claim for false imprisonment against the clerk?

(A) No, because it was unusual for anyone to be using the library late on a Friday afternoon.

Incorrect. The fact that it was unusual for anyone to be using the library at the time the clerk locked the door might lead a fact finder to conclude that the clerk was not negligent in failing to detect the lawyer. However, because false imprisonment is an intentional tort, the reasonableness of the clerk's conduct is irrelevant. If the clerk had intended to lock the lawyer in the library, the lawyer would have a claim for false imprisonment even if it was unusual for anyone to be using the library at the time. Under these facts, however, the clerk did not intend to lock the lawyer in the library, so the lawyer does not have a viable claim for false imprisonment.

(B) No, because the clerk did not intend to confine the lawyer.

Correct. Intent to confine the claimant (or to commit some other intentional tort) is essential to establishing liability for false imprisonment. There is no evidence that the clerk had such an intent.

(C) Yes, because the clerk should have checked to make sure no one was in the library before the clerk locked the door.

Incorrect. Whether a reasonable person in the clerk's position would have checked before locking the door is irrelevant to a claim for false imprisonment. False imprisonment is an intentional tort requiring intent to confine the claimant (or to commit some other intentional tort). What a reasonable person would have done is relevant to a negligence claim, but not to a false imprisonment claim.

(D) Yes, because the lawyer was aware of being confined.

Incorrect. In cases involving false imprisonment, courts often hold that the plaintiff must have been aware of the confinement at the time of the imprisonment or else must have sustained actual harm. It is also essential, however, that the defendant have had an intent to confine the plaintiff (or to commit some other intentional tort). If the clerk had had such an intent, the lawyer's awareness that she was confined might have completed the prima facie case, but the clerk had no such intent.

5. A woman signed up for a bowling class. Before allowing the woman to bowl, the instructor required her to sign a waiver explicitly stating that she assumed all risk of injuries that she might suffer in connection with the class, including injuries due to negligence or any other fault. After she signed the waiver, the woman was injured when the instructor negligently dropped a bowling ball on the woman's foot.

The woman brought a negligence action against the instructor. The instructor has filed a motion for summary judgment based on the waiver.

What is the woman's best argument in opposition to the instructor's motion?

(A) Bowling is an inherently dangerous activity.

Incorrect. Bowling is not inherently dangerous; virtually no one is seriously injured while bowling. Even if bowling were inherently dangerous, that characterization would support an argument for permitting recreational participants who appreciate the risks of the activity to assume the risks by signing a waiver rather than constituting a reason for ignoring the waiver.

(B) In circumstances like these, it is against public policy to enforce agreements that insulate people from the consequences of their own negligence.

Correct. Waivers are most easily justified when an activity poses inherent risks that are familiar to the participants and cannot be entirely eliminated without removing the pleasure from the activity. The risk that materialized here is not inherent to bowling but could arise whenever someone is careless while holding a heavy object. A court might find that it is against public policy to permit individuals or businesses to insulate themselves from the deterrent incentives provided by the threat of negligence liability. For that reason, the court might find that the waiver did not present the woman with a fair choice and could hold the waiver ineffective.

(C) It was unreasonable to require the woman to sign the waiver before she was allowed to bowl.

Incorrect. Although the court might find that the waiver did not present the woman with a fair choice and therefore hold the waiver to be no bar when the harm was due to the instructor's negligence, asking the woman to sign the waiver was not in itself negligent or unreasonable. For example, the waiver might have barred recovery against the instructor if the woman were injured by the negligence of another class participant, or the court might have decided that the waiver was not inconsistent with public policy given the recreational nature of the activity.

(D) When she signed the form, the woman could not foresee that the instructor would drop a bowling ball on her foot.

Incorrect. Pre-injury waivers are often enforced despite the fact that the precise injury that materializes is virtually never foreseen with a high level of specificity at the time of the signing of the waiver. The problem here is that the risk that materialized was not inherent to the enjoyment of bowling.

6. A boater, caught in a sudden storm and reasonably fearing that her boat would capsize, drove the boat up to a pier, exited the boat, and tied the boat to the pier. The pier was clearly marked with "NO TRESPASSING" signs. The owner of the pier ran up to the boater and told her that the boat could not remain tied to the pier. The boater offered to pay the owner for the use of the pier. Regardless, over the boater's protest, the owner untied the boat and pushed it away from the pier. The boat was lost at sea.

Is the boater likely to prevail in an action against the owner to recover the value of the boat?

(A) No, because the owner told the boater that she could not tie the boat to the pier.

Incorrect. The boater was privileged to trespass on the owner's property under the doctrine of private necessity, because the boater's property was at risk. Because the boater's intrusion onto the pier was privileged, the owner had no right to exclude her or her boat from the pier. In telling the boater that she could not tie the boat to the pier, the owner was asserting a right that he did not possess. When the owner untied the boat, he committed an unprivileged trespass upon the boater's property, so the owner must pay for the loss of the boat.

(B) No, because there was a possibility that the boat would not be damaged by the storm.

Incorrect. The boater was privileged to trespass on the owner's property under the doctrine of private necessity, because her property was at risk. In order to establish that privilege, the boater need not establish that harm to the boat was inevitable, but only that her actions were reasonable given the circumstances. Because the boater's intrusion onto the pier was privileged, the owner had no right to exclude her or her boat from the pier. When the owner untied the boat, he committed an unprivileged trespass upon the boater's property, so the owner must pay for the loss of the boat.

(C) Yes, because the boater offered to pay the owner for the use of the pier.

Incorrect. The boater is likely to prevail, but it is because the boater was privileged to trespass on the owner's property under the doctrine of private necessity. Because the boater's property was at risk, her intrusion onto the pier was privileged, and the owner had no right to exclude her or her boat from the pier. Whether or not the boater offered to pay the owner is irrelevant to the privilege of private necessity. When the owner untied the boat, he committed an unprivileged trespass upon the boater's property, so the owner must pay for the loss of the boat.

(D) **Yes, because the boater was privileged to enter the owner's property to save her boat.**

Correct. The boater was privileged to trespass on the owner's property under the doctrine of private necessity, because the boater's property was at risk. Because the boater's intrusion onto the pier was privileged, the owner had no right to exclude her or her boat from the pier. When the owner untied the boat, he committed an unprivileged trespass upon the boater's property, so the owner must pay for the loss of the boat.

CONTRACTS MBE QUESTIONS ANALYSES

1. A seller borrowed $5,000 from a bank. Soon thereafter the seller filed for bankruptcy, having paid nothing on his debt to the bank. Five years after the debt had been discharged in bankruptcy, the seller contracted to sell certain goods to a buyer for $5,000. The contract provided that the buyer would pay the $5,000 to the bank. The only debt that the seller ever owed the bank is the $5,000 debt that was discharged in bankruptcy. The seller delivered the goods to the buyer, who accepted them.

If the bank becomes aware of the contract between the seller and the buyer, and the buyer refuses to pay anything to the bank, is the bank likely to succeed in an action against the buyer for $5,000?

(A) No, because the buyer's promise to pay the bank was not supported by consideration.

Incorrect. The buyer and the seller entered into a bargained-for exchange for the sale and purchase of goods. Thus their agreement was supported by consideration. Moreover, a promisee (the seller) can intend that a third party be the beneficiary of the performance the promisee expects to receive from a promisor (the buyer). Because the parties' agreement provided that the buyer would pay to the bank the $5,000 that the buyer had promised to pay for the goods, the bank was an intended beneficiary of the enforceable agreement between the seller and the buyer, and the buyer is obligated to pay the bank.

(B) No, because the seller's debt was discharged in bankruptcy.

Incorrect. The bank was an intended beneficiary of the contract between the buyer and the seller, and the fact of discharge is irrelevant. The seller and the buyer entered into a bargained-for exchange for the sale and purchase of goods. Because their agreement provided that the buyer would pay to the bank the $5,000 that the buyer had promised to pay for the goods, the bank was an intended beneficiary of the enforceable agreement between the seller and the buyer, and the buyer is obligated to pay the bank.

(C) **Yes, because the bank was an intended beneficiary of the contract between the buyer and the seller.**

Correct. The buyer and the seller entered into a bargained-for exchange for the sale and purchase of goods. Because their agreement provided that the buyer would pay to the bank the $5,000 that the

buyer had promised to pay for the goods, the bank was an intended beneficiary of the enforceable agreement between the seller and the buyer, and the buyer is obligated to pay the bank.

(D) Yes, because no consideration is required to support a promise to pay a debt that has been discharged in bankruptcy.

Incorrect. It is true that a promise by a debtor to pay a debt that has been discharged in bankruptcy requires no consideration to be enforceable. In this case, however, the discharge of the seller's debt is irrelevant. Here, the seller and the buyer entered into a bargained-for exchange for the sale and purchase of goods. Because their agreement provided that the buyer would pay to the bank the $5,000 that the buyer had promised to pay for the goods, the bank was an intended beneficiary of the enforceable agreement between the seller and the buyer, and the buyer is obligated to pay the bank.

2. A man sent an email to a friend that stated: "Because you have been a great friend to me, I am going to give you a rare book that I own." The friend replied by an email that said: "Thanks for the rare book. I am going to give you my butterfly collection." The rare book was worth $10,000; the butterfly collection was worth $100. The friend delivered the butterfly collection to the man, but the man refused to deliver the book.

If the friend sues the man to recover the value of the book, how should the court rule?

(A) **For the man, because there was no bargained-for exchange to support his promise.**

Correct. To constitute consideration, a return promise must be bargained for. A return promise is bargained for when it is sought by the promisor in exchange for his promise and is given by the promisee in exchange for that promise. Because the man's promise to give the rare book to the friend did not seek a return promise or performance, the friend's promise to give the man her butterfly collection did not constitute consideration for the man's promise. Accordingly, no contract arose between the parties, and the court should rule in favor of the man.

(B) For the man, because the consideration given for his promise was inadequate.

Incorrect. Instead of giving inadequate consideration, the friend gave no consideration at all. To constitute consideration, a return promise must be bargained for. A return promise is bargained for when it is sought by the promisor in exchange for his promise and is given by the promisee in exchange for that promise. Because the man's promise to give the rare book to the friend did not seek a return promise or performance, the friend's promise to give the man her butterfly collection did not constitute consideration for the man's promise. Accordingly, no contract arose between the parties, and the court should rule in favor of the man.

(C) For the friend, because she gave the butterfly collection to the man in reliance on receiving the book.

Incorrect. Although it is true that a promisee's reliance may provide the basis for the enforcement of a promise in the absence of consideration, that principle is inapplicable here. The man's promise failed to induce reliance by the friend of the type that the man reasonably might have expected when he promised to give her the rare book. In addition, this is not a case in which injustice could only be avoided by the enforcement of the man's promise. The dispositive issue here is whether the friend's promise to give her butterfly collection to the man constituted consideration for the man's promise. Because the man's promise to give the rare book to the friend did not seek a return promise or performance, the friend's promise did not constitute consideration for the man's promise. Accordingly, no contract arose between the parties, and the court should rule in favor of the man.

(D) For the friend, because she conferred a benefit on the man by delivering the butterfly collection.

Incorrect. The fact that a promisee confers a benefit on a promisor does not create an enforceable obligation on the part of the promisor. The dispositive issue here is whether the friend's promise to give her butterfly collection to the man constituted consideration for the man's promise. Because the man's promise to give the rare book to the friend did not seek a return promise or performance, the friend's promise did not constitute consideration for the man's promise. Accordingly, no contract arose between the parties, and the court should rule in favor of the man.

3. A seller sent an email to a potential buyer, offering to sell his house to her for $150,000. The buyer immediately responded via email, asking whether the offer included the house's front porch swing. The seller emailed back: "No, it doesn't." The buyer then ordered a front porch swing and emailed back to the seller: "I accept your offer." The seller refused to sell the house to the buyer, claiming that the offer was no longer open.

Is there a contract for the sale of the house?

(A) No, because the buyer's initial email was a counteroffer.

Incorrect. A reply to an offer that merely requests information regarding the offer constitutes an inquiry rather than a counteroffer. The buyer's response asking whether the seller intended to include the front porch swing in his offer was an inquiry rather than a counteroffer. The buyer's subsequent email stating "I accept your offer" was an acceptance that created a contract between the parties. Therefore, the seller's attempted revocation of his offer was ineffective.

(B) No, because the offer lapsed before the buyer accepted.

Incorrect. An offeree's power of acceptance may terminate due to a lapse of time when the offeree fails to accept the offer within the time stated in the offer or within a reasonable time. In this case, the offer did not include an express time limitation. Therefore, the buyer could accept within a reasonable period of time. The email exchanges between the buyer and the seller demonstrate that the buyer accepted the seller's offer within a reasonable time period. The dispositive issue here is whether the buyer's reply to the seller's offer constituted an acceptance or a counteroffer. A reply to an offer that merely requests information regarding the offer constitutes an inquiry rather than a counteroffer. The buyer's response asking whether the seller intended to include the front porch swing in his offer was an inquiry rather than a counteroffer. The buyer's subsequent email stating "I accept your offer" was an acceptance that created a contract between the parties. Therefore, the seller's attempted revocation of his offer was ineffective.

(C) Yes, because the buyer relied on the offer by ordering the swing.

Incorrect. An offeree's reliance on an offer can create a binding option contract that precludes an offeror from revoking its offer. In this case, however, there is no indication that the buyer's purchase of the swing was the type of act performed in substantial reliance on the offer that the seller reasonably could have expected at the time he communicated his offer. The dispositive issue here is whether the buyer's reply to the seller's offer constituted an acceptance or a counteroffer. A reply to an offer that merely requests information regarding the offer constitutes an inquiry rather than a counteroffer. The buyer's response asking whether the seller intended to include the front porch swing in his offer was an inquiry rather than a counteroffer. The buyer's subsequent email stating "I accept your offer" was an acceptance that created a contract between the parties. Therefore, the seller's attempted revocation of his offer was ineffective.

(D) **Yes, because the buyer's initial email merely asked for information.**

Correct. A reply to an offer that merely requests information regarding the offer constitutes an inquiry rather than a counteroffer. The buyer's response asking whether the seller intended to include the front porch swing in his offer was an inquiry rather than a counteroffer. The buyer's subsequent email stating "I accept your offer" was an acceptance that created a contract between the parties. Therefore, the seller's attempted revocation of his offer was ineffective.

4. On June 15, a teacher accepted a contract for a one-year position teaching math at a public high school at a salary of $50,000, starting in September. On June 22, the school informed the teacher that, due to a change in its planned math curriculum, it no longer needed a full-time math teacher. The school offered instead to employ the teacher as a part-time academic counselor at a salary of $20,000, starting in September. The teacher refused the school's offer. On June 29, the teacher was offered a one-year position to teach math at a nearby private academy for $47,000, starting in September. The teacher, however, decided to spend the year completing work on a graduate degree in mathematics and declined the academy's offer.

If the teacher sues the school for breach of contract, what is her most likely recovery?

(A) $50,000, the full contract amount.

Incorrect. The teacher is entitled to recover damages that will place her in the position she would have been in but for the school's breach. However, an injured party is expected to make reasonable efforts to mitigate the loss resulting from the other party's breach. In the case of a wrongfully discharged employee, the employee is expected to accept an offer of comparable employment. If the employee fails or refuses to do so, the employee's recovery is reduced by the amount of the loss that the employee could have avoided by accepting comparable employment. Here, the teacher's damages of $50,000 should be reduced by the $47,000 she would have earned if she had accepted the comparable teaching position at the private academy. Therefore, the teacher is entitled to recover $3,000 from the school.

(B) $30,000, the full contract amount less the amount the teacher could have earned in the counselor position offered by the school.

Incorrect. The teacher is entitled to recover damages that will place her in the position she would have been in but for the school's breach. However, an injured party is expected to make reasonable efforts to mitigate the loss resulting from the other party's breach. In the case of a wrongfully discharged employee, the employee is expected to accept an offer of comparable employment. If the employee fails or refuses to do so, the employee's recovery is reduced by the amount of the loss that the employee could have avoided by accepting comparable employment. Because it is unlikely that a court would consider the counseling position to be comparable employment, the teacher's damages should not be reduced by the $20,000 she would have earned if she had accepted that position. On the other hand, her damages of $50,000 should be reduced by the $47,000 she would have earned if she had accepted the comparable teaching position at the private academy. Therefore, the teacher is entitled to recover $3,000 from the school.

(C) **$3,000, the full contract amount less the amount the teacher could have earned in the teaching position at the academy.**

> Correct. The teacher is entitled to recover damages that will place her in the position she would have been in but for the school's breach. However, an injured party is expected to make reasonable efforts to mitigate the loss resulting from the other party's breach. In the case of a wrongfully discharged employee, the employee is expected to accept an offer of comparable employment. If the employee fails or refuses to do so, the employee's recovery is reduced by the amount of the loss that the employee could have avoided by accepting comparable employment. Here, the teacher's damages of $50,000 should be reduced by the $47,000 she would have earned if she had accepted the comparable teaching position at the private academy. Therefore, the teacher is entitled to recover $3,000 from the school.

(D) Nothing, because the school notified the teacher of its decision before the teacher had acted in substantial reliance on the contract.

> Incorrect. The teacher and the school entered into an enforceable contract, and the school's unjustified nonperformance constituted a breach of contract. The teacher is therefore entitled to recover damages that will place her in the position she would have been in but for the breach and need not show reliance in order to recover. However, while she is entitled to damages from the breach, an injured party is expected to make reasonable efforts to mitigate the loss resulting from the other party's breach. In the case of a wrongfully discharged employee, the employee is expected to accept an offer of comparable employment. If the employee fails or refuses to do so, the employee's recovery is reduced by the amount of the loss that the employee could have avoided by accepting comparable employment. Here, the teacher's damages of $50,000 should be reduced by the $47,000 she would have earned if she had accepted the comparable teaching position at the private academy. Therefore, the teacher is entitled to recover $3,000 from the school.

5. A buyer purchased a new car from a dealer under a written contract that provided that the price of the car was $20,000 and that the buyer would receive a "trade-in allowance of $7,000 for the buyer's old car." The old car had recently been damaged in an accident. The contract contained a merger clause stating: "This writing constitutes the entire agreement of the parties, and there are no other understandings or agreements not set forth herein." When the buyer took possession of the new car, she delivered the old car to the dealer. At that time, the dealer claimed that the trade-in allowance included an assignment of the buyer's claim against her insurance company for damage to the old car. The buyer refused to provide the assignment.

The dealer sued the buyer to recover the insurance payment. The dealer has offered evidence that the parties agreed during their negotiations for the new car that the dealer was entitled to the insurance payment.

Should the court admit this evidence?

(A) No, because the dealer's acceptance of the old car bars any additional claim by the dealer.

Incorrect. A buyer's mere acceptance of goods does not waive its potential claims against a seller. The dispositive issue here is whether the parol evidence rule will allow the proffered evidence. Under that rule, a merger clause does not conclusively determine that an agreement is completely integrated. Moreover, a finding that an agreement is completely integrated does not necessarily bar the admission of extrinsic evidence. Although extrinsic evidence is inadmissible to supplement or contradict the express terms of a completely integrated agreement, such evidence is admissible to explain the terms of an agreement. In this case, evidence of the parties' discussions during their negotiations is admissible to aid in explaining whether they intended "trade-in allowance" to include an assignment of the buyer's claim against her insurance company.

(B) No, because the merger clause bars any evidence of the parties' prior discussions concerning the trade-in allowance.

Incorrect. Under the UCC's parol evidence rule, a merger clause does not conclusively determine that an agreement is completely integrated. Moreover, a finding that an agreement is completely integrated does not necessarily bar the admission of extrinsic evidence. Although extrinsic evidence is inadmissible to supplement or contradict the express terms of a completely integrated agreement, such evidence is admissible to explain the terms of an agreement. In this case, evidence of the parties' discussions during their negotiations is admissible to aid in explaining whether they intended "trade-in allowance" to include an assignment of the buyer's claim against her insurance company.

(C) Yes, because a merger clause does not bar evidence of fraud.

Incorrect. The UCC's parol evidence rule allows the introduction of extrinsic evidence to establish fraud even if an agreement is completely integrated. Because there is no indication of fraud in this case, however, the fraud exception is irrelevant. The dispositive issue here is whether the parol evidence rule will allow the proffered evidence. Under that rule, a merger clause does not conclusively determine that an agreement is completely integrated. Moreover, a finding that an agreement is completely integrated does not necessarily bar the admission of extrinsic evidence. Although extrinsic evidence is inadmissible to supplement or contradict the express terms of a completely integrated agreement, such evidence is admissible to explain the terms of an agreement. In this case, evidence of the parties' discussions during their negotiations is admissible to aid in explaining whether they intended "trade-in allowance" to include an assignment of the buyer's claim against her insurance company.

(D) Yes, because the merger clause does not bar evidence to explain what the parties meant by "trade-in allowance."

Correct. Under the UCC's parol evidence rule, a merger clause does not conclusively establish that an agreement is completely integrated. Moreover, a finding that an agreement is completely integrated does not necessarily bar the admission of extrinsic evidence. Although extrinsic evidence is inadmissible to supplement or contradict the express terms of a completely integrated agreement, such evidence is admissible to explain the terms of an agreement. In this case, evidence of the parties' discussions during their negotiations is admissible to aid in explaining what amount they intended for the trade-in and whether they intended "trade-in allowance" to include an assignment of the buyer's claim against her insurance company.

6. An art collector paid a gallery $1,000 to purchase a framed drawing from the gallery's collection. The price included shipping by the gallery to the collector's home. The gallery's owner used inadequate materials to wrap the drawing. The frame broke during shipment and scratched the drawing, reducing the drawing's value to $300. The collector complained to the gallery owner, who told the collector to take the drawing to a specific art restorer to have the drawing repaired. The collector paid the restorer $400 to repair the drawing, but not all of the scratches could be fixed. The drawing, after being repaired, was worth $700. The gallery owner subsequently refused to pay either for the repairs or for the damage to the drawing.

In an action by the collector against the gallery owner for damages, which of the following awards is most likely?

(A) Nothing.

Incorrect. The gallery's use of inadequate materials to wrap the drawing constituted a breach of warranty. Therefore, the collector is entitled to be placed in the position he would have been in but for the gallery's breach. Awarding the collector nothing would violate the expectation damages principle. Under UCC § 2-714(2), the generally applicable standard for measuring the collector's resulting damages would be the difference between the value of the drawing as accepted and the value of the drawing if it had been as warranted. Repair costs often are used to determine this difference in value, but when repairs fail to restore the goods to their value as warranted, an adjustment is required. The collector is entitled to recover the repair costs ($400) plus the difference between the value of the drawing if it had been as warranted and its value after the repairs ($1,000 - $700 = $300). Accordingly, the collector should recover $700.

(B) $300.

Incorrect. The gallery's use of inadequate materials to wrap the drawing constituted a breach of warranty. Therefore, the collector is entitled to be placed in the position he would have been in but for the gallery's breach. Awarding the collector $300 would violate the expectation damages principle. Under UCC § 2-714(2), the generally applicable standard for measuring the collector's resulting damages would be the difference between the value of the drawing as accepted and the value of the drawing if it had been as warranted. Repair costs often are used to determine this difference in value, but when repairs fail to restore the goods to their value as warranted, an adjustment is required. The collector is entitled to recover the repair costs ($400) plus the difference between the value of the drawing if it had been as warranted and its value after the repairs ($1,000 - $700 = $300). Accordingly, the collector should recover $700.

(C) $400.

Incorrect. The gallery's use of inadequate materials to wrap the drawing constituted a breach of warranty. Therefore, the collector is entitled to be placed in the position he would have been in but for the gallery's breach. Awarding the collector $400 would violate the expectation damages principle. Under UCC § 2-714(2), the generally applicable standard for measuring the collector's resulting damages would be the difference between the value of the drawing as accepted and the value of the drawing if it had been as warranted. Repair costs often are used to determine this difference in value, but when repairs fail to restore the goods to their value as warranted, an adjustment is required. The collector is entitled to recover the repair costs ($400) plus the difference between the value of the drawing if it had been as warranted and its value after the repairs ($1,000 - $700 = $300). Accordingly, the collector should recover $700.

(D) **$700.**

Correct. The gallery's use of inadequate materials to wrap the drawing constituted a breach of warranty. Therefore, the collector is entitled to be placed in the position he would have been in but for the gallery's breach. Under UCC § 2-714(2), the generally applicable standard for measuring the collector's resulting damages would be the difference between the value of the drawing as accepted and the

value of the drawing if it had been as warranted. Repair costs often are used to determine this difference in value, but when repairs fail to restore the goods to their value as warranted, a further adjustment is required. Here the repairs failed to restore the drawing to its value as warranted. Therefore, the collector is entitled to recover the repair costs ($400) plus the difference between the value of the drawing if it had been as warranted and its value after the repairs ($1,000 - $700 =$300). Accordingly, the collector should recover $700.

CIVIL PROCEDURE MBE QUESTIONS ANSWERS

[Note: the NCBE has not released explanations for the Civil Procedure questions.]

1. B

2. D

3. B

4. A

5. D

6. A